NEW BEGINNINGS

CELEBRATING BIRTH

TOWER HAMLETS COLLEGE
Learning Centre
Arbour Square
LONDON E1 0PT
Tel: 020 7510 7568

First published in paperback in 2005 by
Evans Brothers Limited
2A Portman Mansions
Chiltern Street
London W1U 6NR

First published 1998
Reprinted 2000 , 2001 , 2004

British Library Cataloguing in Publication Data
Ganeri, Anita
  New beginnings. - (Life times)
  1.Birth customs - Juvenile literature
  2.Mourning customs - Juvenile literature
  I.Title
  392.1'2

ISBN 0237528428

Editor: Nicola Barber
Designer: Neil Sayer
Picture research: Victoria Brooker
Illustrations: Jackie Morris
Production: Jenny Mulvanny
Consultant: Alison Seaman, Deputy Director of the National Society's RE Centre.

Printed by New Era in Hong Kong

Cover pictures:
(Left) A Muslim father and his new-born baby
(Top right) A Hindu naming ceremony
(Middle right) Baptism in the Orthodox Christian Church
(Bottom right) A page from the Sikh holy book; the *Guru Granth Sahib*

VISIT OUR WEBSITE
Evans
www.evansbooks.co.uk

Acknowledgements

Cover (left) Peter Sanders (top right) Ann and Bury Peerless (middle) M. Harney/Hutchison Library (bottom right) Judy Harrison/Format **page 3** Peter Sanders **page 6** Ann & Bury Peerless **page 7** Bipinchandra J Mistry **page 8** Bipinchandra J Mistry **page 11** (top) JHC Wilson/Robert Harding Picture Library (bottom) Hutchison Library **page 13** (top) Circa Photo Library (bottom) Christine Osborne Pictures **page 14** (top and bottom) Judy Harrison/Format **page 15** (top) Judy Harrison/Format (bottom) Ann & Bury Peerless **page 16** (top) Trip/I Genut (bottom) Trip/I Genut **page 17** Miriam Reik/Format **page 18** Hutchison Library **page 19** (top) Ancient Art and Architecture Collection (bottom) Trip/I Genut **page 20** (top) D.Rose (bottom) Trip/H Rogers **page 21** (top) D. Rose (bottom) D. Rose **page 22** (left) M. Harney/Hutchison Library (right) Kunstmuseum, Basle, Switzerland/Peter Willl/Bridgeman Art Library **page 24** Peter Sanders **page 25** (top) Peter Sanders (bottom) Circa Photo Library **page 26** (top) Trip/ H Rogers (bottom) Paul Harris/Tony Stone Images

NEW BEGINNINGS

CELEBRATING BIRTH

ANITA GANERI

Evans

EVANS BROTHERS LIMITED

INTRODUCTION

In each of the world's six major religions, the most important times in a person's life are marked by special ceremonies. These are a bit like signposts on the journey through life, guiding a person from one stage of their life to the next. They also give people the chance to share their beliefs and their joys or sorrows, whether in celebrating a baby's birth, the change from child to adult, a wedding, or marking and remembering a person's death. For each occasion, there are prayers to be said, presents to give and receive, festive food to eat and stories to tell. Customs and ceremonies vary in different parts of the world. This book looks at just some of them.

CELEBRATING BIRTH

This book examines how people from the Hindu, Buddhist, Sikh, Jewish, Christian and Muslim faiths welcome a new-born baby into the world. You can find out how a baby's name is chosen and the meanings of popular names. You can also read about some very special birthdays.

In this book dates are written with BCE and CE, instead of BC and AD which are based on the Christian calendar. BCE means 'Before the Common Era' and it replaces BC (Before Christ). CE means 'in the Common Era' and it replaces AD (Anno Domini 'in the year of our Lord').

This is the Hindu sacred symbol 'Om'. It expresses all the secrets of the universe.

This wheel is a Buddhist symbol. Its eight spokes stand for eight points of the Buddha's teaching.

This Sikh symbol is called the 'Ik onkar'. It means 'There is only one God'.

The Star of David is a Jewish symbol. It appears on the flag of Israel.

The cross is a Christian symbol. It reminds Christians of how Jesus died on a cross.

The star and crescent moon are symbols of Islam.

CONTENTS

Honey and horoscopes   6

The birth of the Buddha   10

A welcome in the gurdwara   12

A covenant with God   16

Being baptised   20

The call to prayer   24

HONEY AND HOROSCOPES

In the Hindu religion, important times in a person's life are marked by 16 special ceremonies, called samskaras. These are performed in front of a sacred fire, while priests say prayers and read from the holy books. The first samskaras happen even before a baby is born, to give it the best possible start in life.

The baby is born

The birth of a baby is a happy time in a Hindu household. Soon after the baby is born, it is bathed and the sacred word, 'Om', is written in honey on its tongue, using a golden pen. 'Om' is a very holy word, recited at the beginning of prayers, blessings and meditation. It is believed to hold all the secrets of the universe.

At a Hindu naming ceremony, the father tells the priest the baby's name. The priest is wearing saffron robes, the holy colour of Hinduism.

Choosing a name

Twelve days after the baby's birth, the priest visits the family to bless and name the baby. The baby lies in its mother's lap, with its father to one side. In front of them is a metal plate spread with grains of rice. Using a piece of gold wire, the father writes the name of the family god and the baby's name and date of birth on the rice grains.

It's a fiddly job! Then he whispers the baby's name into its right ear. The priest blesses the baby and shares out sweets and other offerings of food that he has blessed.

Casting a horoscope

Before the naming ceremony, the priest works out a horoscope for the baby, based on the position of the stars and planets at the time of its birth. From this, he reads the baby's future and suggests a suitable name.

This is the horoscope of a baby boy, written in Sanskrit, the ancient language of India.

A priest draws up a horoscope.

Some Hindu names

Many children are named after Hindu gods and goddesses, or have names with other religious meanings.

Boys' names
Suresh - another name for the great god, Shiva
Rabindra - son of Indra, the Lord of Heaven
Ram Kumar - son of the god, Rama
Sudarshan - another name for the blue god, Krishna

Girls' names
Vandana - prayer or homage
Radha - the name of Krishna's wife
Sita - the wife of Lord Rama
Lakshmi - the goddess of wealth and good fortune

The cycle of life

Hindus believe that when you die, your soul is reborn in another body, human or animal. You can be reborn many times, unless you break free from the cycle and reach moksha, or salvation. This is when your soul joins with the great soul, Brahman (God). It depends on your actions, and the results of your actions, in your present life. If you act well, you will be reborn in a higher form, closer to moksha. If you act badly, you will move further away. This process is called karma. This is the belief that all actions have their effects, good or bad.

This baby is having its first haircut. This is done to remove any bad karma. A prayer is said to wish the baby a long, happy and healthy life.

Showing the Sun

A few months after the naming ceremony, another samskara takes place, early in the morning. After praying to the family gods, the father takes his baby outside to see the rays of the rising Sun. The Sun is all-important, as the giver of life itself.

First haircut

Before the baby boy is a year old, the family gathers for another special event. First the priests perform a puja, or prayer ceremony. They sit in front of the sacred fire, reciting passages from the holy books. Then they draw a pattern in red dye showing the planets and the gods. The baby's parents make an offering – of water, flowers and incense – to each of these gods. Then the priests pour ghee (butter) on to the fire to make it blaze brightly. The puja ends with a joyful bhajan, or hymn. Everyone joins in.

After this the baby's hair is shaved off and collected for burning. This is believed to remove any bad karma from the baby's past lives (see box). The fire carries the offering of the hair up to the gods and wipes away evil.

The birth of the blue god

The blue god, Krishna, is one of the best-loved Hindu gods. His birthday is at midnight on the night of the full Moon in August. It is celebrated all over India with a festival called Janmashtami. This is the story of Krishna's birth.

Krishna's mother was a royal princess but the blue god did not grow up as a prince. His wicked uncle, the king, hated the child and vowed to kill him. Just in time, the gods warned Krishna's mother:

"Send your son across the river to live with Nanda, the cowherd."

So Vasudeva, Krishna's father, took his son to the banks of the Yamuna River. But the river was a raging torrent. How could they get across? Vasudeva put Krishna's basket down as he thought what to do.

Then Krishna, the blue god, poked a tiny foot out of his basket and dangled it into the water. At once the mighty river grew calm and parted, making a path for them to cross. For Krishna was no ordinary child.

THE BIRTH OF THE BUDDHA

Buddhists do not have set ceremonies to mark a baby's birth. Parents may take their babies to a temple to be blessed by the monks. For Buddhists, the happiest birthday of all is that of Prince Siddhartha Gautama. He went on to become the Buddha, whose teachings all Buddhists follow.

Greeted by the gods

In Nepal, about 2500 years ago, a baby was born in a grove of trees. A bright, full Moon shone in the sky. The gods showered the baby with sweet-smelling petals and poured scented water from heaven to bathe him. Then, as an earthquake shook the ground, the baby took seven steps forwards. The trees in the grove burst into flower. Blind people could see and lame people could walk again. Siddhartha Gautama, the Buddha-to-be, was born.

Soon afterwards Siddhartha's mother, Queen Maya, died. Siddhartha grew up in his father's luxurious palace. A wise man gave his father a warning.

"Your son will become a great ruler or a great holy man," he said, "depending on how much suffering he sees in the world."

The king was determined that his son should rule after him. So he kept him safe inside the palace, surrounded by beautiful things.

One day, Siddhartha sneaked out of the palace, against his father's wishes. He saw three terrible sights – an old man, a sick man and a dead man. How badly they had suffered! Then he saw a monk, happy with his simple life. Siddhartha knew what to do. That night he left the palace for good, put on monk's robes and set off to follow this way of life.

Six years later, as he sat meditating under a tree, Siddhartha felt he understood the truth about suffering. He became the Buddha, a name which means 'awake' or 'enlightened', one of the greatest holy people of all. He spent the rest of his life travelling around India, teaching people a better, wiser way to live.

Buddhist monks meditate, just as the Buddha did.

Birthday bathday

In Japan, the Buddha's birthday is celebrated on 8 April with a festival called Hana Matsuri. Japanese people visit the temple to pour bowls of sweet tea over a statue of the Buddha. This reminds them of the Buddha's first bath (see page 10).

People pour sweet tea over a statue of the Buddha.

A WELCOME IN THE GURDWARA

For Sikhs, family life is very important. A baby is seen as a precious gift from God. To celebrate a baby's birth, the parents give boxes of sweets as presents to their friends and relations. In return, they receive gifts of money, new clothes and lengths of cloth for winding into turbans.

Words of prayer

Soon after the baby is born, the words of the Mool Mantar prayer (see box) are whispered in its ear. This is an important prayer. It sums up what the Sikhs believe about God.

The Mool Mantar

This prayer was composed by Guru Nanak, the founder of the Sikh religion.
'There is only one God
  Whose name is Truth
God the creator
  is without fear
  is without hate
  is timeless and without shape
  is beyond death, the
    enlightened one
and is understood through God's
    grace.'

A visit to the gurdwara

A few weeks after birth, parents take the baby to the gurdwara, the temple where Sikhs meet to worship. They want to thank God for the baby and to choose its name. They take with them a beautiful, embroidered silk cloth, called a romalla. It will be placed over the *Guru Granth Sahib*, the holy book of the Sikhs, to cover it when it is not being used. (You can read more about this book on page 14.) The baby's naming ceremony usually takes place at the end of a normal service in the gurdwara.

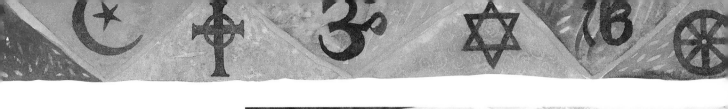

A close-up of a romalla, beautifully embroidered with red and gold thread

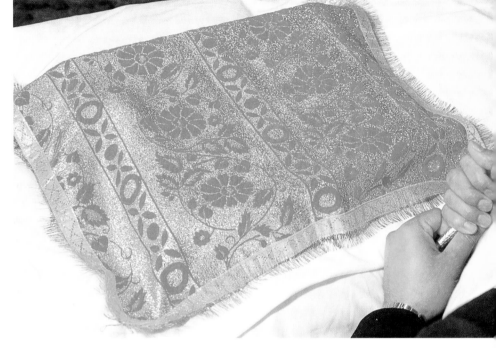

When it is not being read, the Guru Granth Sahib *is covered by a romalla of silk or velvet.*

The Sikh symbol

This Sikh symbol is called the 'Ik onkar' which means 'There is only one God', the first words of the Mool Mantar prayer. It is sometimes embroidered on romalla cloths.

The Guru Granth Sahib

The Sikhs' holy book is called the *Guru Granth Sahib*. It is a collection of hymns and prayers, written hundreds of years ago by the Sikh gurus, or teachers, and other holy people. In the gurdwara, the *Guru Granth Sahib* is treated with great respect. An appointed reader, called a granthi, looks after it and reads from it during services. It is placed on a raised throne under a canopy. When not in use, it is wrapped up in a romalla cloth.

Reading the Guru Granth Sahib

The Guru Granth Sahib *is written in Gurmukhi. This is the script used to write Punjabi, the Sikh language.*

Choosing a name

In the gurdwara, the parents and baby stand before the sacred book. An Ardas, a prayer, is said. Then the granthi opens the *Guru Granth Sahib* at random and reads the first word on the left-hand page. The parents choose a name for their baby which begins with the same letter as that word. They tell the granthi who announces the name to the congregation. In reply, and to show that they all agree, everyone shouts "Sat sri akal" which means "God is truth".

Joining in

At the end of the ceremony, everyone receives a portion of karah parshad, a sweet made from flour, sugar and butter. Sharing the food shows that everyone is equal in God's eyes. Sometimes a sweet, sugary mixture, called amrit, is dripped on to the baby's tongue, to give the baby a welcome into the Sikh community.

There is great celebration if a baby is born at the time of the Sikh winter festival of Lohri. The baby is bounced in a pile of sweets or popcorn, and sweets are given to friends and relatives.

Guru Nanak's birthday

Every year, in November, Sikhs all over the world celebrate the birthday of Guru Nanak, the founder of the Sikh religion. He was born in a small village in India in 1469. A special festival, called a gurpurb, is held in his honour. The most important part of the festival is the reading of the *Guru Granth Sahib*, non-stop from beginning to end. There is also a colourful procession through the streets, carrying a copy of the *Guru Granth Sahib* on a decorated platform called a palki.

Guru Nanak, the founder of the Sikh religion. When he was about 30 years old, God told him to go out and teach people the right way to live. He spent the rest of his life preaching and teaching.

A COVENANT WITH GOD

Jews do not believe in rebirth, as Hindus and Buddhists do. They believe that each life is a gift from God, to be lived according to God's commandments. According to Jewish law, anyone with a Jewish mother is a Jew, whether they follow the customs and practices of Jewish religion or not.

Brit Milah

Eight days after a baby boy is born a ceremony is held, called the Brit Milah. This can take place at home or in the hospital where the baby was born. Sometimes only men and boys are present. Sometimes the baby's mother watches too.

First, the baby is placed on a chair, known as Elijah's chair. Elijah was a Jewish prophet and a protector of children.

The father carries the baby on a cushion, ready for the Brit Milah ceremony. He says that he is presenting his son for circumcision, in keeping with God's wishes.

This seat is called Elijah's chair. The words on it mean welcome. The baby is placed here to gain Elijah's protection.

Then the baby is placed on his godfather's knee while a simple operation is carried out to cut a small piece of skin from his penis. This is called circumcision. It is performed by a specially trained Jew, called a mohel. It is quickly over.

A prayer

During the circumcision, the baby's father says a prayer:

"Blessed are you, Lord our God, King of the Universe, Who has blessed us with his commandments, and ordered us to enter my son into the promise made by Abraham."

Then the baby is given his name and more prayers are said to bless the child. Everyone drinks some wine – even the baby is given a drop – and a party is held to celebrate.

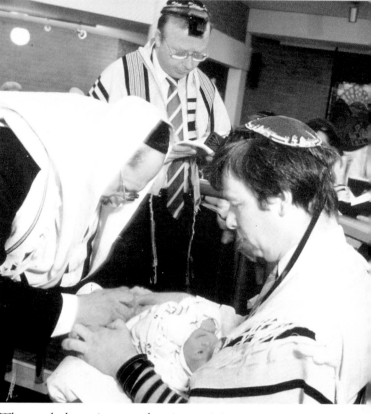

The mohel carries out the circumcision.

Jewish names

As well as their ordinary names, Jewish children are also given Jewish names, often of important Jews from history.

Boys' names
David - King of Israel in the 10th century BCE
Samuel - Jewish prophet and judge
Jacob - the son of Abraham's son, Isaac
Aaron - brother of Moses. Jews believe that Moses was given the *Torah* by God.

Girls' names
Ruth - King David's great grandmother
Miriam - sister of Aaron
Sarah - Abraham's wife
Rebecca - Isaac's wife
Esther - a Persian queen who lived more than 2300 years ago. She saved the Jews living in Persia from death.

The Ten Commandments

The most important rules for Jews to follow are called the Ten Commandments. They believe that these were given by God to Moses.

1. I am the Lord your God.
2. You must have no other gods.
3. You must not misuse my name.
4. Keep the Shabbat day holy.
5. Respect your father and mother.
6. Do not kill.
7. Do not commit adultery.
8. Do not steal.
9. Do not tell lies.
10. Do not be jealous of other people.

Copies of the Torah *are handwritten in Hebrew on special scrolls. Writing out a* Torah *takes about a year. Hebrew is the sacred language of the Jews.*

God's Chosen People

The Brit Milah ceremony is very ancient. It dates back more than 4000 years to the time of the prophet, Abraham, one of the first Jews. Abraham made a special agreement with God, called a covenant. By circumcising their sons, Jewish fathers are entering them into the same covenant with God. The words Brit Milah mean 'covenant' and 'circumcision'.

The birth of a daughter

There is no Brit Milah when a baby girl is born. Instead, she is taken to the synagogue on the first Shabbat (Saturday) after her birth. Her father is called up to the bimah, the raised platform at the front of synagogue. This is where the *Torah*, the Jewish scriptures, are read. Being called up is a great honour. While the father stands at the bimah, his daughter's name is announced to the congregation.

In the synagogue, the sacred Torah scrolls are kept in a special cupboard, called the Ark. This is the holiest part of the synagogue.

Five silver shekels

Another ceremony may be held when a first-born baby boy is about a month old. His father pays five shekels (silver coins) to the synagogue. This dates back to a time long ago in Israel. All first-born boys were given to God in thanks. They were sent to the Temple in Jerusalem to serve as priests or helpers. Later, it became the custom for parents to pay a sum of money in place of their son. Today, the money is usually donated to charity.

Shekels are still used in Israel.

BEING BAPTISED

When a Christian baby is born, its parents take it to church to be baptised. A service is held at which the baby is accepted into the Christian faith and given a name. Some close friends or relations are chosen to be the baby's godparents. They promise to help support and look after the child as it grows up in the Christian faith.

A baby is baptised at the font.

A shell is sometimes used to scoop water over the baby's head. This is a reminder that the first Christians were baptised by the river or the seashore.

Washing away sins

For the baptism, the parents and godparents stand near the font, a special container which holds holy water. In old churches, the font is often at the back of the church. It reminds worshippers entering the church that baptism is the first step on their journey through life. The priest, or minister, asks the parents and godparents to promise to look after the baby and to help them follow the teachings of Jesus Christ. Then he or she

pours some holy water over the baby's head and makes the sign of the cross on its forehead. The water is meant to wash away the baby's sin. The cross is the symbol of the Christian faith.

Baptising the baby

As the priest pours the water and makes the sign of the cross, he says the baby's name, together with the following words:

"I baptise you in the name of the Father, and of the Son, and of the Holy Spirit. I sign you with the Cross, the sign of Christ."

Baptism is sometimes called Christening when a person becomes a member of the Christian family. The baby's first name is also known as its Christian name.

A Paschal candle. It is decorated with a cross and two Greek letters which stand for Jesus Christ.

The priest lights the candles used at the baptism from the Paschal candle.

The light of the world

In some churches, during the baptism, the priest hands a candle to the baby's parents. This is lit from the Paschal, or Easter, candle, near the altar. It is a symbol of Jesus as the light that will help to guide the baby through life. The priest gives the candle to a parent or godparent saying, "Receive this light. This is to show that you have passed from darkness to light." Everyone replies "Shine like a light in the world, to the glory of God the Father."

After the service, there is a party for friends and family. Some people save the top layer of their wedding cake to use at the party.

Chrismation

Orthodox Christians have an extra ceremony at the baptism. This is called Chrismation. The priest draws a cross in holy oil, or chrism, on the baby's head and chest. This is believed to protect the baby and give it strength. The oil is a symbol of the Holy Spirit, the invisible part of God which is believed to be present in everything.

This is a baptism in an Orthodox Church in Moscow. The small chest next to the font holds the bottles of holy oil, or chrism.

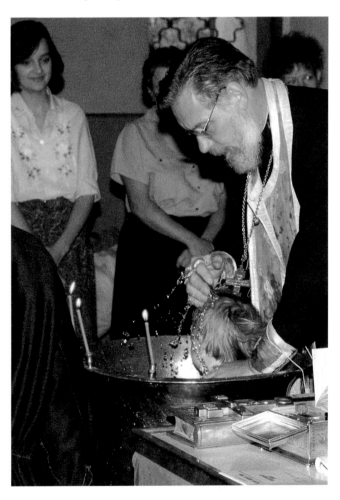

Saints' names

Many Christian children are named after saints. For example:

Boys' names
Christopher - patron saint of travellers
Antony - patron saint of lost objects
Dominic - patron saint of astronomers
Joseph - patron saint of carpenters

Girls' names
Teresa - patron saint of lacemakers
Anne - patron saint of grandmothers
Barbara - patron saint of architects
Catherine - patron saint of students

St Christopher

The birth of Christ

At Christmas, Christians all over the world celebrate the birth of Jesus Christ almost 2000 years ago. Christians believe Jesus is the Son of God, and follow his teachings and example.

Jesus's mother, Mary, and her husband, Joseph, had travelled to the small town of Bethlehem to pay their taxes. When they arrived, the town was crowded and they had to sleep in a stable. It was here that Jesus was born. News of Jesus's birth spread quickly, for the scriptures had told of a baby who would become the saviour of the world. The first visitors were shepherds who had been tending their flocks in the fields nearby. Angels told them about the baby and they wanted to see him for themselves. Next came the three wise men, bringing gifts of gold, frankincense and myrrh. They had followed a star to the stable.

Jesus's birthday is traditionally celebrated on 25 December, though no one knows exactly when he was born. Orthodox Christians celebrate Christmas on 6 January, the day on which the three wise men are said to have visited the stable.

THE CALL TO PRAYER

For Muslim parents, children are a gift from Allah (God), and looking after a baby is a special responsibility. From an early age, children are taught to be good Muslims, learning about their faith, working hard and caring for others.

First words

The first words that a Muslim baby hears are those of the Adhan, or call to prayer, whispered in its right ear. These are the words that sound out every day from the mosque, calling Muslims to prayer:

"Allah is the greatest.
I bear witness that there is no God but Allah
I bear witness that Muhammad is the messenger of Allah.
Come to prayer
Come to safety
Allah is the greatest."

After this another prayer called the iqamah is whispered in the baby's left ear. This is usually done by the baby's father, or by the imam – the person who leads the prayers in the mosque.

This father is whispering the words of the Adhan into his new-born baby's ear.

A sweet start

Sometimes a tiny amount of sugar or honey is placed on the baby's tongue, and a prayer is said giving thanks to Allah. No one knows exactly why this is done. Some people say it links the sweet words with a sweet taste.

Names and gifts

When the baby is seven days old, the aqiqah ceremony is held. First the baby's hair is shaved off. Then the hair is weighed and the weight of the hair is given in silver to the poor. Often, money is given instead. Giving to the poor is one of the main beliefs of Islam (see page 27). At this ceremony, the baby is also given its name (see box below). All Muslim names have a meaning. Choosing a good name is very important!

Muslims praying in a mosque. Muslims must pray five times a day. This is one of the Five Pillars of Islam (see page 27).

Choosing a name

Muhammad was the final prophet, or messenger, of Allah who first taught the religion of Islam in the 7th century CE (see page 27). Many Muslim children are named after him or after someone in his family, for example Amina, his mother, or Ibrahim, his son. Others are given one of the 99 names that Muslims use for Allah, for example Rashid, which means 'guide'.

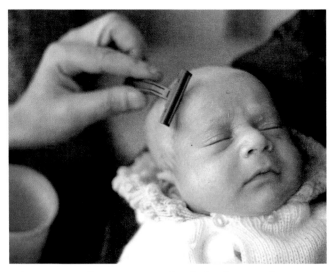

At its aqiqah ceremony, the baby has its hair shaved off.

Reading and studying the Qur'an is very important for Muslim boys and girls.

Time for a feast

After the aqiqah ceremony, the family hold a feast for their friends and neighbours. Traditionally, in Muslim countries two sheep or goats were killed for the feast if the baby was a boy; one if a girl was born. One-third of the meat was given to the poor. Today, though, it is often easier for people to give money instead.

The Bismillah

In some Muslim countries a ceremony, called the Bismillah, is held when a child is four or five years old. The child recites the first few verses of the *Qur'an*, the Muslim holy book, which have been learned by heart. The *Qur'an* is written in Arabic, the language spoken by Muhammad. The 'Bismillah' is said at the beginning of a task or a meal to ask for Allah's blessing. It means 'In the name of Allah, the merciful'.

The Bismillah, written in Arabic

The Qur'an is written in Arabic, the language spoken by Muhammad.

The Five Pillars of Islam

The five main beliefs of Islam are called pillars because they help to 'support' Islam, just as real pillars support a building. They help Muslims to be aware of Allah in everything they do.

1. Shahadah, or the statement of faith. This says that: "There is no other God but Allah, and Muhammad is his prophet."
2. Salah, or prayer. Muslims must pray five times a day, at set times, facing the holy city of Makkah.
3. Zakah, or giving money to the poor. Muslims believe that this is their duty.
4. Sawm, or fasting. Muslims do not eat or drink from dawn until sunset during the Islamic month of Ramadan.
5. Hajj, or pilgrimage. Muslims try to make a pilgrimage to Makkah at least once in their lives.

Muhammad's early life

The prophet Muhammad was born in Makkah, Saudi Arabia, in 570 CE. His father, Abdullah, died before he was born. While Muhammad was still a baby his mother, Amina, sent him to be looked after by a foster-mother. That was the custom in those days. The woman who cared for Muhammad was called Halimah. She lived in a nearby village. She was very happy to take Muhammad home with her and loved him as her own son. Some years later, Muhammad went back to Makkah to live with his mother. But Amina died when he was just six years old. So Muhammad was brought up by his grandfather and, later, by his uncle. He learned to work hard and, when he grew up, he became a merchant like his uncle.

FACT FILES

 **Hinduism**

- **Numbers of Hindus:** *c.*732 million
- **Where began:** India (*c.* 2500 BCE)
- **Founder figure:** None
- **Major deities:** Thousands of gods and goddesses representing different aspects of Brahman, the great soul. The three most important gods are Brahma the creator, Vishnu the protector, and Shiva the destroyer.
- **Places of worship:** Mandirs (temples), shrines
- **Holy books:** *Vedas, Upanishads, Ramayana, Mahabharata*

Buddhism

- **Numbers of Buddhists:** *c.* 314 million
- **Where began:** Nepal/India (6th century BCE)
- **Founder figure:** Siddhartha Gautama, who became known as the Buddha
- **Major deities:** None, the Buddha did not want people to worship him as a god.
- **Places of worship:** Viharas (monasteries or temples), stupas (shrines)
- **Holy books:** *Tripitaka (Pali Canon), Diamond Sutra* and many others

 Sikhism

- **Numbers of Sikhs:** *c.* 18 million
- **Where began:** India (15th century CE)
- **Founder figure:** Guru Nanak
- **Major deities:** One God whose word was brought to people by ten earthly gurus, or teachers.
- **Places of worship:** Gurdwaras (temples)
- **Holy book:** *Guru Granth Sahib*

Judaism

- **Number of Jews:** *c.* 17 million
- **Where began:** Middle East (*c.* 2000 BCE)
- **Important figures:** Abraham, Isaac, Jacob, Moses
- **Major deities:** One God, the creator who cares for all people.
- **Places of worship:** Synagogues
- **Holy books:** *Tenakh* (Hebrew *Bible*), *Torah* (the first five books of the *Tenakh*), *Talmud*

Christianity

- **Numbers of Christians:** *c.* 2000 million
- **Where began:** Middle East (1st century CE)
- **Important figure:** Jesus Christ
- **Major deities:** One God, in three aspects - as the Father (creator of the world), as the Son (Jesus Christ), and as the Holy Spirit
- **Places of worship:** Churches, cathedrals, chapels
- **Holy books:** *Bible* (Old and New Testaments)

Islam

- **Numbers of Muslims:** *c.* 1000 million
- **Where began:** Saudi Arabia (*c.* 610 CE)
- **Important figure:** The prophet, Muhammad
- **Major deities:** One God, Allah, who revealed his wishes to the prophet Muhammad.
- **Places of worship:** Mosques
- **Holy books:** The *Qur'an*

GLOSSARY

Adhan The words that call Muslims to prayer.

Allah The Arabic word for God.

amrit A special mixture of sugar and water used at Sikh ceremonies.

aqiqah A ceremony that takes places when a Muslim baby is about a week old. This is when the baby is given its name.

baptism A ceremony at which a person becomes a full member of the Christian Church. They are sprinkled or bathed in water as a sign that they are cleansed from sin.

bhajan A Hindu hymn or song of praise.

bimah A raised platform in the front of a synagogue from where the *Torah* is read.

Brit Milah The ceremony at which a Jewish baby boy is circumcised.

Chrismation Part of the baptism ceremony in an Orthodox church.

circumcision The cutting of a small piece of skin from a boy's penis. Jewish and Muslim boys are circumcised.

covenant A special agreement between God and the Jews.

font A container in a church which contains holy water for baptisms.

granthi A Sikh who is appointed to look after and read from the *Guru Granth Sahib*.

gurdwara A Sikh place of worship.

gurpurb A Sikh festival which celebrates the birth or death of a Sikh guru (teacher).

Guru Granth Sahib The holy book of the Sikhs.

horoscope A chart showing the position of the stars and planets at the time of a baby's birth.

Ik onkar A sacred Sikh symbol which means 'There is only one God'.

imam A Muslim person who leads the prayers in the mosque.

karah parshad A type of sweet food shared out at a Sikh ceremony.

karma Your actions and their results.

meditation Thinking deeply about something.

mohel A Jewish man trained to perform a circumcision.

moksha Freedom from being born over and over again.

Mool Mantar A very important Sikh prayer.

mosque A Muslim place of worship.

Om A sacred Hindu symbol and sound. It is thought to express all the secrets of the universe.

Paschal Another word for Easter.

puja A Hindu ceremony of worship.

Qur'an The holy book of the Muslims.

romalla An embroidered cloth which covers the *Guru Granth Sahib* when it is not being read.

samskara A ceremony which marks a special time in a Hindu's life. There are 16 samskaras in total.

Sanskrit An ancient Indian language. The Hindu sacred books are written in Sanskrit.

Shabbat The Jewish day of rest or worship. It lasts from sunset on Friday to sunset on Saturday.

shekel A Jewish silver coin.

Torah The Jewish holy book.

INDEX

Abraham 18
Adhan 24
Amina 27
aqiqah ceremony 25, 26

baptism 20-2
Bismillah 26
Brahman 8
Brit Milah 16-18
Buddhist ceremonies 10-11

chrism (holy oil) 22
Chrismation 22
Christian ceremonies 20-3
circumcision 16-18

Elijah's chair 16

Five Pillars of Islam 25, 27
fonts 20

godparents 20-1
granthis 14
Gurmukhi 14
Guru Granth Sahib 12, 13, 14, 15

Hajj (pilgrimage) 27
Hana Matsuri 11
Hindu ceremonies 6-9
horoscopes 7

Ik onkar 13

Jesus Christ 20, 21, 23
Jewish ceremonies 16-19
Joseph 23

karah parshad 15
karma 8
Krishna 9

Makkah 27
Mary 23
Maya, Queen 10
mohels 17
moksha 8
Mool Mantar 12, 13
Moses 18
Muhammad, Prophet 24, 25, 26, 27
Muslim ceremonies 24-7

Nanak, Guru 12, 15

'Om' 6

Paschal (Easter) candles 21

Qu'ran 26, 27

Ramadan 27
romalla cloths 12, 13

samskaras 6, 8
Sanskrit 7
shekels 19
Siddhartha Gautama, the Buddha 10-11
Sikh ceremonies 12-15

Ten Commandments 18
Torah 18, 19

Reading	Writing	Listening	Speaking
Choosing suitable section headings from a list Sentence completion Identification of information in the text– *True/False/Not Given*	IELTS Task 1	IELTS Section 1	IELTS Part 2
Identification of information in the text– *True/False/Not Given* Classification Multiple-choice	IELTS Task 2	IELTS Section 2	IELTS Part 2
Locating information Identification of information in the text– *True/False/Not Given* Multiple-choice	IELTS Task 1	IELTS Section 3	1 IELTS Part 1 2 IELTS Part 2 3 IELTS Part 3
Summary completion Identification of writer's views/claims– *Yes/No/Not Given*	IELTS Task 2	IELTS Section 4	1 IELTS Part 1 2 IELTS Part 2 3 IELTS Part 3
Summary completion Multiple-choice Short-answer questions	IELTS Task 1	IELTS Section 1	IELTS Part 3
Locating information Identification of information in the text– *True/False/Not Given* Flow-chart completion	IELTS Task 1	IELTS Section 2	IELTS Part 2
Matching Sentence completion Multiple-choice	IELTS Task 1	IELTS Section 3	1 IELTS Part 3 2 IELTS Part 2
Sentence completion Table completion Multiple-choice	IELTS Task 2 IELTS Task 1	IELTS Section 4	IELTS Part 2
Sentence completion Classification Multiple-choice	IELTS Task 2	IELTS Section 3	1 IELTS Part 2 2 IELTS Part 3
Summary completion Matching	IELTS Task 2	IELTS Section 2	1 IELTS Part 3 2 IELTS Part 2
Locating information Sentence completion Multiple-choice	IELTS Task 2	IELTS Section 1	IELTS Part 2
Summary completion Identification of information in the text– *True/False/Not Given*	IELTS Task 2	IELTS Section 2	1 IELTS Part 1 2 IELTS Part 2
Locating information Identification of writer's views/claims *Yes/No/Not Given* Multiple-choice	IELTS Task 1	IELTS Section 3	IELTS Part 2
Locating information Identification of information in the text– *True/False/Not Given* Sentence completion Multiple-choice	IELTS Task 1	IELTS Section 4	IELTS Part 3
Grammar reference Page 219	Listening scripts Page 227	Sample answer sheets Page 238	

3

Introduction

Welcome to *Ready for IELTS*, a course which is designed to help you prepare for the IELTS Academic exam.

The book aims to help students with a global IELTS band score of 5 to progress to a band score of 6.5/7. Students with a minimum score of 4/5 in any aspect of the exam can also use this book to help them achieve a global band score up to 6.5/7. For example, to achieve a global band score of 5 upwards a candidate would need minimum scores of 4, 5, 5, 5 (in any order) in the four modules of Listening, Academic Reading, Academic Writing and Speaking.

The book contains a wide range of activities aimed at improving your English and developing the language and skills you need to improve your band score. As well as providing thorough practice in reading, writing, listening and speaking, each unit of *Ready for IELTS* includes one or more *Language focus* sections, which analyze the main grammar areas that are required for the exam, together with *Vocabulary* slots and regular *Word building* sections.

Throughout the book you will find the following boxes, which are designed to help you when performing the different tasks:

- **What to expect in the exam:** these contain useful information on what you should be prepared to see, hear or do in a particular type of task in the exam.

- **How to go about it:** these give advice and guidelines on how to deal with different types of tasks and specific questions.

- **Don't forget!:** these provide a reminder of important points to bear in mind when answering a particular type of question.

Further information and advice is included in the four supplementary *'Ready for ... '* units, one for each of the four parts of the exam. These are found at regular intervals in the book and can be used at appropriate moments during the course.

At the end of each unit there is a two page *Review* of the language covered in the unit. As a quick revision guide along with the *Wordlists* and *Grammar Reference*, you may want to refer back to the *Review* sections as you progress through the book.

At the end of the book in the *Grammar reference* you will find detailed explanations of the grammar areas seen in the units. There is also an extensive *Wordlist*, based on the vocabulary in each unit, and comprehensive checklists for the writing and speaking.

In each unit you will find practice in: the reading test using full passages, either Task 1 or Task 2 of the academic writing test, one or more of the parts of the speaking test and one section of the listening test. Each section of the listening test is covered in turn throughout the book, so there is the equivalent of three and a half full listening tests in the main units with an additional example of each section in the *Ready for Listening* section.

Overview of the examination

The IELTS Academic exam consists of four tests: Listening, Academic Reading, Academic Writing and Speaking. For more information and advice on each module, see the appropriate *'Ready for ...'* unit, as well as the relevant sections in the main units of the book.

IELTS Listening   approximately 30 minutes

The Listening test has 40 questions and lasts approximately 30 minutes. You hear each section once only and you answer the questions in the question booklet as you listen. At the end of the test you have ten minutes to transfer your answers to the answer sheet.

Section 1	A conversation between two people. Its subject is concerned with social issues.
Section 2	A monologue or a conversation between two people. Its subject is concerned with social issues.
Section 3	A conversation involving up to four people. The situation is related to education and training.
Section 4	A monologue. The context is related to education and training.

Question types

Multiple-choice

Short-answer

Sentence completion

Notes/form/summary/flow-chart completion

Labelling a diagram/plan/map

Classification

Matching

MACMILLAN EXAMS

Ready for

IELTS

coursebook

Sam McCarter

Contents Map

	Unit	Language focus	Vocabulary
1	We are all friends now Page 6	1 Present simple, present continuous and past simple 2 Likes and dislikes	1 Describing people 2 Verbs of movement
2	Technology – now and then Page 18	1 Past simple and present perfect 2 Habit in the past Adverbs of frequency	Verbs of cause and effect Word building: Qualifying adjectives
3	Thrill seekers Page 30	1 Comparison 2 Adjectives with prepositions	Sports Word building: Adjectives ending in -ing/-ed
	Ready for Listening Page 42		
4	Global problems and opportunities Page 48	1 Countable and uncountable nouns 2 Making suggestions	1 General category nouns 2 Developing ideas by expanding the meaning of adjectives
5	The future Page 60	Ways of looking at the future	1 Adjective/noun collocations 2 Verbs of prediction Word building: Forming adjectives from nouns
6	Fruits and seeds Page 72	Transitive and intransitive verbs	1 Conservation 2 Describing sequences
	Ready for Reading Page 84		
7	The world of work and training Page 92	Conditionals 1	1 Work 2 Collocations
8	The history of geography Page 104	Referring in a text	1 Nouns relating to places 2 Verbs relating to changes in maps
9	What is beauty? Page 116	Modal verbs for evaluating	Beauty Word building: Prefixes over- and under-
	Ready for Writing Page 128		
10	Is it art? Page 140	Defining and non-defining clauses	Art
11	Psychology and sociology Page 152	Conditionals 2	The family Word building: Suffixes -hood and -ship
12	Travelling around the world Page 164	Articles	Adjectives with multiple meaning
	Ready for Speaking Page 176		
13	The importance of infrastructure Page 182	Concession	Nouns related to systems Word building: Modal verbs to adjectives
14	Money and happiness Page 194	Substitution and ellipsis	Money matters Word building: Values and beliefs
	Additional material Page 206	Checklists page 209	Wordlist Page 211

IELTS Academic Reading   1 hour

In the Academic Reading test there are three passages, which are from various sources like books, journals, magazines and newspapers. The passages do not require specialist knowledge for you to understand them, and at least one of the three passages contains a detailed logical argument.

Question types
Choosing suitable paragraph headings from a list
Identification of information using 'True/False/Not Given' statements
Identification of the writer's claims using 'Yes/No/Not Given' statements
Multiple-choice
Short-answer
Sentence completion
Notes/summary/flow-chart/table completion
Labelling a diagram
Classification
Matching

IELTS Academic Writing   1 hour

The Academic Writing test lasts one hour and there are two tasks. You are advised to spend 20 minutes on Task 1 and asked to write at least 150 words. For Task 2 you are advised to spend 40 minutes and asked to write at least 250 words.

Task	Task type
1	Candidates are asked to describe data, presented as a graph, chart or table, or a diagram such as a map or process, using their own words.
2	Candidates are given a question containing a point of view, argument or problem.

The instructions in the questions follow these patterns:

Discuss the advantages and disadvantages of …

Discuss both these views and give your own opinion.

To what extent do you agree or disagree?

You may also be asked a specific question such as:

What do you consider to be the major influence?

What do you think are the causes of this problem and what solutions can you suggest?

IELTS Speaking   11–14 minutes

The IELTS Speaking test lasts between 11 and 14 minutes and consists of three parts. The exam is recorded.

Part	Task type
1	Candidates are asked questions about a variety of familiar topics such as their family, their job/studies or their interests. Part 1 lasts four to five minutes.
2	Candidates talk about a given topic for one to two minutes. You are given one minute to think about the topic and make notes.
3	Candidates have a discussion with the examiner linked to the topic in Part 2. Part 3 lasts between four to five minutes.

Sam McCarter

Vocabulary 1: Describing people

1 ◯ With a partner, describe what is happening in each of the photographs. Then discuss the questions below.

- Do the photographs give you any clues about the personalities of the people in them?
- Which, if any, of the people appeal to you as friends? Why?

2 Match the people in each photograph with one or more of the adjectives below. Give at least one reason for each choice.

Example:

The student in picture 5 looks very hard-working and conscientious, because he seems to be studying hard.

| hard-working | artistic | supportive | adventurous | talkative | chatty |
| sporty | creative | wise | considerate | conscientious | helpful | dynamic |

3 ◯ 'People generally judge other people just by their appearance without knowing them'. Do you think this is true? Why/Why not? Do you do this yourself?

4 For **1–14** below, decide what the adjective is for each noun. There may be more than one possible answer.

	Noun	Adjective		Noun	Adjective
1	respect	______________	**8**	sociability	______________
2	ambition	______________	**9**	calmness	______________
3	care	______________	**10**	punctuality	______________
4	sense of humour	______________	**11**	reliability	______________
5	talent	______________	**12**	loyalty	______________
6	generosity	______________	**13**	honesty	______________
7	cheerfulness	______________	**14**	patience	______________

5 Work in pairs. Each of the sentences **1–12** below describe people. Match each sentence to an adjective from exercise 4.

1 He tells jokes all the time and makes us all laugh.
2 She rarely loses her temper with anyone, which is why I like her so much.
3 She is never sad. She is always smiling and positive about everything.
4 He plays the piano exceptionally well. I hope to be as good as him one day.
5 She is a shrewd businesswoman with a strong desire to succeed in everything she does.
6 She loves being around people all the time, chatting and making new friends.
7 He is valued and appreciated by everyone who knows him.
8 She gives a lot of money away to charities and to people who need it.
9 He is a faithful friend, and always supports me when things go wrong.
10 When she was younger she devoted her time to looking after seriously ill people.
11 You can trust him with anything. He never lets anyone down.
12 He's never late for work, no matter what happens.

6 Think of a friend who has one or more of the qualities above. With a partner, describe the friend by explaining the qualities they have.

7 How do you think your friends see you? Write down three adjectives from exercise 4 or look at the Wordlist on page 211. Show the words to your partner and ask each other: *Why do you think you are ... ?*

8 Is it possible to make loyal and sincere friends on social networking sites on the Internet? Why/Why not?

Is the Internet a safe place to make friends? Why/Why not?

Reading
IELTS Reading Passage

What to expect in the exam

- IELTS Reading has three reading passages and 40 questions.
- You should spend about 20 minutes on each passage.
- See the introduction to Ready for Reading on page 84 for information about the different types of passages and questions in IELTS Reading.

1 You are going to read a passage with three sets of questions. Read the title and the subheading of the passage. Decide what kind of 'sites' they are talking about – are they commercial, social, or financial websites?

2 ⬤ How important is it to make friends at a new college or university? Why? How do you think social networks at a university can help students in their studies?

3 ⬤ Skim (see Ready for Reading on page 84) questions **1–6** below. These give you a summary of the passage. With a partner, discuss what you think the passage is about by using words like *Facebook, social networking, face to face, research and social integration* to help you.

How to go about it

- Read the title and skim the whole passage to get an overall idea of the content. Spend no more than two minutes skimming the passage at this stage.

- Learn to analyze the headings quickly. Look at heading (i). Put a box around *result*. Does it mean 'outcome'? Would you expect to find results at the beginning, middle or end of the passage?

- For heading (ii), put a box around the word *aims*. What tense do you expect to see in the paragraph? What words are similar to *aim*: *goal, plan, hope, want*?

- For heading (iii), there is no noun like *aim* or *result*, but can you translate the word *what* into a noun? Is it *methods, ways, premises*?

- Use the same methods with headings iv–ix. You will not need to use all of the headings.

- When you have finished, always check the sequence of the headings you have chosen to make sure it makes sense.

READING PASSAGE

You should spend about 20 minutes on **Questions 1–13**, which are based on the reading passage below.

Questions 1–6

The reading passage has six sections, **A–F**.

Choose the correct heading for each section from the list of headings below.

List of Headings

i   The expected result of the project

ii Further aims of the research project

iii What the research project is based on

iv The use of expertise from countries around the world

v   A need to concentrate on academic integration

vi A lack of knowledge about the effect of social networking on student retention

vii An emphasis until now on academic rather than social integration

viii The reason for using Facebook to recruit students

ix Increasing the chance of withdrawal

---

1 Section **A**

2 Section **B**

3 Section **C**

4 Section **D**

5 Section **E**

6 Section **F**

Face-to-face or Facebook?
Can online networking sites help new students settle into university?

A Can online networking sites such as Facebook and MySpace, help new students settle into university social and academic life and minimize the chance of them withdrawing from their courses?

Researchers at the University of Leicester are now looking for first-year University of Leicester students who use Facebook to help their pioneering research into this issue. They should not be too difficult to recruit. The reason for this is that student use of the online networking site Facebook is running at a phenomenal level, with almost 10,000 present and past students and staff participating.

Currently, 95 per cent of 16–18 year olds intending to go to university are using social networking sites like Facebook and MySpace.

B 'Yet we know little about how this phenomenon impacts on the student experience and, in particular, if and how it helps them integrate into university life,' commented Jane Wellens, Education Developer in the University of Leicester's Staff Development Centre. She is working with Dr Clare Madge, of the Department of Geography, Tristram Hooley, of CRAC, the Career Development Organisation, and Julia Meek, an independent evaluation consultant.

'The expectations and online experience of the latest and next generations of students requires universities to think carefully about how, and whether, to use these new technologies and meeting spaces to enhance the social aspects of student integration into university life,' she further commented.

C Academic and social integration into university life are key factors influencing individual students' experiences and the likelihood of their withdrawing from their student courses. Until now most research in the field has concentrated on academic support rather than integration into the wider social world of the university.

Students are now so used to using social networking sites that one university in the US has actually been running sessions to encourage students to build up face-to-face networks. One aspect of the Leicester project is to explore whether there are differences in the longevity and nature of university friendships that students establish face-to-face compared with those they make online through social networking sites.

D The Leicester project builds on internationally acclaimed work the University has already started on teaching and learning online. 'We recently used Facebook as a means of encouraging students on an online module to get to know one another,' Jane Wellens said. 'This raised many issues such as where the boundary between public and private space is, and how comfortable students (and staff) of different ages feel regarding the use of such technology.'

The Leicester project also draws on internationally recognised expertise by this specific team of researchers in online research methodologies. As Clare Madge of the Department of Geography at the University of Leicester stated: 'This project will be using both an online questionnaire and virtual interviews, and will innovate in the use of Facebook itself as a site to conduct virtual interviews'.

E What Dr Wellens and her colleagues hope to establish from the new research project is how Leicester students are using Facebook as part of their social and learning experience and whether joining the University's Facebook network before they come to Leicester helps students to settle down more easily into university life.

They will also be looking to see if there is any way that university support services and academic departments can use the online social networking sites to help students integrate into university life, and how the sites might be reshaping our everyday lives in terms of the importance of place-based versus virtual networking.

F Research results are expected to influence university policies at Leicester and beyond. 'It may affect the way the University uses its Facebook network,' said Dr Wellens. 'One outcome might be that the University would use these sites to bring new students together before their arrival, or to bring together current and new students to provide peer support. It will also ascertain students' views about the ways in which the University and its staff should, or shouldn't, use Facebook for academic purposes.'

Questions 7–10

Complete the sentences below.

Choose **NO MORE THAN TWO WORDS** from the passage for each answer.

7 Access to Facebook by students is happening at a ....

8 Few details exist on how much networking sites help students fit into ....

9 Most research has in the past focused on ....

10 One aim of the project is to determine if the length and nature of .... made online or face-to-face vary.

Questions 11–13

Do the following statements agree with the information in the reading passage?

Write:

TRUE	if the statement agrees with the information
FALSE	if the statement contradicts the information
NOT GIVEN	if there is no information on this

11 The only research methodology used at Leicester will be virtual interviews.

12 The Leicester team will focus on research from the UK rather the USA or Europe.

13 One possible development in the future is that existing students will help those who have just started university for the first time.

Reacting to the text

Do you think using websites such as Facebook to help students integrate into university life is a good idea? Why/Why not?

In terms of socializing, do these sites reduce or increase social contact?

Language focus 1: Present simple, present continuous and past simple

1 Scan (see Ready for Reading on page 84) the reading passage on page 9 as quickly as you can to find the following:

1 *This raised many issues such as where the boundary between ...*
2 *Student use of the online networking site Facebook is running at a phenomenal level ...*
3 *Yet we know little about how this phenomenon impacts on the student experience ...*
4 *The Leicester project builds on internationally acclaimed work ...*

2 In each of the sentences above, underline the main verbs and decide whether the present simple, present continuous or past simple tense is used.

3 Match the tenses in exercise 2 with an appropriate explanation **a–d**.

a These events/actions occur routinely and repeatedly.
b An action which is still going on and is not finished yet.
c The event occurred in the past at a definite time.
d This is always true, like a fact or a state.

Read more about the present simple, present continuous and past simple in the Grammar reference on page 219.

4 Complete sentences **1–6** below by putting the verb in brackets into the present simple, present continuous or past simple.

1 A mentor (help) new students integrate into university life. That is their function.
2 Fewer older people (participate) in social websites then compared to now.
3 The research (impact) on the way the new students were helped on their arrival at the university.
4 When I was young, my parents (influence) my attitude to education enormously.
5 Researchers (now recruit) students for academic research.
6 Each time I go on the net, I (feel) that the amount of information is overwhelming.

5 Scan the reading passage on page 9 and find the main verb in each sentence in exercise 4. Are they in the same tenses as in exercise 4? If not, what tense are they in?

What to expect in the exam

- In IELTS Listening Section 1 you will hear a conversation between two people once only. The recording tells you what the conversation is about. In this case it's a young woman answering an advert looking for help at a charity event.
- You will be given time to look at the questions before you begin and in the middle of the recording.
- At the end of the section you will be given time to check your answers.
- You will hear an example.
- See the introduction to Ready for Listening on page 42 for information about the different types of questions in IELTS Listening.

1 Look at questions **1–8** and predict whether the answer is a noun, name, number or adjective.

2 Which numbers do you find difficult to understand? Write down 5 sets of numbers, for example, *6633, 6363, 3663, 677 331, 3553*. Give them to a partner and ask him/her to dictate the numbers to you slowly and then quickly in any order. Write down the numbers you hear.

3 What letters do you find difficult to understand? Write them down then give them to a partner and ask him/her to dictate the letters to you in any order, for example, f-p-t-f-g-j-l-m-f-b-d. Write down the letters you hear.

4 Look at questions **9** and **10**. If you wanted someone to help you organize an event, what qualities would you want the person to have? Use the following questions to help you exclude some possibilities and predict the answer.

Is it desirable to:
- take risks or to be timid?
- be adaptable or obstinate?
- be on time or sometimes to be late?
- get on with people or dislike people?
- be good at sport or to be lazy?

How to go about it

- Underline the words in the questions that warn you that the answer is coming soon. Try to predict the answers.
- If the answer can be a word(s) or a number, read the questions to check which is required.
- Practise transferring your answers to an answer sheet. Be careful that you do not create mistakes during the transfer.
- Read the instructions carefully and note word limits.

1.1 **SECTION 1 Questions 1–10**

Questions 1–4
Complete the notes below.
Write no more than **ONE WORD AND/OR A NUMBER** for each answer.

Notes on Volunteering

Example	Answer
Event:	**Charity**

Venue: 1 .... Hall
Days: Friday to Sunday
Dates: 15th–17th 2 ....
Opening Time: 10 am
Closing time: 3 .... pm
Type of helpers now required: 4 ....

Questions 5–8

Complete the form below.

Write no more than **ONE WORD AND/OR A NUMBER** for each answer.

> Name: Andrea **5** ....
>
> Address: 90 **6** .... Mansions,
>
>   62 Park Avenue, London, SW1 4PQ
>
> Telephone: **7** ....
>
> Telephone in the: **8** ....

Questions 9 and 10

Choose **TWO** letters, **A–E**.

Which **TWO** types of people are mentioned as desirable?

A adventurous

B inflexible

C punctual

D friendly

E sporty

5 ⬤ Have you ever been in a situation where you had to explain your qualities or strengths? Describe the situation to a partner.

Language focus 2: Likes and dislikes

1 In the conversation in the listening practice, Andrea explains what kind of person she is by saying what she likes.
I like working with other people.
Why does she use the *- ing* form of the verb after *like*?

2 Work in pairs. For **1–7** below, decide which sentences are correct.

  1 Gabriella likes swimming a lot.
  2 John likes to get there on time. He doesn't like lateness.
  3 Would you like joining our study group?
  4 Why did you hate playing football as a child?
  5 Do you really dislike being in this country?
  6 My grandparents loved looking after us as kids.
  7 As Joseph is independent, he enjoys to do things alone.

Ⓖ Read more about likes and dislikes in the Grammar reference on page 219.

3 For sentences **1–9** below, put the verb in brackets into the correct form. More than one answer may be correct.

  1 Most of my friends dislike (play) computer games.
  2 I'd like (live) near the sea as the air is fresh.
  3 Certain animals hate (be) around people.
  4 He likes (keep) the garden tidy, even though it takes a lot of time.
  5 He enjoys (take) long walks on his own along the seashore.
  6 As she is punctual herself, she likes other people (be) on time.

  7 Sarah loves (socialize) with other people rather than (stay) at home alone.
  8 He can't stand (play) sport.
  9 Wouldn't you prefer (see) this film at the cinema?

4 Rewrite sentences **1–8** below using the verb in brackets. Do not change the meaning.

  1 The idea of living in the countryside appeals to me. (I'd like)
  2 Nowadays people don't seem to take any pleasure in doing certain sports. (dislike)
  3 Adrian cleans the kitchen every morning. (like)
  4 She gets enormous enjoyment from shopping. (enjoy)
  5 Pedro has a hatred of playing video games. (can't stand)
  6 He expects honesty in people he knows. (like)
  7 She wants to see the film on DVD at home, not in the cinema. (would prefer)
  8 He really likes to mingle with other people at parties. (love)

5 ⬤ Work in pairs. Ask your partner about two sports he/she likes doing and two sports he/she doesn't like doing. Use the questions below and ask for reasons and examples.

Why do you like/enjoy/dislike … ?
Why don't you like/enjoy … ?

6 ⬤ Are the sports your partner talked about popular in your country? Is the popularity of these sports increasing or decreasing? Why?

Speaking
IELTS Part 2

What to expect in the exam

- There are three parts in IELTS Speaking. In Part 2 you are asked to talk about a person, event, place, object, film, documentary etc …
- You will have to talk about the topic for one to two minutes.
- You will be given one minute to think about what you are going to say and make notes.

1 Look at the photographs below. Choose at least two adjectives to describe each of the adults. Use the adjectives in Vocabulary 1 on page 6.

How to go about it

- If you are asked to talk about a person, name the person. Try to visualize the person and an activity they do which you like.
- Use the minute you have to make brief notes. Develop your notes as you speak.
- Try to use the following words as you explain: *for example …, when/ if…, because…, and so…* .

2 Decide which person appeals to you most. Look at the adjectives you chose for the person and make notes for the following:

- what kind of person they are generally
- what he/she did when he/she was younger
- why he/she appeals to you
- what activities he/she is doing now

3 ⬤ Use your notes to tell your partner about the person.

4 Look at the following Part 2 task card. Decide which tense you are going to use for each part of the topic.

> Describe a person you would like to be similar to.
>
> You should say:
>
> who this person is
>
> what they are like generally
>
> what qualities this person has
>
> and explain why you would like to be similar to this person.

5 Spend one minute making brief notes.

6 ⬤ Work in pairs. Take turns talking about the topic, using your notes to guide you. You should speak for up to two minutes; time each other using a stopwatch.

Vocabulary 2: Verbs of movement

1 Work in pairs. Match the parts of the graph **1–10** with the verbs **a–j**.

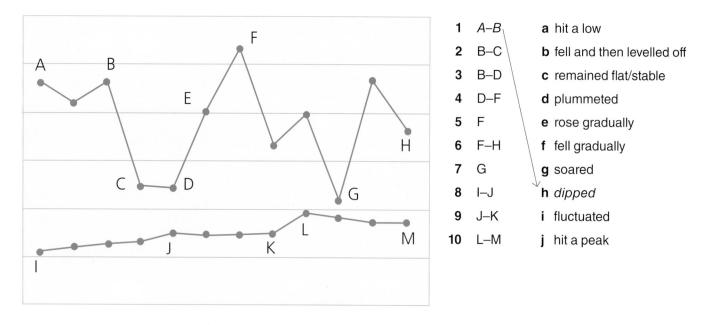

1	A–B	**a**	hit a low
2	B–C	**b**	fell and then levelled off
3	B–D	**c**	remained flat/stable
4	D–F	**d**	plummeted
5	F	**e**	rose gradually
6	F–H	**f**	fell gradually
7	G	**g**	soared
8	I–J	**h**	*dipped*
9	J–K	**i**	fluctuated
10	L–M	**j**	hit a peak

2 For sentences **1–10** below, use the verbs in exercise 1 to replace the underlined text.

1 The price of laptops <u>dropped followed by a period of stability</u>.
2 Numbers <u>reached a high</u> in the year 2009.
3 The amount of money spent <u>fell slightly and then quickly recovered</u>.
4 Visitor numbers to the website <u>plunged</u> in the first quarter of the year.
5 Book purchases <u>increased slowly but surely</u> over the year.
6 The number of students applying to the university <u>stabilized</u> over the decade.
7 Attendance at the conference <u>decreased steadily</u> last year.
8 The growth rate <u>was erratic</u> during the previous year.
9 Member numbers <u>reached their lowest point</u> in March.
10 Car sales <u>rocketed</u> over the period.

3 To add variety to your writing you can use nouns instead of verbs to describe movement. Look at the nouns in the box below and decide which ones are not correct.

> a drop   a plunge   a bottom out   an increase   stabilization
> fluctuations   a decline   a rocket   a soar   a plummet   a rise
> a dip   a fall   a level off   a climb   a peak   a surge

4 Rewrite the sentences from exercise 2 using nouns instead of verbs. Use the following structure: *There was a* (+ adjective) + noun + *in* … . For two of the sentences this is not possible. Make any other necessary changes.

Example:

There was a drop in the price of laptops followed by a period of stability.

Writing:
IELTS Task 1

What to expect in the exam

- In IELTS Writing Task 1 you will be asked to describe some data (graph, chart or table) or a diagram.
- You are asked to write at least 150 words.
- You should spend about 20 minutes on this task.

How to go about it

- Study the data carefully, noting any special features.
- Make sure you summarize rather than just list data.
- Always write an overview of the data. This can come after the introduction, or at the end as a conclusion.

1 Work in pairs. Read the Task 1 question below and the three introductions **a–c** which follow. Decide which is the best introduction and why.

WRITING TASK 1

You should spend about 20 minutes on this task.

> *The graph below provides a breakdown of the UK weekly market share of visits to three social networking websites between March 2007 and March 2008.*
>
> *Summarise the information by selecting and reporting the main features, and make comparisons where relevant.*

Write at least 150 words.

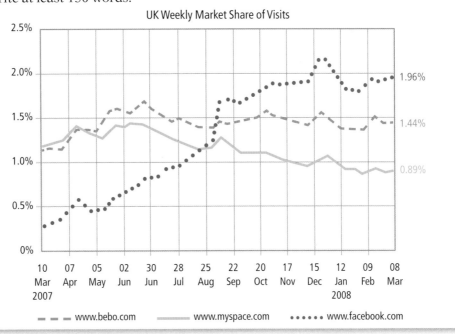

UK Weekly Market Share of Visits

- – – – www.bebo.com
- ——— www.myspace.com
- •••••• www.facebook.com

a The graph below shows in percentage terms the UK weekly market share of visits to three websites between March 2007 and March 2008.

b The chart below shows the percentage of hits to three websites over the period of a year.

c The chart illustrates the market share of hits to various social networking sites in the UK on a weekly basis over one year to March 2008.

2 Complete the gaps in the following model answer for the task with the correct form of a suitable verb. There may be more than one possible answer.

The graph **1** _____ the proportion of hits to three social networking sites on a weekly basis from 10th March 2007 to 8th March 2008.

Generally speaking, the trends in the market share of the three sites **2** _____ . The most viewed site **3** _____ clearly www.facebook.com, whose share of the market **4** _____ dramatically from approximately 0.25 per cent on 10th March 2007 to 1.96 per cent on 8th March 2008. This **5** _____ nearly an eightfold increase over the period. It **6** _____ noticeable that the market share of Facebook **7** _____ a high of around 2.2 per cent during December 2008, with peaks being hit by the other two sites during the same period.

The market share of hits to the bebo site, meanwhile, **8** _____ at a slower pace from about 1.2 to 1.44 per cent, a rise of approximately 40 per cent. In contrast to the other two websites, the market share of www.myspace.com **9** _____ , decreasing from approximately the same level as www.bebo.com on 10th March 2007 to 0.89 per cent.

3 Now cover the model answer above and make notes about what you remember about it. Then use your notes to write your own answer to the question.

Vocabulary

1 Match nouns **1–8** with an explanation **a–h**.

1	honesty	**a**	is about being happy and optimistic
2	punctuality	**b**	is about having a special gift or skill to do something
3	generosity	**c**	is about one's dreams and desires
4	cheerfulness	**d**	is about being able to depend on someone
5	reliability	**e**	is about being on time
6	ambition	**f**	is about enjoying the company of others
7	talent	**g**	is not just about money; it's about being kind as well
8	sociability	**h**	is about not telling lies

2 Complete the gaps in the following extracts from IELTS Speaking Part 2 with a suitable adjective. Then decide what the candidates were asked to describe.

'The person that I would like to be similar to is my father. At first he appears very serious, but he has a very **1** _____ side to him. He loves to make people laugh. His stories are usually about people and they are very funny, but he never says anything bad about the people. He is a very **2** _____ person and always takes everyone's feelings into consideration.'

'My elder brother is the sort of person who is always **3** _____ ; he is never late for anything, no matter how unimportant it is. He says that being on time when you are meeting someone is about showing them respect. So as you can imagine he is highly **4** _____ amongst his friends.'

'What really appeals to me about my grandfather is that he is very **5** _____ , as he has many gifts. He's very **6** _____ and he's always drawing. He can make anything with his hands and he can play the piano and violin as well. And when we were children he was very **7** _____ when he explained things to us; I never remember him losing his temper. I can honestly say that I have never met anyone as **8** _____ . You can depend on him for anything.'

Present simple, present continuous and past simple

1 Sentences **1–12** relate to four people: Sonja, Wei, Ahmed and Tony. Three sentences relate to each person. Read the sentences and decide which relate to each person.

1 As a child she dreamt of working as an air hostess, or a job dealing with people.

2 He built his own computer when he was in his teens.

3 When she was a child her grandfather taught her to paint.

4 Sonja can't stand chatting on computers; she enjoys socializing face to face.

5 Now she's working as a tour guide.

6 He is currently conducting research for a book on modern Chinese writers.

7 She is drawing a sketch, which she plans to turn into an oil painting soon.

8 Wei is very artistic and spends all her time in her studio painting and drawing.

9 He loves reading and any intellectual hobbies like music and philosophy.

10 He's very talented and is creating his own website at the moment.

11 Tony is a doctor of literature; he studied a huge amount of Chinese literature for his PhD.

12 Ahmed likes to spend his time and money on technology.

2 Decide whether each sentence **1–12** in exercise 1 tells you:

    a what activity the people are involved in at the moment

    b about their state of mind and habits

    c about their past

Writing

1 Complete sentences **1–10** with a word from the box below. Make any necessary changes.

surge	breakdown	fluctuate	remain steady	trend
decline	plummet	downward	show	noticeable

    1 The most _____ feature of the chart was the sharp fall in theatre attendances.

    2 The graph _____ the increase in the market share of Facebook compared to the other two sites.

    3 Shopper numbers _____ over most of the year, but the last three months were less erratic.

    4 There was a _____ in visitors to the site during the holiday period with numbers almost doubling.

    5 The amount of energy used _____ throughout the first nine months and then it began to increase.

    6 Sales _____ in September, hitting a low for the year.

    7 There was a gradual _____ in profits over last year.

    8 The trend for two of the sites was upward, with the other being clearly _____.

    9 There was very little difference in the _____ in sales for all five companies, with the exception of Sewell Ltd.

    10 The chart provides a _____ of the number of passenger miles travelled according to different modes of transport.

2 Use the words in **1–8** below to create sentences that provide a suitable overview for a Task 1 question. Make any necessary changes to the words.

Example:

book sales overall rise period

Overall book sales rose during the period.

    1 trend attendances clear upward

    2 increase student numbers over the year

    3 market share fall overall past decade

    4 trend cost train journeys flat generally speaking

    5 trend prices downward overall

    6 miles covered shoppers declined

    7 price of grain steady rise in the last six months

    8 clear downward trend flights abroad

②Technology–now and then

Vocabulary: Verbs of cause and effect

1 ⬤ Work in pairs. Look at the photographs and discuss the questions below.

- Name each item. What do you know about each one? What do they all have in common?
- Choose three of the items and decide how they have shaped people's lives.
- Which do you think have a direct influence on people's lives today? Give reasons and examples.

2 In academic writing sentences with nouns are more common than sentences with verbs. For some verbs the noun form is the same as the verb, for example, *influence*. You can also make nouns from verbs by adding endings like: *-ment, -ion* and *-ing*. Decide what the noun form is for each of the verbs **1–16** below. Which verb does not follow any of these patterns?

1 improve	*improvement*		**9** damage	_____
2 destroy	_____		**10** ruin	_____
3 shape	_____		**11** produce	_____
4 result	_____		**12** foster	_____
5 affect	_____		**13** advance	_____
6 harm	_____		**14** deteriorate	_____
7 enhance	_____		**15** achieve	_____
8 promote	_____		**16** attract	_____

3   Work in pairs. The verbs and nouns in exercise 2 can be used to describe changes in something. Decide if you would use each verb and noun to describe a positive change, a negative change, or a neutral change (one that is neither positive nor negative).

4   Rewrite sentences **1–9** below so that they contain the verb in brackets. Make any other necessary changes.

Example:

The use of mobile phones is having a dramatic effect on the way we communicate. (affect)

The use of mobile phones is dramatically affecting the way we communicate.

1   The demand for fuel is bringing about the destruction of the way of life of the inhabitants of rainforests. (destroy)
2   People constantly debate whether television has a positive or negative influence on society. (influence)
3   The company restructuring will lead to a significant improvement in profits. (improve)
4   Climate change has led to the ruin of many crops. (ruin)
5   The fire did not do as much harm to the mountainside as people first thought. (harm)
6   The conflict resulted in a sharp deterioration in relations between the two countries. (deteriorate)
7   The affair caused enormous damage to his reputation. (damage)
8   Artificial intelligence is having a huge impact on the development of technology. (impact)
9   Many people like Einstein and Newton changed the shape of the world. (shape)

5   For sentences **1–6** below, complete the gaps using the nouns in exercise 2.

1   Advertising companies increase sales through the _____tion of goods on TV.
2   Some pessimists argue that the human race's love of technology will eventually cause the _____tion of society.
3   _____ments in technology have gathered pace in recent years as the speed of computers has increased.
4   The greatest human _____ment is the invention of the wheel, not the computer.
5   What is the _____tion of the latest electronic gadgets for consumers?
6   Why is the _____ing of new ideas so crucial for developing new products?

Listening

IELTS Section 2

What to expect in the exam

- In IELTS Listening Section 2 you will hear a monologue (one person speaking), but sometimes you may hear one person answering questions. The topic is usually of general interest and there can be two or three sets of questions.
- You will be given time to look at the questions before you begin and in the middle of the recording.
- At the end of the section, you will be given time to check your answers.

The items listed in questions **16–20** on page 20 are in the order they appear in the monologue. You will probably not hear the same words and phrases, so you will have to listen for synonyms or paraphrases. Look at the adjectives listed in **A–F** and think of at least one synonym for each.

1.2 **SECTION 2** Questions 11–20

Questions 11–15

Choose the correct letter, **A**, **B** or **C**.

How to go about it

- You can use the questions to prepare yourself for the answers. For example, look at question 11, you can use the question to be ready to listen for 'how many prize winners there were'.
- If the different sections of the questions have headings, skim the headings and questions to get a general idea of the monologue.
- Underline words in the stem of the multiple-choice questions and alternatives which you think will help you listen for the answer. Most of the words you need to listen for are paraphrases or synonyms of these words.
- Do not underline the whole of the stem of the multiple-choice question. Mark only words like nouns, names, verbs or function words like *because*, which you think will tell you the answer is about to come.

Penwood Museum Competition

11 In the sixth summer show competition, there were

   A five prize winners.

   B four prize winners.

   C three prize winners.

12 The theme of this year's competition is

   A involving young people in the museum's activities.

   B forming better links between local people and the museum.

   C improving the local community's access to art appreciation.

13 The competition was open to those aged

   A 13–19.

   B 15–19.

   C 13–18.

14 During the preparation for the entry the competitors were

   A able to use the museum's educational facilities.

   B not permitted to use the museum's educational facilities.

   C allowed to buy any of the equipment they needed.

15 According to the speaker, the prize-winning exhibit has

   A had no influence at all on attendances.

   B led to a big reduction in attendances.

   C brought about an increase in attendances.

Questions 16–20

The Video Commentaries

What did the older people say about each piece of equipment?

Choose **FIVE** answers from the box and write the correct letter, **A–F** next to questions 16–20.

Comments
A too large
B boring
C more convenient
D exciting
E well-constructed
F still looked fashionable

Equipment

16 early wooden-framed TV   ....

17 early radios   ....

18 microwave ovens   ....

19 laptops   ....

20 old cameras   ....

How to go about it

- Some IELTS reading passages do not have a title. For these passages, look at the last question which will be a multiple-choice question. There are usually four alternatives. One alternative covers the whole passage and the others generally relate to parts of the passage, so they will give you an idea of what the passage is about.
- Skim the passage and the questions as quickly as you can. Remember the questions will give you a summary of the content of the passage.

READING PASSAGE

You should spend about 20 minutes on **Questions 1–13**, which are based on the reading passage below.

The long period of the Bronze Age in China, which began around 2000 B.C., saw the growth and maturity of a civilization that would be sustained in its essential aspects for another 2,000 years. In the early stages of this development, the process of urbanization went hand in hand with the establishment of a social order. In China, as in other societies, the mechanism that generated social cohesion, and at a later stage statecraft, was ritualization. As most of the paraphernalia for early rituals were made in bronze and as rituals carried such an important social function, it is perhaps possible to read into the forms and decorations of these objects some of the central concerns of the societies (at least the upper sectors of the societies) that produced them.

There were probably a number of early centers of bronze technology, but the area along the Yellow River in present-day Henan Province emerged as the center of the most advanced and literate cultures of the time and became the seat of the political and military power of the Shang dynasty (ca. 1600–1050 B.C.), the earliest archaeologically recorded dynasty in Chinese history. The Shang dynasty was conquered by the people of Zhou, who came from farther up the Yellow River in the area of Xi'an in Shaanxi Province. In the first years of the Zhou dynasty (ca. 1046–256 B.C.), known as the Western Zhou (ca. 1046–771 B.C.), the ruling house of Zhou exercised a certain degree of 'imperial' power over most of central China. With the move of the capital to Luoyang in 771 B.C., however, the power of the Zhou rulers declined and the country divided into a number of nearly autonomous feudal states with nominal allegiance to the emperor. The second phase of the Zhou dynasty, known as the Eastern Zhou (771–256 B.C.), is subdivided into two periods, the Spring and Autumn period (770–ca. 475 B.C.) and the Warring States period (ca. 475–221 B.C.). During the Warring States period, seven major states contended for supreme control of the country, ending with the unification of China under the Qin in 221 B.C.

Although there is uncertainty as to when metallurgy began in China, there is reason to believe that early bronze-working developed autonomously, independent of outside influences. The era of the Shang and the Zhou dynasties is generally known as the Bronze Age of China, because bronze, an alloy of copper and tin, used to fashion weapons, parts of chariots, and ritual vessels, played an important role in the material culture of the time. Iron appeared in China toward the end of the period, during the Eastern Zhou dynasty.

One of the most distinctive and characteristic images decorating Shang-dynasty bronze vessels is the so-called taotie. The primary attribute of this frontal animal-like mask is a prominent pair of eyes, often protruding in high relief. Between the eyes is a nose, often with nostrils at the base. Taotie can also include jaws and fangs, horns, ears, and eyebrows. Many versions include a split animal-like body with legs and tail, each flank shown in profile on either side of the mask. While following a general form, the appearance and specific components of taotie masks varied by period and place of production. Other common motifs for Shang ritual bronze vessels were dragons, birds, bovine creatures, and a variety of geometric patterns. Currently, the significance of the taotie, as well as the other decorative motifs, in Shang society is unknown.

Jade, along with bronze, represents the highest achievement of Bronze Age material culture. In many respects, the Shang dynasty can be regarded as the culmination of 2,000 years of the art of jade carving. Shang craftsmen had full command of the artistic and technical language developed in the diverse late Neolithic cultures that had a jade-working tradition. On the other hand, some developments in Shang and Zhou jade carving can be regarded as evidence of decline. While Bronze Age jade workers no doubt had better tools – if only the advantage of metal ones – the great patience and skill of the earlier period seem to be lacking.

If the precise function of ritual jades in the late Neolithic is indeterminate, such is not the case in the Bronze Age. Written records and archaeological evidence inform us that jades were used in sacrificial offerings to gods and ancestors, in burial rites, for recording treaties between states, and in formal ceremonies at the courts of kings.

How to go about it

For questions **1–6**:
- Look for words and paraphrases of words that will help you scan for the answer.

For questions **7–12**:
- Find the words *bronze*, *taotie* and *jade* in the passage and put a box around them, so you can see them easily.
- Read the statements and underline the information to scan for.
- Scan the passage for words and paraphrases of words in the questions.

For question **13**:
- Look for the title that focuses on all the information in the text and not just part of it.

Questions 1–6

Do the following statements agree with the information given in the reading passage?

Write:

TRUE	if the statement agrees with the information
FALSE	if the statement contradicts the information
NOT GIVEN	if there is no information on this

1 As the migration of people to towns and cities took place, Chinese society became more unified.

2 According to evidence that has been unearthed, the Zhou people lost power to the Shang.

3 At the end of the Zhou dynasty, there were nine powers seeking to rule China.

4 Iron was introduced to China from outside.

5 There was only one type of taotie.

6 There is some proof that later jade carving was superior to earlier examples.

Questions 7–12

Classify the following descriptions as relating to

    A Bronze

    B Taotie

    C Jade

List of Descriptions

7 Its decoration depended on when and where it was made.

8 Its meaning in one period of history is still a mystery.

9 Its decoration illustrates issues with which the elite in China dealt with.

10 It was not worked with the same degree of sophistication as in previous times.

11 It sprang up spontaneously without any help from beyond China.

12 The time when it was first produced is not known.

Question 13

Choose the correct letter **A**, **B**, **C** or **D**.

Which of the following is the most suitable title for the reading passage?

    A The importance of jade carvings

    B The Chinese Bronze Age

    C The decline of the Bronze Age

    D How iron was introduced to China

Reacting to the text

'History has nothing to teach us, so there is no point dwelling on the past.'

Do you agree with the statement? Does ancient history have any relevance today?

Language focus 1: Past simple and present perfect

1 Look at the verb tenses in the reading passage on page 21 and answer the following questions:

- Which tense is used more often: the past simple or the present perfect? Why do you think this is?

- Which is more common, the active or the passive voice? Why?

Read more about how the tenses are used in the Grammar reference on page 220.

2 For sentences **1–8** below, decide if the verb in brackets should be active or passive. Then put it into the past simple.

  1 The invention of the plough (revolutionize) agriculture.
  2 What (contribute) to the rapid pace of change in the world in the 20th century?
  3 The impact of a comet (lead) to the extinction of the dinosaurs.
  4 Chess first (play) in India.
  5 The radio (invent) in Italy by Marconi.
  6 When people (create) cities, it (shape) the way the human race (live) forever.
  7 Before the advent of mechanized transport, people (travel) for days between countries.
  8 The mountainous landscape in Greece (influence) the development of ancient city states.

3 For sentences **1–8** below, underline the correct verb form in brackets.

  1 Not long ago, I (began/have begun/was begun) to study another language.
  2 When we (were/have been) young, we (had/didn't have/haven't had) many toys, but children nowadays (became/have become/have been become) used to having lots of toys and games.
  3 Recently, companies (started/have started/have been started) thinking about moving into space tourism.
  4 In the middle of the 20th century, new materials like plastic (transformed/have transformed/have been transformed) kitchenware.

5 I first (went/have gone/have been gone) to South America in the early seventies, but I (never visited/have never visited/have never been visited) Asia.

6 (Did you ever see/Have you ever seen/Did you ever seen) the Northern Lights?

7 In the past five years, survival rates for people with certain illnesses (improved/have improved/have been improved).

8 Yesterday, I (did/have done/have been done) something I (did not do/have not done/have not been done) before. I (spent/have spent/have been spent) the whole day reading a novel.

4 Write five statements about yourself, using the structure *I have never … , but I …* and the time phrases below.

    The day before yesterday …

    Three days/weeks ago …

    Last week/month/year …

    The week before last …

Example:

I have never been to a gym/the theatre on my own, but yesterday I went to the cinema for the first time by myself.

5 Work in pairs. Tell your partner your sentences. Then ask each other questions to find out more details. Use the following words in your questions: *when, why, why not, what, how, how long.*

Word building: Qualifying adjectives

1 In IELTS Writing Task 2, IELTS Speaking Part 3 and IELTS Listening it is important
be able to qualify ideas and recognize when ideas are being qualified. In the listening
practice on page 20 you heard people using adjectives like *too big, stylish* and *handy* to
make positive or negative comments about objects. For each adjective **1–12** below, write
the opposite form in the correct column of the table.

	in-/im-	un-	-less
1 convenient	*inconvenient*		
2 practical			
3 important			
4 necessary			
5 significant			
6 harmful			
7 valuable			
8 useful			
9 effective			
10 appealing			
11 worthwhile			
12 inspiring			

2 Decide which of the words below are synonyms for the word *important*.

crucial   pointless   vital   essential   empty   key   critical

3 Decide which of the words below is a synonym for the word *unimportant*.

trivial   harmless   worthless   insignificant

4 For sentences **1–6** below, decide which adjective from exercise 1 can be used to replace
the <u>underlined</u> words. Make any necessary changes.

Example:

Many of the early technologies we take for granted are <u>those that we cannot do without</u>.

necessary

1 Some ideas from the 1950s were <u>not very sensible
or easy to use</u>.

2 Using hydrogen cars to combat global warming is a
solution <u>that produces the desired result</u>.

3 Underground transport systems built in the 19th
century are still <u>easy to use</u> for commuters.

4 The coordination skills learnt when doing practical
work like making things by hand proved to be
<u>extremely useful</u> for young people.

5 Instead of being an activity <u>which does no harm</u>,
playing computer games can cause emotional
damage to young players.

6 The work of people like Louis Daguerre, who
shaped the world of cinema, can only be considered
as <u>stimulating and motivating</u> to later generations.

Language focus 2: Habit in the past

1 Look at the following statements from the listening practice on page 20.

They remembered how they would all go round to ... ,

... all of whom used to have one ...

Statements **a–c** below explain the reasons why we use *would* and *used to* to talk about the past. Decide which statements describe why they are used in the examples above.

a Like the simple past, *would* and *used to* show repeated actions/activities that no longer happen.

b *Would* is used for reminiscing about the past.

c *Used to* is used to talk about states that no longer exist, while *would* is only used to describe repeated actions/activities. *Would* is not usually used in negative or *yes/no* questions.

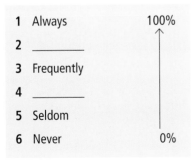 Read more about *would* and *used* to in the Grammar reference on page 220.

2 For **1–8** below decide which sentences are correct. Then decide why the incorrect sentences are wrong.

1 I would work at the post office during holidays when I was young.

2 Students used to play silly games, but they would never hurt anyone.

3 My father would work as a lawyer, but he didn't do it for long.

4 People in my hometown would hold lots of parties at all times of the year.

5 My uncle used to mend machinery and would even build his own car.

6 My brothers and sisters didn't use to go to university. They went straight into work after secondary school.

7 As a rule, people left their doors unlocked; there never used to be any break-ins.

8 People didn't use to throw things out rather than mending them, as they do now.

Adverbs of frequency

1 Look at the following sentence from the listening practice on page 20 and underline the adverb of frequency. Decide where this word fits in the line below showing adverbs of frequency.

They remembered how they would sometimes all go round to someone's house to watch TV as a special treat.

1	Always	100%
2	_____	
3	Frequently	
4	_____	
5	Seldom	
6	Never	0%

2 Complete the remaining gap in the line with a suitable adverb of frequency.

3 Decide where on the line you can add the words in the box below.

occasionally	often	not often	normally
regularly	hardly ever	rarely	commonly

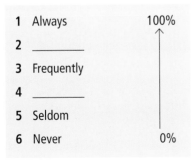 Read more about adverbs of frequency in the Grammar reference on page 220.

4 For questions **1–8** below, decide if the adverb of frequency in *italics* is suitable. Replace the adverbs that are not suitable.

1 I *always* read the newspaper in the morning. I only read it in the afternoon.

2 I would *sometimes* play games with my friends in the summer evenings. We used to meet up about five times a week.

3 I have *never* liked any computer games, but as a teenager I would play board games.

4 Governments *seldom* listen to their people. It happens only once in a while.

5 Where I come from, people *usually* tend to greet each other in the street each time they meet, but sometimes they don't.

6 In some parts of the world people have *hardly* ever left their villages, maybe only once in a lifetime.

7 When I was a child I *often* used to watch my grandfather working; as a rule nearly every day.

8 At school, I would *always* do my homework on time. I was never late.

5 Write a sentence about your childhood and early life for each of the sentence beginnings below.

Example:

I would ...

I would go to the river near my home rather than sit at home all day in front of a machine.

1 I used to ...

2 I would sometimes ...

3 I used to always ...

4 I would hardly ever ...

1 Work in pairs. Look at the following Part 2 task card and make notes.

> Describe something which you have made.
>
> You should say:
>
> what it was
>
> when you made it
>
> how you felt about making it
>
> and explain why you made it.

2 Compare your notes with another pair. Consider the following:

- The number of words in your notes

- Are your notes easy to read at a glance? Why/Why not?

3 ◯ Work in pairs. Take turns talking about the topic, using your notes to guide you. You should speak for up to two minutes; time each other using a stopwatch. When your partner has finished speaking, give him/her feedback using the checklist on page 210.

Writing:
IELTS Task 2

What to expect in the exam

- In IELTS Writing Task 2 you will be asked to write an essay about a topic of general interest.
- You are asked to write at least 250 words.
- You should spend about 40 minutes on this task.

1 Work in pairs. Read the Task 2 question below and answer questions **1–10** which follow.

How to go about it

- Two different views are expressed in the question. On a piece of paper, make two columns A and B. Choose one of the views and write a list of ideas in column A in one to two minutes. Do not exclude any ideas. Then write a list of opposing views in column B. Select one or two ideas from each column.

- Express your own opinions by either balancing the two views or supporting one view.

- Write an introduction that paraphrases the question. Keep the introduction brief - two to three sentences is enough.

WRITING TASK 2

You should spend about 40 minutes on this task.

Write about the following topic:

> *Some people fear that technology is gradually taking over control of our lives, while others think that it has led to many positive developments in all aspects of their lives.*
>
> *Discuss both these views and give your own opinion.*

Give reasons for your answer and include any relevant examples from your own knowledge or experience.

Write at least 250 words.

1 Is it crucial to write more than 250 words?
2 Do you need to give reasons and examples to support your answer? Should the examples be personal or abstract?
3 Can you give results, causes and effects and express reservations to support your answer?
4 Is there an upper and lower limit to the number of paragraphs you can write?
5 How many parts are there in the above question?
6 How many ideas do you need to write about?
7 Can you state your opinion in the first paragraph?
8 How long should each paragraph be?
9 Is there only one way to answer the question?
10 What are complex sentences? How do you write them?

2 Work in pairs. Look at the following introductions to an answer to the question. Decide which two are suitable and why.

1 *Technology is now used in all areas of our lives: the home, at work and in education. Most people use computers every day.*

2 *Some people fear that technology is gradually taking control of our lives. Others think that it has led to many positive developments in all areas of their lives.*

3 *In some people's eyes the influence of technology over our lives is beneficial and yet to others it is harmful. The arguments on both sides are valid, but there is, in my opinion, little to be anxious about regarding the use of technology.*

4 *As with any development, people worry about how new technology will affect their lives. There are, however, many people who see the benefits of technology, and so are in favour of its use.*

3 The paragraph below continues the argument from one of the introductory paragraphs in exercise 2. Read the paragraph and match it to an introduction.

To some people technology appears to be controlling people's lives. **However,** I feel the overwhelming effect is beneficial, **because** technology **like** computers, mobile phones etc. has brought enormous improvements to many people's lives worldwide. Take, **for example,** the impact technology has had on communication. Computers have revolutionized the way items **such as** letters, messages and packages are sent. A quick message, **for instance,** can be transmitted between New York and Beijing in seconds either by text message or by email. **Moreover,** very large files such as reports and even whole books that were once sent by post can now be transmitted **in order to** save time and money. **As a result,** the economy benefits.

4 Put each of the linking words in **bold** in exercise 3 into the correct box in the table below.

	Example	Reason	Result	Additional information	Purpose	Contrast
Adverb						
Conjunction						
Other						

5 Decide what other words can be used to indicate examples and add them to the table.

6 Decide which words in the box below can be used to replace the words in exercise 3 and 4 and add them to the table.

but	although	since	as	similarly	furthermore
consequently	despite	so	therefore	accordingly	
what is more	also	and so	to		

7 Write your own answer for the Task 2 question in exercise 1. When you have finished, check your answer using the checklist on page 209.

Vocabulary

Complete the gaps in **1–8** below with a suitable word. There may be more than one possible answer.

1 How have young people been _____ by video games?

2 What do you think has been the greatest _____ in the world in recent years?

3 Who do you think has done the most to _____ the world in the past 50 years?

4 What is the _____ of overusing computers?

5 Has technology _____ the way we live?

6 What has been the most crucial _____ in your life in the past year?

7 Do you believe that as human beings we are _____ the planet?

8 What do you think you can do to _____ your career?

Word building

1 Complete the following qualifying adjectives from page 24.

1 c _____ t

2 s _____ t

3 u _____ g

4 n _____ y

5 w _____ s

6 a _____ g

7 h _____ s

8 i _____ e

9 c _____ l

10 i _____ t

2 For **1–6** below, underline the correct adjective in *italics*.

1 The restrictions on car movements are *harmless/harmful* to the economy.

2 In some ways using technology is dangerous, but by and large it is very *useful/detrimental*.

3 Many people thought the film was rather *inspiring/dull,* but the critics felt it was just very ordinary.

4 Training courses need to teach relevant practical skills, but in most cases they are totally *practical/impractical*.

5 Learning to read efficiently is *crucial/unimportant* in today's world, but unfortunately not enough is being done to improve people's skills.

6 Do you think it is *necessary/inconvenient* to know how things work or are made? Or is it unnecessary in the modern world?

Past simple and present perfect

In three of the sentences below the <u>underlined</u> phrases need to change places. Decide which three sentences need to be changed and correct them. Make any necessary changes.

Example:

I <u>have listened</u> to the radio yesterday, but I <u>didn't listen</u> to it this morning.

I <u>listened</u> to the radio yesterday, but I <u>haven't listened</u> to it this morning.

1 I <u>have played</u> the piano yesterday at home, but I <u>didn't play</u> it today yet.

2 I <u>have never eaten</u> dates, but I <u>had</u> figs for the first time a few days ago.

3 More new inventions <u>have been created</u> since 1900 than <u>were created</u> at any time before then.

4 Although the latest developments in technology <u>affected</u> the way we live, I think the wheel <u>has made</u> a greater impact when it was invented.

5 Many people throughout the ancient world <u>developed</u> ideas that <u>have influenced</u> modern education more than is realized.

6 My grandfather <u>has designed</u> a new type of car engine when he was in his twenties. I <u>designed</u> one too as part of the engineering course I'm doing.

Habit in the past

In the following extract from IELTS Speaking Part 2, <u>underline</u> the five mistakes in the verbs and verb phrases in *italics*. Then decide what the candidate was asked to describe.

'The place I'd like to describe is my hometown, where I lived until I was ten years old. I **1** *hadn't visited* my hometown for the last 15 years. So recently I **2** *decided* to pay a short visit. I can't say that I **3** *would know* what to expect. Fields where I **4** *would play* with my friends **5** *were now covered* with buildings and the school I **6** *would attend* is no longer there. It **7** *has been turned into* a supermarket. A lot of famous people **8** *used to attend* the school, so I am surprised that permission **9** *was given* to knock it down.

If I remember rightly, it **10** *would rain* a lot when I was a child, but **11** *it has never seemed* to annoy us kids. We **12** *have just carried on* regardless.

Spelling check

As quickly as you can, look at the following lists of words and ⓒircle the correct spelling.

1	convenent	convenient	convenient
2	whorthwhile	worthwhile	worthwile
3	appealing	apealing	apealling
4	ineffectiv	inefective	ineffective
5	useful	usfull	usefull
6	unecessary	unnecessary	unnecesary
7	impractical	inpractical	impracticel

③ Thrill seekers

Vocabulary: Sports

1 ⬭ With a partner, describe what is happening in each of the photographs. Then discuss the questions below.

- Do any of these activities appeal to you? Why/Why not?
- Which activity do you think is the most exciting/popular/risky?
- What is the attraction of extreme sports compared with activities such as playing computer games or reading?

2 For **1–8** in the table below decide what sport is connected with the place and the equipment. There may be more than one possible answer.

Sport	Place	Equipment
1	pitch	ball/goal
2	ring	gloves/shorts
3	track	shoes/spikes
4	gym	weights
5	pool	costume
6	sea reefs	oxygen tank
7	court	racquet/ball
8	course	clubs/irons

3 Work in pairs. Give at least one example of each type of sport in **1–10** below. You may use a dictionary to help you, if necessary.

1 motor	**3** water	**5** racquet	**7** winter	**9** outdoor
2 field	**4** combat	**6** equestrian	**8** indoor	**10** team

Listening
IELTS Section 3

What to expect in the exam

- In IELTS Listening Section 3 there can be two or more speakers having a discussion about a subject of an academic nature. You need to concentrate and learn to recognize who is speaking.
- At the beginning of the recording the topic of the conversation is mentioned.
- You will be given time to look at the questions before you begin and in the middle of the recording.
- At the end of the section you will be given time to check your answers.

How to go about it

Skim the questions to get an idea of the content of what you will hear.

Mark any specific information in tables, for example, numbers, nouns, headings etc.

- Try to decide the type of word that is required, for example, noun, verb etc. Also try to decide whether nouns are singular or plural.

- Check the number of words required.

- Do not write any words from the questions on the answer sheet. For example, if the question is, 'in the ....' and the correct answer is answer is *morning*, the answer *in the morning* would be wrong.

🔘 1.3 **SECTION 3 Questions 21–30**

Question 21

Choose the correct letter, **A**, **B** or **C**.

21 The initial purpose of the case study was to look only at the club's

    A health and safety policy.

    B sporting achievements.

    C management structure.

Questions 22–25

Complete the notes below.

Write **NO MORE THAN TWO WORDS AND/OR A NUMBER** for each answer.

Stars Club Case Study

Club background

- 600 members overall
- 23 staff including **22** .... workers

So far interviewed around **23** ....

Face-to-face interviews preferable to a questionnaire

Would be able to ask for **24** .... where necessary

Good administration/very focused managers

Management group has team **25** ....

Being there is an exhilarating experience

Questions 26–30

Complete the table below.

Write **NO MORE THAN TWO WORDS** for each answer.

Reasons for Club's Success

Reasons	Comments by researchers	Purpose
funding from government, private **26** .... and	crucial	to pay for facilities, **27** .... and time off work
quality of **28**	professional	encouraging people to reach their **29** ....
motivation and **30** .... of athletes	thrilling	to become the best in their field

Language focus 1: Comparison

1 Look at the following extract from the listening practice on page 31.

a *... what's made it (the club) more successful than other local clubs ...*

This can be rewritten as:

b *... why it (the club) has had more success than other local clubs*

or

c *... why it (the club) has succeeded more than ...*

Look at sentences **a–c** above and decide whether each one uses a noun, verb or adjective to make a comparison. Why is the comparative of the adjective formed with the word *more*?

🔘 Read more about comparison in the Grammar reference on page 220.

2 Complete the table below.

Adjective	Comparative	Superlative
		the worst
	better	
noisy		
wet		
tasty		
cheap		
lively		
appetizing		

3 For **1–8** below, put the word in brackets into the correct comparative or superlative form.

1 It's much (easy) to find places to do specialist sports outside cities and towns.

2 Activities like bowling are far (popular) among older age groups.

3 Which sport do you think is (energetic) of all?

4 People who do some physical activity are supposed to be (happy) than less active people.

5 It is becoming (difficult) for people to organize their lives around leisure activities nowadays.

6 Is work (stressful) aspect of modern life?

7 Is mental activity (important) than physical activity?

8 People don't realize that racing drivers are (fit) individuals in sport.

4 Work in pairs. Look at sentences **1–8** in exercise 3 and decide what the noun is for each adjective.

5 Rewrite sentences **1–8** in exercise 3 using a noun instead of an adjective. Make any necessary changes.

Example:

1 It's much (easy) to find places to do specialist sports outside cities and towns.

Places to do specialist sports can be found with more ease outside cities and towns.

6 The questionnaire below contains some mistakes. Rewrite the questions that are incorrect.

Do you agree that ...

1 football is exciting than swimming?

2 athletics is the most boring activity to watch on TV?

3 extreme sports like sky-diving are dangerouser than hiking?

4 you need to be fiter to go cycling than walking?

5 table tennis is not most exciting sport in the world?

6 people are lazier nowadays than they were in the past?

7 rowing is a sport only for richest people?

8 tennis is more exhilarating than skiing?

9 watching sport on TV or the Internet is less exciting than seeing it live?

10 racquet sports like squash and tennis are tiring than many other sports?

7 🔘 Use the questionnaire to interview other students in your class. Ask for reasons and examples. If someone agrees with a statement, put a tick (✓) next to the question.

Word building: Adjectives ending in *-ing / -ed*

In the listening practice on page 31, Marcello says:

It's a really exhilarating experience being there. I can't wait to go in every day.

The adjective *exhilarating* comes from the verb *exhilarate*. There are two types of adjectives that can be made from the verb:

- Verb + *-ing*: *exhilarating*   *Something is **exhilarating** if it makes me feel **exhilarated**.*

- Verb + *-ed*: *exhilarated*   *I feel **exhilarated** because something is **exhilarating**.*

Adjectives ending in *-ing/-ed* like *exhilarating* and *exhilarated* are used to evaluate or express an opinion about something. Like the speaker in the listening practice you can use adjectives like this in your speaking and writing to express your judgement about an idea, event, experience etc.

1 For **1–8** below, <u>underline</u> the correct adjective in *italics*.

    1 Do you find sports like mountaineering and parkour *thrilling/thrilled* to watch?

    2 Do you think people get *irritating/irritated* by the constant encouragement to do something physical?

    3 Why do you think people are *interesting/ interested* in extreme sports?

    4 Do you think sports stars are as *motivating/motivated* for young people now as in the past?

    5 What makes funfair rides like roller coasters *exciting/excited*?

    6 Are you the sort of person who considers sports programmes on TV *annoying/annoyed,* or do you get *annoying/annoyed* by other types of programmes?

    7 Do you think extreme sports are more *challenging/challenged* than other sports?

    8 Do you feel *invigorated/invigorating* when you do any type of energetic activity?

2 ⬭ Work in pairs. Choose three questions from exercise 1 to ask your partner. Take turns asking and answering the questions. Give reasons and examples in your answers.

3 Work in pairs. For **1–8** below, use a form of the word in brackets (noun, verb or adjective) to complete the sentences.

    1 It is rare to see a whole stadium (electrify) by a player's performance.

    2 These days I don't think young people feel (challenge) enough physically at school or work.

    3 Where I come from people find football more (interest) than other sports.

    4 Some sports like snowboarding and skateboarding seem to hold some (fascinate) for young people.

    5 Being (motivate) to take up some activity, however gentle, is not always easy.

    6 The thrill of modern computer games is as (excite) as some real sports.

    7 People often feel (refresh) after doing strenuous physical exercise.

    8 Other people may find as much (excite) in reading a book as in climbing a mountain.

Speaking
IELTS Part 1

What to expect in the exam

- In IELTS Speaking Part 1 you will be asked about familiar topics, for example, common pastimes in your country now compared with the past.
- In Part 1 the discussion is more personal and less abstract than in Parts 2 and 3.

1   Make examiner's questions from the following lists of words.

    1   what/kinds/sports/popular/your country?

    2   they/as popular/used be/in past?

    3   are/same games/popular/as in past?

    4   do/young people/more physical activities/extreme sports/now past?

    5   what/makes/these games/interesting/people?

    6   sports/challenging/now than/they in the past

    7   young people/challenged more/nowadays in the past?

2   ◯   Work in pairs. Take turns playing the role of the examiner and the candidate. Ask and answer the questions. Try to use some of the adjectives from the Word building section on page 33.

Reading
IELTS Reading Passage

Don't forget!

- If there is no title, look at the last question to get an idea of the content of the passage.

What to expect in the exam

- IELTS reading passages may be unique but they follow certain patterns like cause and effect, problem and solution, historical development and argument and explanation. The patterns that you will come across in IELTS are limited, but the content is unlimited.
- To achieve a high score you need to learn to be familiar with and recognize how writers organize information as this helps you see the patterns of organization of reading passages, for example, cause and effect. See Ready for Reading on page 91.

Work in pairs. Look at the photograph. Describe what kinds of rides you would expect to find in an amusement park or fairground.

READING PASSAGE

You should spend about 20 minutes on **Questions 1–13**, which are based on the reading passage below.

Readers can join a unique experiment to discover what goes on in our brains and bodies at the fairground.
Roger Highfield reports.

A   For decades, thrill-seekers have happily queued to experience a few seconds of the adrenaline-spiking, intestine-twisting thrills of roller coaster and other funfair joy rides. Nowadays, people also spend hours living out the virtual excitement of computer games.

B   An experiment will soon lay bare the science of thrills and help to build the foundation of the next generation of funfair rides and sensational computer games. Brendan Walker, a self-proclaimed 'thrill engineer', is curating this extraordinary venture where people can become a guinea pig. Fairground: Thrill Laboratory, at the Science Museum's Dana Centre, will include three different rides over three weeks – the Booster, to measure the physiology of excitement and thrill; a ghost train, to measure fear and the tingle of anticipation; and Miami Trip, a gentler ride designed to explore pleasure.

C One of the collaborators in the thrill lab is Prof Tom Rodden. Its impetus is the blurring of the boundary between the real and the digital worlds, he explained: today, trainers count footsteps, wrist watches can measure heart rate, satellites can detect where we are and, all the while, computer games are being played in the streets not just the living room, and computer accessories such as joysticks are being replaced with real-world objects such as tennis racquets.

D Doctors already understand the broad effects of joy rides. As a roller coaster puts the body through weightlessness, high gravitational forces and acceleration, the brain struggles to make sense of conflicting and changing signals from the senses. There are effects on the vestibular system, located in the inner ear, that detects position and motion, and on the somatic nervous system, which controls voluntary systems in the body, such as heartbeat.

E Added to the confusion of these signals are the messages from the eye, which may be different from those of the other systems. This can lead to peculiar effects such as the vection illusion (think of when you are stopped at a traffic light and the car next to you edges forward – you feel as though you are moving).

F Overall the brain responds to an exhilarating ride by triggering the release of a potent cocktail of biochemicals to deal with the body's stress, including more adrenaline (epinephrine) and norepinephrine which can suppress pain and boost the glow of euphoria that follows. The result can be pleasure but can also be nausea. Military and Nasa researchers have studied the problem for half a century, calling it 'simulator sickness'.

G But engineers and scientists have not figured out how to fool the senses at the same rate at the same time. They still don't know for sure who might get sick. Meanwhile, the latest rides are pushing the boundaries of endurance. The human body cannot take much more of a G-force than the latest rollercoasters, so we need to understand more about what distinguishes a spine-tingling thrill from a gut-emptying fright to ensure the experience is memorable for the right reasons.

H At the thrill lab volunteers will be asked to try the fairground rides while hooked up to special equipment. This includes an accelerometer that measures the G-force their body is subjected to; a measure of blood oxygen levels; measures of skin conductance (sweating) and an ECG monitor that keeps track of their heart rate. In addition, a helmet-mounted video camera will film their expressions, from the first gasp to the last scream. As with astronauts and test pilots, information will be beamed in real time to a computer. And measurements will be displayed publicly. Aside from providing amusement for onlookers, participants can relive their terrifying experiences.

I This study will help designers of amusement parks to squeeze more shrieks out of people by creating the illusion of imminent death, said Prof Rodden. Equally, the next generation of rides will sense when too many people feel nauseous and wind down accordingly. In short, they will be able to distinguish terror from titillation. This work will also help computer games to escape the boundaries of the Xbox and PlayStation. Steve Benford, of the mixed-reality lab at the University of Nottingham, believes that the thrill lab will help to design more immersive rides and games, 'real-time adaptive spaces.'

How to go about it

or questions **1–6**:

Read the instructions carefully. In this instance, you can use any letter more than once.

Check if any of the information in the phrases looks as if it might fit together in the same paragraph.

Check if any pieces of information will follow other information in the list.

Questions 1–6

The reading passage has nine paragraphs, **A–I**.

Which paragraph contains the following information?

NB You may use any letter more than once.

1 the impact on the human auditory system

2 what the lab experiments will show onlookers

3 the purpose of having different test rides

4 the various types of medical apparatus employed to monitor the research

5 the substances produced in reaction to thrilling rides

6 specific assistance to those designing amusement parks in the future

Questions 7–12

Do the following statements agree with the information given in the reading passage?

Write:

> **TRUE**   if the statement agrees with the information
>
> **FALSE**   if the statement contradicts the information
>
> **NOT GIVEN**   if there is no information on this

7 More people now get thrills from computer games than fairground rides.

8 The brain has difficulty understanding the messages sent from the senses during rollercoaster rides.

9 Simulator sickness has been under investigation by a large number of researchers.

10 The most recent rollercoasters take the human body further than their G-force limits.

11 The lab volunteers will consist of equal numbers of men and women.

12 Future rides will be able to adapt to people's reactions.

Question 13

Choose the correct letter **A**, **B**, **C**, or **D**.

13 Which of the following is the most suitable title for the reading passage?

   A Roller coasters and their effects on the brain

   B What makes fairground rides so thrilling?

   C The equipment used to test the efficacy of funfair rides

   D How the brain copes with fear in response to funfair rides

⬭ Reacting to the text

Do you find roller coasters 'thrilling'? Why/Why not?

Why do you think people enjoy extreme rides?

Language focus 2: Adjectives with prepositions

1 For **1–10** below, underline the correct preposition in *italics* .

   1 I am very keen *about/on/for* swimming, especially first thing in the morning.
   2 Some people are addicted *by/with/to* sports, they spend all their time glued to the TV.
   3 He's mad *for/to/about* parachuting. It's something I personally can't understand.
   4 I'm not interested *in/by/with* going to the gym.
   5 I easily get bored *in/about/with* doing nothing.
   6 I can't say I'm indifferent *in/to/about* sport, but I don't like spending my time watching it.
   7 I used to be very enthusiastic *on/about/with* team sports, but not any more.
   8 I'm not sure I'm capable *to/for/of* running for long distances.
   9 I'm really passionate *for/about/on* travelling around the world and meeting fellow hockey enthusiasts.

10 I am fond *about/to/of* travelling but my brother is fanatical *for/about/with* visiting new places.

   ⬭ Read more about adjectives with prepositions in the Grammar reference on page 221.

2 Work in pairs. Match the sentence beginnings **1–7** with the endings **a–g**. It is possible to match two of the sentence beginnings with more than one ending.

1	I am mad	a	to any kind of physical activity.
2	I am not keen	b	about playing computer games.
3	I am bored	c	on team sports.
4	I am interested	d	in walking in the countryside.
5	I am passionate	e	with watching sport on TV.
6	I am fond	f	about doing all kinds of exercise.
7	I am indifferent	g	of reading the sports pages in the newspaper.

3 Look at questions **1–6** in the table below and <u>underline</u> the answer which is most suitable for you. If none are suitable, write your own answer in the 'other' box.

1 Which sport do you like the most?	football	horse-riding	swimming	other:
2 Who do you prefer doing it with?	a colleague	a friend	nobody	other:
3 How often do like doing it?	once a week	twice a week	three times a week	other:
4 When do you normally like to do it?	mornings	afternoons	evenings	other:
5 How would you describe your attitude to the sport?	interested	enthusiastic	addicted	other:
6 Why do you enjoy doing it?	challenging	exciting	exhilarating	other:

4 ⬭ Explain your answers to a partner using the adjectives and prepositions in exercise 1.

Speaking
IELTS Part 2

1 Look at the following Part 2 task card. Make notes to prepare your answer using the adjectives and questions and answers in the Language focus 2 exercises on page 36 to help you.

> Describe a sporting activity you like.
>
> You should say:
>
>   when you first played it
>
>   who you do it with
>
>   where you do it
>
> and explain why you enjoy doing it.

2 ⬭ Work in pairs. Take turns talking about the topic, using your notes to guide you. You should speak for up to two minutes; time each other using a stopwatch. When your partner has finished speaking, give him/her the feedback using the checklist on page 210.

Speaking
IELTS Part 3

What to expect in the exam

- In IELTS Speaking Part 3 you will have a discussion with the examiner, which is linked to the topic of Part 2. However, the questions will be more abstract and you need to talk about general ideas, not about yourself and your own experiences as in Parts 1 and 2.

1 ⬭ Decide which three of the following phrases describe the main reasons for people doing sport. Then discuss your answers with a partner, giving reasons and examples.

1 to keep fit

2 so they can lose weight

3 so that they can make friends

4 in order to help them relax

5 so as to get an adrenaline rush

6 in order to escape from the real world

2 <u>Underline</u> the words in **1–6** above that indicate purpose. Then use these phrases to write your own sentences explaining why you do sporting activities.

3 It is important to give variety to what you say. Rephrase items **1–6** using the following structure: *because they + want/would like/would rather/would rather not/like to … .* Make any necessary changes.

How to go about it

- You need to develop your ideas by using simple signposts such as 'purpose' words.
- Give reasons and examples.

4 ⬭ Work in pairs. Look at the Part 3 questions below and choose one or two questions from each. Briefly discuss them using the expressions of purpose in exercise 1. Then take turns asking each other the questions. When your partner has finished speaking, give him/her feedback using the checklist on page 210.

Physical activity

Do you think that doing physical activity is important nowadays?

What are the advantages and disadvantages of doing any kind of physical activity?

Are people less active than they were in the past? Why/Why not?

In what ways can people be encouraged to adopt a less sedentary and more active lifestyle?

Benefits of sport

What are the social benefits of doing sporting activities?

Are we more risk averse than we were in the past, that is, do we seek to avoid risks nowadays?

How can the lives of young people be made more challenging?

What are the benefits to the individual and society of people being involved in extreme sports? Why?

Writing:
IELTS Task 1

1 Look at the following Task 1 question. Then write the answers to questions **1–9** below in full sentences.

WRITING TASK 1

You should spend about 20 minutes on this task.

The table below shows the percentage of adults aged 16 and over who participated in various activities in the four weeks prior to interview in the United Kingdom in 2002.

Summarise the information by selecting and reporting the main features, and make comparisons where relevant.

Write at least 150 words.

Participation in various sporting activities

	Males (%)	Females (%)	Total (%) (average)
Walking	49	41	45
Cue sports (eg. billards)	19	4	11
Cycling	15	8	11
Swimming	13	16	15
Football	10	0	5
Weight training	9	3	6
Keep fit/Yoga	7	17	12
At least one activity [1]	71	57	64

[1] Includes other items not separately listed.

1 Did fewer women than men go swimming?

2 Was there a far greater proportion of men than women involved in walking?

3 Were males less likely to take part in sporting activities?

4 Did nearly twice as many women as men go cycling?

5 Does the table compare data about male and female involvement in a selection of activities in the United Kingdom in 2002?

6 Did ten per cent of men play football, while no women played?

7 Compared with males, did more than twice as many females go to keep fit/yoga classes?

8 Was football the least popular activity overall?

9 Overall, were males more involved in physical activity than females?

2 Work in pairs. Match each of your answers to the questions in exercise 1 to section **a**, **b** or **c** below.

a the introduction   **b** the overview   **c** specific data

3 <u>Underline</u> the words and phrases used to make comparisons in questions **1–9** in exercise 1.

4 Rewrite sentences **1–6** using the words and phrases in the box below. Make any necessary changes.

a smaller proportion of	a third of the number of	40% of
three-quarters half	five times the number of	over 50%

Example:

Twice as many cars were sold in June compared to March.

Half as many cars were sold in March compared to June.

1 The football match was attended by three times as many spectators as the rugby match.

2 The sports department was visited by only 20 per cent of the shoppers in February 2009 when compared to February 2008.

3 More than four out of every ten competitors were from the main city.

4 The bulk of players were from overseas rather than home-grown.

5 A quarter of the members of the sports club paid by cash rather than credit card.

6 The team lost just under half of the games they played last season.

Don't forget!

- Make sure your introduction does not just copy the instructions.
- Write a clear overview.
- Select data and compare specific data, but do not just write a list.

5 Write an answer for the Task 1 question below using the comparative structures in Language focus 1 on page 32 and the words and phrases in exercise 4. When you have finished, check your answer using the checklist on page 209.

WRITING TASK 1

You should spend about 20 minutes on this task.

The table below gives information about the participation of 11–14 year-olds by gender in extreme sports in the UK in 2003.

Summarise the information by selecting and reporting the main features, and make comparisons where relevant.

Write at least 150 words.

Extreme sports that 11–14 year-olds participated in, by gender, 2003

	Male (%)	Female (%)	Total (%) (average)
Mountain biking	22.7	13.3	**18.1**
Snowboarding	8.1	4.0	**6.1**
Mountain Climbing	10.6	9.3	**10.0**
Skateboarding	27.5	13.8	**20.8**
Rollerblading	21.7	31.7	**26.6**

③ Review

Vocabulary

1   Decide if the sports in the box below are indoor sports, outdoor sports or both. Then put them in the correct column in the table.

> golf   snowboarding   boxing   squash
> football   baseball   rugby   running

Indoor	Oudoor	Both

2   Decide which of the sports in exercise 1 require each piece of equipment **1–9** below?

1 a ball	**6** a board
2 a wall	**7** gloves
3 clubs	**8** a racquet
4 a net	**9** a bat
5 goal posts	**10** spikes

Comparison

1   Rewrite sentences **1–6** below using an adjective made from the noun underlined.

Example:

People's lives have less excitement nowadays than in previous generations.

People's lives are less exciting nowadays than in previous generations.

1   Does windsurfing involve greater expense than ordinary surfing?
2   I find that watching sport has greater appeal for me than taking part.
3   Which sport presents a greater challenge than any other?
4   Which sport has the best safety on record?
5   As they are old, the facilities have less value than those at other clubs.
6   The club has more success than similar organizations.

2   Write a full sentence for each list of words in **1–8** below.

1   India/not/be/big/Africa
2   Pacific Ocean/be/wide/Atlantic Ocean
3   mountaineers/not/earn/much/footballers
4   football matches/attract/far great/numbers/squash tournaments
5   parkour/seem/much/risky/skateboarding
6   many sports/demand/stamina/intellect
7   active/life/be/considerable/harmful/sedentary lifestyle
8   private cars/make/much/noise/lorries

Adjectives with prepositions

Complete sentences **1–7** with a suitable adjective. There may be more than one possible answer.

1 Are you _____ on listening to sports commentaries on the radio?

2 Are you _____ in meeting famous sports people?

3 He has enormous stamina. He is _____ of running for hours.

4 Sport is like a drug to some people. They are completely _____ to doing it or watching it.

5 Some people do not find sport interesting. They are completely _____ to it.

6 I like adventure films, but I wouldn't say I was wildly _____ about them!

7 I get easily _____ with watching sport on TV.

Word building

1 For **1–8** below, <u>underline</u> the adjectives and decide if they are correct. Correct any mistakes.

   1 I found that I was fascinated by the skill required in the game of baseball.

   2 It was clear that he was very motivating and wanted to go back to the gym.

   3 We were all thrilled by the pace of the football game.

   4 Is the noise of the motorbikes in motorsports irritated for you?

   5 I was very interesting in trying out snowboarding for the first time.

   6 She was excited to watch in the horse race, especially when she overtook everyone.

   7 I wasn't annoyed at all by the fact that the rugby team lost; it was a good game.

   8 I was not really challenging by the game of tennis, but I enjoyed it nonetheless.

2 Match **1–5** below with **a–e** to complete the IELTS Speaking Part 1 answers.

   1 I really find skiing thrilling.

   2 I love playing football and rugby,

   3 I'm mad about baseball, especially live matches.

   4 I am very keen on indoor sports,

   5 I'm really enthusiastic about extreme sports like hang-gliding.

   a Some people are frightened of heights, but I find flying fascinating.

   b I find being in the stadium electrifying.

   c as they are very fast moving team sports and they're challenging mentally and physically.

   d because where I grew up the weather was too cold to play outside. So I became interested in badminton and squash.

   e It's so exciting racing down a mountain slope at high speed.

3 The IELTS Speaking Part 1 statements in exercise 2 are personal, but in Part 3 you need to talk about abstract ideas. Choose a statement in exercise 3 and write three or four sentences about the sport in an abstract way.

   Example:

   I'm mad about baseball, especially live matches. I find being in the stadium electrifying.

   People generally like baseball because they find the atmosphere in the stadium electrifying.

   The atmosphere in the stadium at baseball games is often electrifying.

   It is thrilling to watch baseball in a packed stadium.

Introduction

The IELTS Listening module has 40 questions and lasts approximately 30 minutes. There are four sections with ten questions in each.

The first two sections are of a social nature. Section 1 is a conversation between two people and Section 2 is usually a monologue. However, Section 2 can also be a conversation between two people. Sections 3 and 4 are connected with education and training. Section 3 is a conversation involving up to four people and Section 4 is a monologue.

You hear each section once only and answer the questions in the question booklet as you listen. You are given time to check your answers at the end of each section. At the end of the test you have ten minutes to transfer your answers to the answer sheet. A brief description is given at the beginning of each section. At the beginning of section 1 an example is always given.

The questions types used are:

- multiple choice
- short-answer questions
- sentence completion
- labelling a diagram/plan/map
- notes/form/summary/flow-chart completion
- classification
- matching

Section 1

Section 1 is a conversation between two speakers in a social setting (for example, enrolling in a club or buying something), which involves the exchange of information like personal details.

The section is divided into two parts. You will be given time to look at the questions before each part.

1 ◉ 1.4 Listen and follow the instructions.

SECTION 1   Questions 1–10

Questions 1–6

Complete the form below.

Write **NO MORE THAN TWO WORDS AND/OR A NUMBER** for each answer.

Details for book search

Example	Answer
Department	Book Search

Title	**1** ....
Author	Dayne **2** ....
ISBN number	978-0- **3** ....
Paperback book	

Only published in	**4** ....
No longer in print	
Book category	**5** .... fiction
Search types:	
Gold	£25
Silver	**6** £ ....

Questions 7–10

Complete the sentences below.

Write **NO MORE THAN TWO WORDS AND/OR A NUMBER** for each answer.

7 The caller's mobile number is 08967 ....

8 Her email address is .... thompson9z@yahoo.fr.

9 Her address is .... Chaucer House, Ludlow Park Drive, Richmond, SW20 9RL.

10 She doesn't want to receive any emails about ....

2 Work in pairs. Look at the listening script on page 228 and check your answers. <u>Underline</u> the words in the questions which show the answer is about to be given. Match these words with the answers in the script.

3 ⬭ With your partner, discuss the type of questions you have problems with, for example, writing down numbers, words with plural endings, or answers which are close together or far apart. Compare them with another pair of students. Keep a record of the problem areas and think about them while you are studying by yourself and before you do a test.

Section 2

In Section 2 you will hear a monologue of a social nature like a radio broadcast or a talk about a place, but be aware than you may also hear a conversation between two people.

There may be two or three types of question. The recording is divided into two parts, but you will be given time to look at the questions before each part.

1 In questions **11–16** on page 44, decide which you think you should listen for first: items **A–G** or the parts of the cinema **11–16**.

2 Work in pairs. Decide what synonyms you might hear for the words in **A–G**.

3 For questions **17–20**, <u>underline</u> the word(s) which show the answer is about to be given.

4　◉　1.5　Listen and follow the instructions.

SECTION 2　Questions 11–20

Questions 11–16

Which change has been made to each part of the cinema?

Choose **SIX** answers from the box and write the correct letter, **A–G,** next to questions **11–16**.

Regal Cinema Complex
A enlarged
B replaced
C still closed
D thoroughly cleaned
E split up
F brightened up
G moved

Part of the cinema

11　facade　　　..........

12　auditorium　..........

13　foyer　　　..........

14　bar　　　　..........

15　roof terrace　..........

16　cinema shop　.........

Questions 17–20

Choose the correct letter **A**, **B** or **C**.

17　The renovated cinema will open again from

　A　14th July.

　B　4th July.

　C　14th June.

18　Which group will receive free tickets during the first week of opening?

　A　Pensioners who attend any evening session.

　B　Young people aged 17–25.

　C　Children who arrive for a matinee performance.

19　On Wednesdays the reduction on ticket prices for cinema members will be

　A　25%.

　B　50%.

　C　33%.

20　A new development at the cinema is the

　A　cinematography classes.

　B　weekly workshops.

　C　monthly talks.

5 Work in pairs. Look at the listening script on page 229 and check your answers. Find the synonyms for the words or phrases in questions **11–16**. Were any of the words you chose in exercise 2 used?

Section 3

In Section 3 you will hear a conversation between two to four people on a topic connected with education or training like preparing for a tutorial or receiving feedback on an assignment.

There may be only one type of question or up to three. The recording is divided into two parts, but you will be given time to look at the questions before each part.

1 Work in pairs. For question **21**, decide which words in the stem help prepare you for the answer. Decide what synonyms might you hear for each.

2 For questions **22–24**, decide which aspects of research you think are most likely to be still undecided at the beginning of a research project. Then think of synonyms for the words in **A–G**.

3 For questions **25–30**, decide which answers are numbers and which answers could be plural.

4 ◉ 1.6 Listen and follow the instructions.

SECTION 3   Questions 21–30

Question 21

Choose the correct letter **A**, **B** or **C**.

21 Zahra's talk is on electronic gadgets that people

 A find very annoying to have to listen to.

 B bought in the recent past.

 C feel they have to carry with them.

Questions 22–24

Choose **THREE** letters, **A–G**.

Which **THREE** of the following elements of conducting Zahra's research are mentioned as not yet decided?

 A length of the questionnaire

 B pictures to use

 C volume of data

 D duration of interviews

 E period of research

 F age of interviewees

 G exact aims

Questions 25–30

Complete the table below.

Write **NO MORE THAN THREE WORDS AND/OR A NUMBER** for each answer.

Questionnaire on gadgets

Tim's electronic gadgets	Use	Score
Mobile	Excluding phoning mainly for sending • texts • **25**	10
Laptop	Typing assignments and **26**	**27** ....
iPod	Just listening to music	**28** ....
Future newspaper reader	Eventually for **29**	**30** ....

5   Work in pairs. Look at the listening script on page 229 to check if any of the words or phrases you chose for exercise 2 were used.

Section 4

In Section 4 you will hear a talk or lecture of an educational/academic nature. You do not need any specialist knowledge to understand the talk.

There may be only one type of question or up to three. There is no break in the middle, but there is a pause of a few seconds. You will be given time to look at all of the questions before you begin.

1   Work in pairs. For questions **31–35**, decide which words in the stem indicate the answer is about to be given. Then think of paraphrases for the alternatives **A–C**.

2   For questions **36–40**, study the diagram carefully and make sure you know the sequence the information is given in.

3   ◉ 1.7   Listen and follow the instructions.

SECTION 4   Questions 31–40

Questions 31–35

Choose the correct letter **A**, **B** or **C**.

Cloud-seeding to provide rain

31   Boreholes provide water for

    A   industrial use.

    B   agricultural purposes.

    C   domestic consumption.

32   According to the speaker, in the past people have tried to induce rain by

    A   supernatural means.

    B   using fires.

    C   special dances.

33 There is some proof that seeding clouds increases rainfall by

    A 15%.

    B 55%.

    C 25%.

34 According to the speaker, why do some people not support cloud seeding?

    A The benefits of the practice are limited.

    B The costs of the equipment are too great.

    C The effects of playing with nature are unknown.

35 The country that is most keen on cloud seeding is

    A Russia.

    B China.

    C the USA.

Questions 36-40

Write **NO MORE THAN TWO WORDS** for each answer.

How cloud seeding works

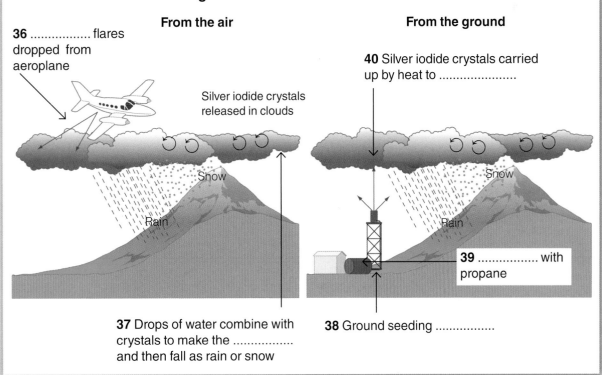

From the air

36 .... flares dropped from aeroplane

Silver iodide crystals released in clouds

Snow

Rain

37 Drops of water combine with crystals to make the .... and then fall as rain or snow

From the ground

40 Silver iodide crystals carried up by heat to ....

Snow

Rain

39 .... with propane

38 Ground seeding ....

4 Check your answers in the listening script on page 230.

What to expect in the exam

At the end of Section 4 you will be given ten minutes to transfer your answers from the question booklet to the answer sheet. In order that you do not lose any marks when you are transferring your answers it is important to do the following:

- make sure that you transfer all the answers and put them in the correct boxes
- take great care with spelling, especially with plural words and countable and uncountable nouns
- make sure that you do not copy words from the questions as part of the answers

4 Global problems and opportunities

Vocabulary 1: General category nouns

1 🔾 With a partner, describe each of the photographs. Then discuss the questions below.

- Describe your reaction to each photograph.
- Do you think any of the photographs present any opportunities? Give reasons and examples.
- Do you think problems and difficult situations can present us with opportunities?

2 Nouns such as *situation* and *problem* can help you to organize your ideas when you are writing or speaking and to understand what you are reading about. Which noun can you use in both of the gaps below?

Computer waste is a serious world _____ . It is now accumulating all over the world. The _____ , however can be solved by …

Match each group of adjectives **1–8** with a noun **a–h** that collocates with all of the adjectives in the group.

1 acute/serious/insurmountable	**a**	circumstances
2 golden/excellent/perfect	**b**	problem
3 adverse/unfavourable/trying	**c**	opportunity
4 ideal/dangerous/sticky	**d**	event
5 imaginative/effective/perfect	**e**	issue
6 memorable/festive/state	**f**	occasion
7 significant/political/momentous	**g**	situation
8 burning/controversial/thorny	**h**	solution

3   Complete sentences **1–8** with a word from the box below. Make any necessary changes.

> issue   incident   outcome   problem   possibility
> impression   dilemma   event

1   I would like to describe an amusing _____ from my work.

2   There is a faint _____ that the plan will succeed.

3   All governments face a terrible _____ over funding priorities.

4   A series of significant _____ occurred in the early part of the 19th century, which changed the face of transport for ever.

5   Instead of being seen as a serious _____ , the situation should be thought of as a golden opportunity.

6   Energy costs have been a burning _____ several times in the last few decades.

7   The sight of the natural forest made a profound _____ on me.

8   The _____ of the talks was not totally unexpected.

4   Match each sentence **1–6** with a sentence **a–f**. Use the adjectives and nouns in **a–f** to help you identify the connection.

1   I lost my wallet last week.

2   I went to my sister's wedding.

3   After leaving college, I found myself with lots of free time.

4   Both sides refuse to talk to each other.

5   Experimentation on animals is controversial.

6   I was offered a scholarship to go to university.

a   It was too good an opportunity to miss.

b   It is a rather awkward situation.

c   It is a divisive issue that arouses passion.

d   It was the happiest event of her life.

e   These were the perfect circumstances to write my first novel.

f   It was an annoying incident, which I reported to the police.

5   ⬤   Work in pairs. Choose one or more of the following events and tell your partner what happened:

- an amusing incident from your work
- a golden opportunity you missed
- an event that made a profound impression on you

Listening
IELTS Section 4

What to expect in the exam

- In IELTS Listening Section 4 you will hear a monologue once only. It is of an academic nature, but does not require specialist knowledge.
- You are told at the beginning of the recording what the topic is about. Sometimes there is a heading for the questions or part of the questions.
- There is a short pause in the middle of the monologue.
- Section 4 is slightly more difficult than Section 3.

How to go about it

- Skim the questions quickly to get an idea of the content.
- Underline words, dates etc. that will help to show that the answer is coming.
- Sometimes, the answers come close together and sometimes there is a big gap between them. Make sure you do not lose concentration.
- When you have to complete gaps, check the number of words or numbers that you need to write and decide what type of words are required: nouns (singular or plural, countable or uncountable), verbs, adjectives or adverbs.

⬤   Work in pairs. Describe the railway system in your country. Say when it was first introduced and how efficient it is.

1.8 SECTION 4 Questions 31–40

Questions 31–37

Complete the table below.

Write **NO MORE THAN TWO WORDS** for each answer.

Date	Modern railway developments
1803	William Jessop's **31** .... is considered to be the first one ever built.
1804	The achievements of Richard Trevithick passed mainly **32** ....
1812	The Salamanca was the first commercially successful **33** ....
1825	The Darlington to Stockton railway was at first constructed to carry **34** .... Carrying **35** .... was considered unimportant.
1831	The Liverpool to Manchester line was the first modern railway, because it carried merchandise and **36** .... on a fixed timetable. **37** .... were felt to be hindering the growth of the cities and towns in the area.

Questions 38–40

Choose **THREE** letters, **A–F**.

Which **THREE** of the following consequences of the opening of the new Liverpool to Manchester railway are mentioned?

    A Coal became scarce

    B Cotton prices rose

    C Passenger numbers rose

    D The volume of goods transported went up

    E No new canals were built

    F Canal charges fell

Language focus 1: Countable and uncountable nouns

1 At the beginning of the listening practice on page 50 you heard the phrases below. <u>Underline</u> the nouns and decide which are countable and which are uncountable?

... the development of early forms of transport ...
... new opportunities for innovation and progress ...
... in the evolution ...

2 Match each uncountable noun **1–10** with a countable noun **a–j** that is associated with it. What other countable nouns can you add in each category?

1	furniture	**a**	shirts
2	clothing	**b**	chairs
3	luggage	**c**	oranges
4	cash	**d**	flats
5	fruit	**e**	goods
6	accommodation	**f**	coins
7	media	**g**	burglaries
8	merchandise	**h**	magazines
9	crime	**i**	bottles
10	litter	**j**	suitcases

G Read more about countable and uncountable nouns in the Grammar reference on page 221.

3 For sentences **1–8**, replace the words in *italics* with a word or phrase from the box below. Make any necessary changes to the verb.

> suggestions   machines   information   behaviour
> musical instruments   robberies and thefts   language
> litter

1 *Cans and bottles* are an eyesore on any city street.
2 *Some machinery* is expensive to maintain.
3 *The actions* of football hooligans cost the public large amounts of money.
4 *Details* about the damage appeared in the newspaper.
5 *Crime* is surprisingly on the decrease.
6 *Music* is played by many people as a means of relaxation.

7 *Advice* from the right person about which career path to follow is vital.
8 *The words and phrases* all children pick up follow fairly similar patterns.

4 Expand the notes below into sentences. Put the nouns into the singular or plural and use the correct form of the verb.

1 many business now demand lot work employee
2 people expect good weather when go holiday
3 theatre audience decline generally but audience for new musical extremely small last night
4 increased use public transport bus train good environment
5 with increase price paper book newspaper become expensive
6 coffee tea commodity which see fall in value recently
7 entertainment like horror and violent film should ban
8 electronic goods refrigerators cause considerable harm planet

5 For sentences **1–8** below, <u>underline</u> the correct word in *italics*.

1 There is now no need for people to throw away *equipment/equipments* like *computer/computers*.
2 The *weather/weathers* deteriorated rapidly with severe *storm/storms* forecast.
3 *Information/Informations* like bank *detail/details* should not be revealed for security reasons.
4 *Business/Businesses* done on the Internet can save *business/businesses* large amounts of money.
5 People frequently travel with a huge amount of *luggage/luggages*, when only a small number of *case/cases* is allowed on board.
6 *Furniture/Furnitures* is made by skilled craftsmen working in *wood/woods* from different *tree/trees*.
7 *Waste/Wastes* such as *litter/litters* ought to be recycled, not thrown away.
8 People sometimes need to do other *job/jobs* besides their permanent *work/works* to earn more *money/moneys*.

Speaking
IELTS Part 1

1 In IELTS Speaking Part 1 you may be asked to talk about the natural resources in your country such as oil and metal, or food products such as tea and coffee. Look at the examiner's questions below. <u>Underline</u> the countable nouns and ⊙ircle the uncountable nouns.

   1 Describe the main types of food resources that are produced in your country.
   2 What goods are manufactured in your home country?
   3 What types of food are produced in your country?
   4 What produce is exported/imported?
   5 What is the staple food in your country?
   6 What commodities are produced in your country?
   7 Is the merchandise sold in the shops in your country the same as in other countries you have visited?
   8 What crops are grown in your country?

2 ◯ Work in pairs. Choose three or four of the questions in exercise 1. Take turns asking and answering the questions. Pay particular attention to the nouns and verbs.

Reading

IELTS Reading Passage

○ What are the three most shocking environmental catastrophes that you have heard or read about in the media recently? Do you think financial penalties are a way to stop such incidents? Why/Why not?

READING PASSAGE

You should spend about 20 minutes on **Questions 1–13**, which are based on the reading passage below.

Why plastic is the scourge of sea life

A 'plastic soup' of waste floating in the Pacific Ocean is growing at an alarming rate, and now covers an area twice the size of the continental United States, scientists have said.

The vast expanse of debris – in effect the world's largest rubbish dump – is held in place by swirling underwater currents. This drifting 'soup' stretches from about 500 nautical miles off the Californian coast, across the northern Pacific, past Hawaii and almost as far as Japan.

Charles Moore, an American oceanographer who discovered the 'Great Pacific Garbage Patch', or 'trash vortex', believes that about 100 million tons of flotsam are circulating in the region. Marcus Eriksen, a research director of the US-based Algalita Marine Research Foundation, which Mr Moore founded, said yesterday: 'The original idea that people had was that it was an island of plastic garbage that you could almost walk on. It is not quite like that. It is almost like a plastic soup. It is endless for an area that is maybe twice the size as continental United States.'

The 'soup' is actually two linked areas, either side of the islands of Hawaii, known as the Western and Eastern Pacific Garbage Patches. About one-fifth of the debris – which includes everything from footballs and kayaks to Lego blocks and carrier bags – is thrown off ships or oil platforms. The rest comes from land.

Mr Moore, a former sailor, came across the sea of waste by chance in 1997, while taking a short cut home from a Los Angeles to Hawaii yacht race. He had steered his craft into the 'North Pacific gyre' – a vortex where the ocean circulates slowly because of little wind and extreme high pressure systems. Usually sailors avoid it.

He was astonished to find himself surrounded by rubbish, day after day, thousands of miles from land. 'Every time I came on deck, there was trash floating by,' he said in an interview. 'How could we have fouled such a huge area? How could this go on for a week?'

Mr Moore, the heir to a family fortune from the oil industry, subsequently sold his business interests and became an environmental activist. He warned yesterday that unless consumers cut back on their use of disposable plastics, the plastic stew would double in size over the next decade.

Professor David Karl, an oceanographer at the University of Hawaii, said more research was needed to establish the size and nature of the plastic soup, but that there was 'no reason to doubt' Algalita's findings.

'After all, the plastic trash is going somewhere and it is about time we got a full accounting of the distribution of plastic in the marine ecosystem and especially its fate and impact on marine ecosystems.'

Professor Karl is co-ordinating an expedition with Algalita in search of the garbage patch later this year and believes the expanse of debris actually represents a new habitat. Historically, rubbish that ends up in oceanic gyres has biodegraded. But modern plastics are so durable that objects half-a-century old have been found in the north Pacific dump. 'Every little piece of plastic manufactured in the past 50 years that made it into the ocean is still out there somewhere,' said Tony Andrady, a chemist with the US-based Research Triangle Institute.

Mr Moore said that because the sea of rubbish is translucent and lies just below the water's surface, it is not detectable in satellite photographs. 'You only see it from the bows of ships,' he said.

According to the UN Environment Programme, plastic debris causes the deaths of more than a million seabirds every year, as well as more than 100,000 marine mammals. Syringes, cigarette lighters and toothbrushes have been found inside the stomachs of dead seabirds, which mistake them for food.

Plastic is believed to constitute 90 per cent of all rubbish floating in the oceans. The UN Environment Programme estimated in 2006 that every square mile of ocean contains 46,000 pieces of floating plastic.

Dr Eriksen said the slowly rotating mass of rubbish-laden water poses a risk to human health too. Hundreds of millions of tiny plastic pellets, or nurdles – the raw materials for the plastic industry – are lost or spilled every year, working their way into the sea. These pollutants act as chemical sponges attracting man-made chemicals such as hydrocarbons and the pesticide DDT. They then enter the food chain. 'What goes into the ocean goes into these animals and onto your dinner plate. It's that simple,' said Dr Eriksen.

Questions 1–9

Complete the summary using the list of words, **A–Q**, below.

Research has shown that the increase in the amount of **1** .... in the Pacific Ocean is disturbing. According to one estimate, there are millions of tons of rubbish floating in the region. The plastic rubbish covers an area approximately **2** .... that of the USA. Some of the garbage comes from ships and oil rigs, but the vast **3** .... is not from the sea. The 'North Pacific gyre', which sailors tend to keep away from, was already **4** .... in the late nineties with predictions of the size of the plastic soup **5** .... twofold in the following ten years. An expedition is being arranged to find the sea junk which Professor Karl thinks is a new living **6** .... While in the past rubbish in the sea broke up, today's plastic is so **7** .... that some pieces half a century old have been found. And the problems all this plastic junk causes? Thousands of sea **8** .... are killed every year and the plastic is now a threat to human food **9** ....

A polluted	**B** junk	**C** short-lived
D majority	**E** increasing	**F** cleaner
G twice	**H** thrice	**I** consumption
J link	**K** creatures	**L** produce
M minority	**N** long-lasting	**O** decreasing
P environment	**Q** world	

Questions 10–13

Do the following statements agree with the claims of the writer in the reading passage?

Write:

YES   if the statement agrees with the claims of the writer

NO   if the statement contradicts the claims of the writer

NOT GIVEN if it is impossible to say what the writer thinks about this

10 The plastic soup is the biggest collection of waste on the planet.

11 The soup is made of three areas connected together.

12 The amount of plastic waste in the sea will remain roughly stable.

13 Most of the rubbish in the sea appears to be made up of plastic.

⬭ Reacting to the text

Were you surprised by the scale of the ocean pollution described in the passage?
Do you think anything can be done to deal with the situation, or are we fighting a losing battle?

How to go about it

or questions **1–9**:

• Decide whether the summary relates to one part or the whole of the passage. This summary relates to the whole passage and does not have a title, so look at the title of the passage and then skim the passage.

• Skim the summary without looking at the wordlist.

• Decide what type of word is needed for each space and think of your own word. The answers can be all nouns, or a mixture of nouns, verbs, adjectives and adverbs.

• Skim the wordlist and try to answer where you can, using grammar and collocation to help you.

• Check your answers with the passage. Sometimes the answers in the summary are in a different order from the passage.

or questions **10–13**:

• Yes/No/Not Given questions check the views or claims of the writer. Underline the words in the questions that will help you scan for the information in the passage.

Language focus 2: Making suggestions

1 ⬭ Work in pairs. The reading passage on page 52 describes a major environmental problem. Decide which one of the following suggestions is the best solution to the problem.

1 The United Nations Environment Programme could be given powers to fine nations who cause pollution.
2 The most important step is to prevent the situation from becoming worse by introducing heavy punishments for pollution, including imprisonment.
3 Countries on the Pacific Rim should seize the opportunity to start a clean up programme.
4 Ships ought to be sent to the area to remove the waste from the water.

2 <u>Underline</u> the words used to make a suggestion in each sentence **1–4** in exercise 1. Then decide whether each measure is a strong or tentative (weak) suggestion.

🅖 Read more about making suggestions in the Grammar reference on page 221.

3 ⬭ Work in pairs. Look at the following statements **1–7** about grave concerns that the world faces today. Discuss what you think might be the best solution for each.

1 There is famine in many parts of the world.
2 Poverty has still not been eradicated.
3 Floods are occurring more frequently.
4 Many of the world's waterways have little life in them.
5 Many species of animals are becoming extinct.
6 Many cities are becoming overcrowded.
7 Water is becoming scarce in various regions.

4 Rewrite sentences **a–g** below using the modal verbs in brackets.

Example:

The most important step is to prevent the situation from becoming worse. (should)

The situation should be prevented from becoming worse.

a The best example I can think of is for governments to try to encourage people to return to the countryside. (ought to)
b Another possible course of action is for banks to cancel the international debts of poor countries. (could)
c One suggestion is for governments to provide poorer countries with the skills to feed themselves. (should)
d One possible answer is to oxygenate rivers and reintroduce fish. (could)
e One possibility is to put protection orders on all wild animals. (can)
f There is a slim chance that water desalination plants will work in some regions. (might)
g I think that planting more trees is the best option. (should)

5 Match each suggestion in exercise 4 to a problem in exercise 3.

6 ⬭ Work in pairs. Write one new suggestion for each problem in exercise 3. Then change partners and ask each other questions about the suggestions you have made. Use the following questions:

What do you think is the answer to solve/tackle/ remedy/deal with/eradicate/improve … ?

What do you think can be done to … ?

Vocabulary 2: Developing ideas by expanding the meaning of adjectives

1 When we write and speak we can use words that are similar in meaning to develop or explain our ideas. For **1–7** below, <u>underline</u> the correct verb in *italics*.

1 Some people find buying consumer goods very satisfying. Sometimes, it is just the act of purchasing which *coaxes/pleases* them.
2 Positive health education on TV can be motivating. It can *encourage/frighten* people to improve their lifestyle.
3 The results were alarming. It *frightened/interested* the government so much they actually took some action.
4 The news on TV is sometimes very worrying. It can *trouble/tempt* people all day long.
5 Disaster movies are very appealing to many people. It is the fact that they feel comfortable and safe themselves as they watch that *excites/attracts* them.
6 I found the festivities really interesting. They *bothered/fascinated* me so much that I had to read more about them.
7 The scale of crime in some cities has been so shocking it has *stunned/pleased* even the police.

2 Rewrite **1–7** in exercise 1 by transforming the verb in *italics* into the adjective and the adjective into the verb.

Example:

Some people find buying consumer goods very pleasing. Sometimes, it is just the act of purchasing which satisfies them.

Writing:
IELTS Task 2

1   In Task 2 the instructions ask you to support your ideas by giving reasons and examples, so it is important to know how to link your ideas to form paragraphs. Read the following paragraph on homelessness and decide whether the words that will go in each gap will introduce an example, result, contrast, reason, purpose or concession.

> Many major cities like New York, London or Paris face problems relating to homelessness, mainly **1** _____ there is a shortage of housing and high rents for property. **2** _____ there are many empty properties in these cities, which could be used to alleviate the situation. Governments should **3** _____ encourage property owners to rent out the properties to those without homes. **4** _____ , incentives can be given to owners by giving tax relief or subsidies **5** _____ help release empty properties on to the market. Measures like this would **6** _____ help to alleviate the situation. **7** _____ this is not a complete answer to the problem, it ought to be considered.

2   Complete each gap in the paragraph in exercise 1 with a linking word from the box below.

> | for example   therefore   yet   in order to   because   although   then |

3   Put the linking words and phrases in the box below into the correct column in the table.

> | however   nevertheless   though   nonetheless   although |
> | still   but   yet   even so   while   even if   despite the fact that |
> | much as   in spite of the fact that |

Adverb	Conjunction	Both

4   For sentences **1–5** below, underline the correct word in *italics*. There may be more than possible one answer.

1   People tend to be pessimistic about their present circumstances. *But/However,/Although* I think the human race is eternally optimistic; otherwise, how would we survive?

2   Man-made problems such as the plastic soup in the Pacific Ocean are disastrous, *but/however,/although* perhaps this time we can learn from our mistakes.

3   *While/Although/However,* green technology is certainly beneficial, there are issues that we need to be careful about.

4   *Even so,/Even if/Though* the human race faces problems, there are always opportunities to use them for further development.

5   Many people believe that the changes we see in the world are a result of natural causes. *Even so,/Nonetheless,/Whereas* there is compelling evidence to the contrary.

How to go about it

- Write any ideas that you can think of that relate to the essay topic. Write the ideas at random around the page or vertically down the left hand side.

- Select two or three main ideas and link other ideas from the list to the main ideas. Alternatively, take one idea and think of other nouns and adjectives that relate to it.

5   Work in pairs. Look at the Task 2 question below and make a list of 5–7 ideas for your answer.

WRITING TASK 2

You should spend about 40 minutes on this task.

Write about the following topic:

> *It is generally agreed that the amount of rubbish created by humans today is a worldwide problem. What do you think are the main causes of this situation? What measures can be used to tackle the problem?*

Give reasons for your answer and include any relevant examples from your own knowledge or experience.

Write at least 250 words.

6   As a class, identify the linking words and phrases you would use to develop and connect your ideas.

7   Look at the following ideas relating to the question. Decide whether each column **A** and **B** relates to causes or examples. Then match each item **1–6** in **A** with an item **a–f** in **B**.

A	B
1 lack of education and ignorance	a merchandise, for example, cars/clothes/computers
2 natural causes	b eating/heating/travelling
3 overpopulation	c throwing away waste like plastic bottles/paper
4 unchecked development	d large cities like Mexico City/London
5 increased consumption	e infrastructure for roads/airports
6 energy demands	f disasters such as flooding/avalanches

8   Write your own answer to the question in exercise 5. When you have finished, check your answer using the checklist on page 209.

Speaking
IELTS Part 2

1 Prepare notes for the following Part 2 task card.

> Describe a recent incident where you damaged
> the environment.
>
> You should say:
>
> > when it happened
> >
> > where it happened
> >
> > how you felt about it
>
> and explain what you learnt from this incident.

2 Work in pairs. Take turns talking about the topic, using your notes to guide you. Speak for up to two minutes; time each other using a stopwatch.

Speaking
IELTS Part 3

1 Work in pairs. Look at each Part 3 question below and decide:

- what synonyms you can use for the nouns, verbs and adjectives in each sentence.
- whether you are likely to use uncountable or countable nouns to begin each answer.

How to go about it

- Develop your answers with reasons and examples.
- Try to use synonyms of words in the questions where you can.
- Use words like *but* and *although* to show contrast and concession.
- Make sure you use uncountable and countable nouns with the correct form of the verb.
- Use adjectives to qualify ideas and associated words to develop them.

> **News and events**
>
> Do media like TV and newspapers influence the way people behave? Why?
>
> How can the media encourage people to change their behaviour as regards the environment? Which do you think is the best means of achieving this?
>
> Do you think the future will be any different? Will there be more environmental issues to concern us?
>
> **World problems**
>
> Do you think that people should be concerned about the world's environmental problems?
>
> What do you think individuals can do to tackle world electronic waste like computers, if anything?
>
> Do you think waste created from discarded machines is causing more problems nowadays than in the past?
>
> Do you think mankind faces more dilemmas now than in the past?

2 Work in pairs. Take turns asking and answering the questions above, asking additional questions where necessary. Choose two or more of the bullet points in the 'How to go about it' box above to check as you listen to your partner. Give each other feedback after each role-play.

Vocabulary

1 Decide which noun is being explained in **1–6** below.

1 _____ A situation where you have to make difficult choices.

2 _____ A matter like a problem that you discuss.

3 _____ Something which happens that is usually important or historic; more than just an occasion or an incident.

4 _____ Something which gives you a chance to do something.

5 _____ Something which happens that is minor; it is not a big or important event.

6 _____ A feeling you have about someone or something.

2 Read the following extracts from IELTS Speaking Part 2. Decide whether the nouns in *italics* are correct. Replace the nouns that are not correct.

I would like to describe an incident that happened to me at college. Just before a major presentation on crisis management in environmental disasters I almost had a **1** *crisis* myself. A minor **2** *event* happened which made a lasting **3** *impression* on me. I lost my bag; I was daydreaming and left it in on a bench. My money, keys, mobile and laptop; everything was in it. It was a terrible **4** *problem* to be in. I saw the **5** *possibility* of failing my course flash in front of me. Someone in the distance, another student, saw it happen and came rushing after me. A minor **6** *occasion* perhaps, but it taught me that there are **7** *events* when you meet honest people. All **8** *situations* are, in fact, perfect **9** *opportunities* for making friends.

3 Use the initial letter before each blank space to help you complete the sentences below with an appropriate adjective and verb. Be careful with the form of each verb.

1 The film was s_____ . It s_____ me completely and I couldn't stop thinking about it.

2 When you find a book that is i_____ and it f_____ you, it is difficult to put down.

3 What makes the sea so a_____? I think it a_____ people because it is so soothing.

4 Sorting out problems is so s_____ . It is the relief of removing difficulty from their lives which p_____ people.

5 Some images at the exhibition on the destruction of the environment are so a_____ that it left people extremely f_____ .

6 I don't find government attempts to change behaviour very m_____ . They frighten people rather than e_____ them.

7 The news item about the plastic soup in the Pacific Ocean was w_____ . It t_____ me for days.

Countable and uncountable nouns

For **1–9** below, complete the table with a suitable uncountable noun for the examples of countable nouns that are given.

Uncountable nouns	Countable nouns
1 *litter*	bottles and cans
2	coats and hats
3	notes
4	trunks and cases
5	bananas and pineapples
6	bedsits and rooms
7	wardrobes and beds
8	robberies and muggings
9	journals and films

Making suggestions

Suggest as many solutions as you can to the problem of water shortages in the world. Give the results of the suggestions. Use the following words: should, ought to, might, could, one possibility, one step.

Examples:

Mobile desalination plants could be built and sent in response to emergencies around the world. This would help poor nations who cannot afford to build permanent plants.

One possibility is to train the public to conserve the water supply when they are using water at home. For example, when cleaning their teeth people could turn the tap off while they brush.

Writing

1 For sentences **1–4** below, <u>underline</u> the correct word in *italics*. There may be more than one possible answer.

   1 The steps that need to be taken are unacceptable to some people. *Nevertheless,/Yet/Still* they need to be taken.

   2 *Despite the fact that/In spite of that/However,* there are constant public campaigns to help prevent pollution, the public continue to ignore the warnings.

   3 Immigration is frequently seen as a negative issue, *yet/however,/even so,* it is vital for most modern economies.

   4 *Much as/Although/But* I am against short-term solutions to problems, I think the government should donate food immediately.

2 Look at the two examples below of IELTS Writing Task 2 questions. What are the similarities and differences between them? Think about the topic and how you would organize the answer.

   a Some people feel that water shortages will cause serious problems in the future, while others believe that such shortages are just temporary natural events. What is your opinion?

   b Water shortages are causing serious problems all over the world. What do you think are the main causes of this situation?

(5) The future

Language focus: Ways of looking at the future

1 ⬤ Work in groups. Look at the pictures below. Which represents your view of what the future will look like? Why?

2 ⬤ Work in pairs. Discuss the questions below.

Do you think machines will control our lives in the future? In what ways? Give reasons.

How do you think machines will improve our lives in the future?

Do you think it is possible that machines will control or govern the planet in the future?

3 Read statements **1–6** below and decide whether each is a prediction, plan or fixed schedule.

> **1** We're going to visit a science exhibition this afternoon.

> **2** I'm leaving in 50 minutes.

> **3** I think people will be living on Mars in 20 years.

> **4** By 2050 machines like robots will have taken over our world.

> **5** Civilization as we know it will no longer exist. It will be very advanced technologically.

> **6** The space shuttle to the moon lifts off at 10pm.

4 Match descriptions **a–f** below to sentences **1–6** in exercise 3.

a The present continuous tense is used for fixed arrangements.

b *Going to* is used for intentions or plans.

c The future simple tense is used for predictions or instant decisions.

d The future continuous tense is used for a situation which will be happening at a particular time in the future.

e The future perfect tense is used for a completed action at or before a point of time in the future.

f The present simple tense is used for events that relate to a schedule/timetable.

⬤ Read more about different ways to talk about the future in the Grammar reference on page 222.

5 For **1–5** below, <u>underline</u> the two verb phrases and match them to a description **a–f** in exercise 4.

1 As we're flying tomorrow morning at 8 am, shall I arrange an alarm call for 5 am?

2 Why are the government going to spend less money on technological research in the future? I think it'll do a lot of harm.

3 By tomorrow, we'll have completed the computer project, and it'll be working perfectly.

4 Some people believe robots are going to be the next big techno craze, but it won't last long.

5 When she arrives tomorrow, she'll be carrying a red bag.

6 For **1–5** below, replace the verb that is in the wrong tense.

1 People will be living in space in the year 2050, but will they really have enjoyed it?

2 According to the timetable, the train arrives at noon. I'll sit at the front if you are looking for me.

3 I'm staying at the Braganza Hotel for four days next week, so I'll have met you on Tuesday.

4 The government are going to change the law next month. At least that's their intention, but I bet something is happening to make them change their minds.

5 The public will have become better informed about healthy eating by then, and are thus going to improve their general well-being.

7 Work in pairs. For sentences **1–6** below, decide whether you can rewrite each one using the tense in brackets. Decide what the difference is.

1 I'll be seeing the doctor next Wednesday at 2.00. (present simple)

2 Society is not going to change dramatically by 2030. (future perfect)

3 The ageing population is going to cause more problems in terms of cost in the future. (present continuous)

4 The world will certainly have changed for the better by then. (*going to*)

5 The human race will be living in more closely-knit communities in the future. (simple future)

6 My diary is full, but perhaps I'll be able to meet you on Saturday. (*going to*)

8 Work in pairs. Make predictions about what your life will be like next year, five years from now and ten years from now. Give reasons and examples.

Vocabulary 1: Adjective/noun collocations

1 Work in pairs. For **1–8** below, use an adjective from the box to replace the words in *italics* to make a common collocation. Place the adjective before the noun.

1 a civilization *that is current and contemporary*

2 societies *that live off the land*

3 a culture *that is stronger than other cultures*

4 communities *that are doing well and are successful*

5 the public *that is made up of ordinary people*

6 populations *that live in towns and cities*

7 the elite *that controls and runs a country*

8 a people *that live in a particular region*

general	governing	agricultural	indigenous
modern	dominant	thriving	urban

2 Complete each gap in the paragraph below with one of the noun collocations from exercise 1.

The **1** _____ has widely different views about what life will be like in years to come. Some pessimists predict that **2** _____ as we know it will collapse in the near future, and that people will end up living in **3** _____ just as their ancestors did before the Industrial Revolution. Others think that **4** _____ will increase in size so much that there will be no agricultural land left, and that there will be one **5** _____ rather than the multicultural world of today with a **6** _____ made up of robots controlling everything and everyone.

3 Work in groups. What is your reaction to the predictions in exercise 2? Do you think life will be very different in the near future? Why/Why not?

Speaking
IELTS Part 3

1 Work in pairs. Use the picture below to help you talk about the world in the future. Describe the following:

- what will be happening
- what will happen
- what will have happened

Useful expressions

In 10/20/50/100 years' time ...
Over the next century ...
Before the end of the century ...
By the time we reach the end of the century ...
In the coming decades ...

2 Work in pairs. Look at the Part 3 questions below. Then take turns asking and answering the questions. When you have finished, give each other feedback using the checklist on page 210.

Don't forget!

- In Part 3 you need to talk in more abstract terms.

Robots

Do you think we should be pessimistic about machines like robots taking over our lives? Why?/Why not?

What do you think are the advantages and disadvantages of using machines like robots?

The world in the future

In what ways do you think society will change in the future?

How do you think modern civilization will develop over the next half century?

Do you think humans will be living on another planet in the future? Why/Why not?

Why do think people make predictions about the future?

Listening
IELTS Section 1

1 You will hear someone enquiring about and booking an exhibition. Before you listen to the conversation, check the meaning of the following words and phrases.

1 booking office
2 preview
3 the week after next
4 restrictions
5 sign up for
6 come up
7 register
8 range

1.9　**SECTION 1**　Questions 1–10

Questions 1–6

Complete the notes below.

Write **NO MORE THAN TWO WORDS AND/OR A NUMBER** for each answer.

Notes on Exhibition

Example	*Answer*
Title of Exhibition: Robots: the end of *modern civilization*	

Two free:　1 ....

Day(s) exhibition full:　2 ....

Days chosen by caller:　3 .... and ....

Reference number:　4 ....

Eating facilities

- 15 restaurants
- Including **5** .... cafés
- Local restaurants putting on **6** ....

Questions 7–10

Accommodation

- Halls of Residence £30 a night
- Hotels from about £30 to approximately **7** £ ....

Transport Links

- Within walking distance of the station and **8** .... from the airport
- It is possible to catch bus number **9** ....
- A taxi costs no more than **10** £ ....

2　◯　Do you like going to exhibitions?

Do you like to book in advance or do you like to turn up on the spur of the moment?

Would you go to an exhibition on robots? Why/Why not?

Word building: Forming adjectives from nouns

1 Work in pairs. Make adjectives from the nouns in the box below and add them to the correct column in the table.

| use | luxury | technology | success | population | space |
| beauty | agriculture | tradition | nation | danger | industry |

Adjectives ending -al	Adjectives ending -ous	Adjectives ending -ful

2 For **1–8** below, complete the gaps with a suitable adjective from exercise 1.

1 At the moment some houses in my community are very _____ , but in the future they will not be so big.

2 I cannot say it is a _____ society at the moment, but as the Internet and computers spread that will change.

3 The area where I was brought up is very _____ with lots of trees and stunning gardens, but I think all this beauty will be destroyed by future developments.

4 My home town still survives on the production of _____ crafts, but I think that modern industry is beginning to creep in.

5 We have many _____ monuments, but people forget what important events they signify.

6 _____ office blocks with all the latest modern facilities and expensive furniture will replace old factories and buildings.

7 I come from one of the most _____ regions of the world, and I think it will become even more crowded in the future.

8 My home town is _____ at attracting tourists, but it's not in danger of becoming overwhelmed yet.

3 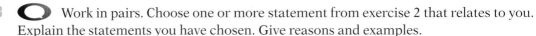 Work in pairs. Choose one or more statement from exercise 2 that relates to you. Explain the statements you have chosen. Give reasons and examples.

Reading
IELTS Reading Passage

Glance quickly at the title, sub-title and the passage as a whole and write down at least five points that you think the text will contain. Then answer the following questions:

• what made you choose the five points you wrote down?

• what do you think the word *pragmatics* might mean in the sub-heading?

READING PASSAGE

You should spend about 20 minutes on **Questions 1–13**, which are based on the reading passage below.

The next big thing in robotics

As Japan builds a new generation of robot companions, U.S. firms focus on pragmatics.

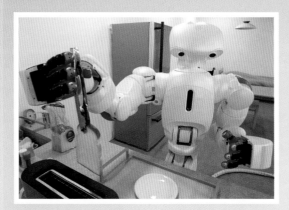

Meet Wakamaru and Roomba, two householdhelper robots with very different pedigrees. Wakamaru, from Mitsubishi Heavy Industries, is a waist-high bot with a canary yellow exterior and limpid eyes. It can recognize 10,000 Japanese words, identify eight family members by face or voice, remind you to make an appointment or make your beds and, if somebody breaks into your house, send photographs of the intruder to your mobile phone. When the machine rolled off the assembly line in 2005, Mitsubishi expected U.S. sales to reach 10,000 models a year, despite the bot's $15,000 price tag. Instead, the company filled only a few dozen orders. Wakamaru is now off the market and being rented out as a receptionist at $1,000 a day.

Roomba, by contrast, looks more like an appliance than a robotic friend. The frisbee-like disc's sole purpose is to vacuum, which it does automatically, thanks to sensors that adjust the settings to suit different floor types, avoid drop-offs like stairs and navigate between table legs and household pets. Starting price: $130. Massachusetts firm iRobotCorp. has sold more than 3 million of the machines.

Wakamaru and Roomba represent radically different approaches to the next big thing in robotics: the use of robot assistants in the office, hospital and home. The Japanese, who have long been fascinated by the robot as android, are concentrating on making machines that look and act like human beings. U.S. firms, on the other hand, have eschewed the flashier android approach and instead are emphasizing products that, like Roomba, are narrowly targeted to specific tasks like mowing lawns, cleaning pools and taking patients' vital signs.

So far, the success of Roomba suggests that the U.S. firms have the upper hand. But the race is only beginning and the stakes are potentially huge. The market for personal and service robots is about $3 billion now, but is expected to reach $15 billion by 2015, according to the Japan Robotics Association and market analysts like ABI Research. In 10 years or so, experts predict, sales of personal robots could surpass sales of industrial robots, now about $4.6 billion a year.

The issue for robot developers is whether the technology of artificial intelligence will allow Japanese developers to fulfill their vision of friendly robots capable of working alongside people. If so, Japan could be in a position to dominate the next phase of robotics. If not, the Americans, with their pragmatic but uninspiring designs, could win the race.

Japan approaches this new market from a position of strength. Over the past 50 years, it has become the undisputed leader in industrial robots, supplying 40 percent of the world market. At the same time, Japanese pop culture has become saturated with images of friendly droids from Manga cartoons and animé, and bots by Sony and Honda are as famous in Tokyo as Jessica Simpson is in Texas. Japan's robot industry — with the help of $100 million in research funding from the government — is driven in large part by the dream of a day when droids will aid humans in almost every aspect of daily life.

There's the egg-shaped PaPeRo — recently rated the most popular bot in Japan by Robot Life magazine — which works select day-care centers, singing songs and reading e-mails to children according to texted instructions from parents. There's Actroid, a mannequinesque gynoid who wows corporate guests with her dynamic facial expressions and cheeky conversation skills (ask her how much she weighs, and she'll tell you what she can bench-press).

Japanese and American firms have their eyes on the same prize: the market for home health care, particularly for the elderly. As baby boomers hit retirement age, the need to monitor and assist seniors will create a surge in demand for personal-care robots, experts say. Since 2001, the Japanese government has spent $210 million on research to meet its goal of deploying robots to support its aging workforce. (It's timeline specifies that bots should be able to straighten a room by the end of this year, make beds by 2013, and help with baths and meals by 2025.) The desire to field human-like robots, however, is an impediment. Honda, for instance, decided to keep its Asimo robot bipedal, even though its two feet are impractical in homes with stairs and clutter. The one field in which Japanese robots have a clear lead requires no practical applications: entertainment robots, a $185 million market that is expected to rise to $3 billion by 2014, according to private research firms.

All this grass-roots robotics innovation has led tech giants to predict that in the next twenty years, robots could be the biggest technological revolution since PCs and the Internet. Whether these robots are cleaning up homes or serving as co-workers, entertainers and friends depends on which vision wins out.

How to go about it

For questions **1–7**:

- Skim the summary to decide whether it relates to the whole passage or part of it.
- This summary does not have a title so look at the title of the passage.
- Check the word limit for each answer.
- Always think about the types of words that are needed, for example, nouns, verbs, adjectives etc.
- Do not write any words on the answer sheet that are paraphrased in the summary.

For questions **8–11**:

- Read the stem and underline any words that you think will be paraphrased.
- Read each alternative as a complete sentence by combining it with the stem.
- Locate the information in the text.

For questions **12 and 13**:

- Use names, numbers and paraphrases of the nouns in the questions to help you locate the answers in the passage.

Questions 1–7

Complete the summary below.

Choose **NO MORE THAN TWO WORDS** from the passage for each answer.

When Wakamaru first appeared on the market, Mitsubishi forecast robot sales in thousands in the US, but sales figures were very low. The robot is now on hire as a **1** .... Roomba, an American robot which was designed only to **2** .... , has sales running into the millions. These two machines symbolize two very **3** .... in the world of robot technology. The Japanese focus is on making machines that behave like **4** .... , while the U.S. are concentrating on robots that do specific tasks. In effect, the choice is between friendly robots working with people or machines that are **5** .... but boring. Japanese and American firms are after the same market: health provision at home, especially for **6** .... Tech giants project that in the coming decades there is a possibility robots will be the most important **7** ....

Questions 8–11

Choose the correct letter **A**, **B**, **C** or **D**.

8 Wakamaru is

    A   the same height as a human being.

    B   shorter than a human being.

    C   heavier than a human being.

    D   quicker than a human being.

9 The purpose of Romba's sensors is to help it

    A   move around objects.

    B   navigate the stairs.

    C   polish different surfaces.

    D   clean household pets.

10 US firms prefer robots

    A   that are very cheap to make.

    B   that can act as companions.

    C   that focus on designated tasks.

    D   that look like humans.

11 The battle in artificial intelligence is between

    A   creating practical robots and friendly robots.

    B   producing cost effective and attractive robots.

    C   building fast and efficient robots.

    D   making elegant and industrial robots.

Questions 12 and 13

Answer the questions below.

Choose **NO MORE THAN TWO WORDS AND/OR A NUMBER** from the passage for each answer.

12 What has Japan's position been in the industrial robots market over the past half century?

13 What was the Japanese government's expenditure on research into using robots to help elderly workers?

⬤ Reacting to the text

Would you like to have a robot in your home? Why/Why not?

How soon do you think robots will be commonplace in people's homes?

Do you think we have anything to fear from the development of robots, or can they only be beneficial? Give reasons and examples.

Vocabulary 2: Verbs of prediction

1 Underline the four verbs in the box below that cannot be used to indicate prediction in an IELTS Writing Task 1 answer.

predict	prophesy	forecast	assume	foretell
project	estimate	anticipate	expect	foresee

2 Decide what the noun and adjective is for the correct verbs in exercise 1.

3 Rewrite sentences **1–8** below using the words which follow each sentence.

Example:

It is predicted that computer sales will account for 20 per cent of the total

... are predicted ...

Computer sales are predicted to account for 20 per cent of the total.

1 By the year 2030 the population will have increased to nearly 70 million.
   ... it is estimated ...

2 Spectator numbers will be rising dramatically towards the end of the year.
   ... are forecast ...

3 The projected sales next month will be lower than this month.
   It is ...

4 It is forecast that passenger numbers will increase substantially.
   The forecast is ...

5 Sales will climb at the rate of 20 per cent a year.
   ... predicted ...

6 Attendances will decline gradually in the next two years.
   ... are anticipated ...

7 Advances in technology are not expected to slow down in the coming years.
   It is expected ...

8 The estimated recovery in ticket purchases will happen in the third quarter.
   ... are estimated ...

Writing:
IELTS Task 1

What to expect in the exam

- Pie charts indicate proportions. They can contain percentages adding up to 100%, as in the example here, or they can contain units in proportions that add up to more than 100. They can show changes over time in different pie charts, or all relate to the same year.

1 Look at the Task 1 question below. Then for **1–12** in the model answer below, put the verb in brackets into the correct tense.

WRITING TASK 1

You should spend about 20 minutes on this task.

> The charts below show the world traffic volume measured in passenger-kilometre-miles.
>
> Summarise the information by selecting and reporting the main features, and make comparisons where relevant.

Write at least 150 words.

World traffic volume

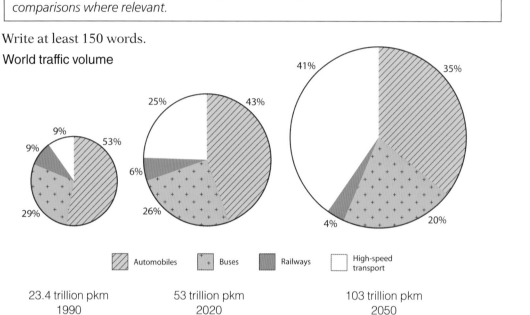

| Automobiles | Buses | Railways | High-speed transport |

23.4 trillion pkm — 1990

53 trillion pkm — 2020

103 trillion pkm — 2050

The pie charts (**1** show) the changes in the proportions of pkm for a range of different forms of transport every thirty years between 1990 and 2050 along with the total number of passenger kilometres.

The most striking feature of the chart (**2** be) the rise in traffic volume from high-speed transport. It (**3** expect) to see a dramatic increase, climbing from just 9% of traffic volume in 1990 to 25%, and then 41% in 2020 and 2050 respectively. By contrast, it (**4** predict) that there will be fewer automobile pkm, which (**5** shrink) from 53% of market share to 43%, and to 35% in 2050.

While railways (**6** see) the most significant fall in traffic volume percentage-wise, it (**7** anticipate) that buses (**8** fare) better. The former (**9** represent) 9% of total traffic volume in 1990, but the projected figure for 2050 (**10** be) just 4%, a drop of more than 50%. This (**11** compare) with traffic volume for buses in 2050 of 20% against 26% in 2020, and 29% in 1990.

It is clear that high speed transport (**12** expect) to increasingly dominate the market.

2 <u>Underline</u> the linking words in the model answer.

3 Find examples in the model answer where the pronouns *it* and *this* and the phrase *the former* are used to connect ideas between sentences. What does each one refer to?

4 For **1–5,** <u>underline</u> two suitable words or phrases in *italics* to link the information. Use the punctuation to help you.

   1 By 2020 it is predicted that more of the total traffic volume of the total 53 trillion pkm will be accounted for by high-speed transport than in 1990 (25% against 9%). *By contrast/While/By comparison* automobiles are expected to account for 43% and 53% in the respective years.

2 In the year 2050 it is projected that high-speed transport will account for 41% of total traffic volume. *By contrast/Whereas/Meanwhile,* bus use is expected to shrink to 20%.

3 In 1960 automobiles accounted for 54% of the traffic volume, *but/whereas/in contrast* high-speed transport represented only 3%.

4 The majority of traffic volume was made up of automobiles in 1990 at 53%. *Meanwhile/But/By contrast,* buses accounted for 29%, with the railways and high-speed transport coming next with 9% each.

5 The proportion of passenger traffic miles accounted for by automobiles is expected to decrease to 43% by 2020, *whereas/whilst/meanwhile* it is forecast that the pkm for railways will shrink by a smaller amount: 29% to 26%.

5 Use the lists of words in **1–4** below to write your own sentences about the pie charts in exercise 1. Add the relevant data from the charts.

    1 high-speed transport account for traffic volume in 1990 while in 2050 forecast represent

    2 estimate proportion traffic volume automobiles 2050 in contrast to 1990

    3 in 1990 automobiles make up bulk passenger kilometres but 2050 this forecast drop to

    4 in 1990 out of a total traffic volume of 23.4 trillion pkm automobiles account for buses, railways and high-speed transport respectively by comparison by 2020 anticipate high speed transport jump automobiles buses railways

6 Write your own answer for the Task 1 question below. When you have finished, check your answer using the checklist on page 209.

WRITING TASK 1

You should spend about 20 minutes on this task.

> *The charts below provide information about energy generation by fuel type in Florida in two separate years.*
>
> *Summarise the information by selecting and reporting the main features, and make comparisons where relevant.*

Write at least 150 words.

Energy generation by fuel type

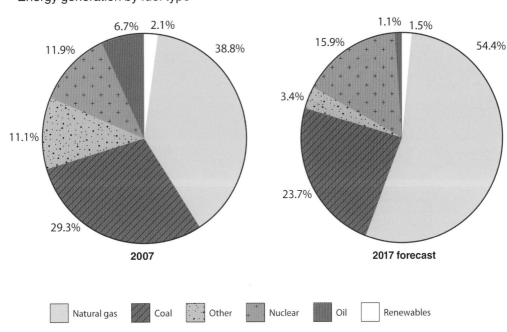

(5) Review

Vocabulary

1 For **1–8** below, replace the <u>underlined</u> phrases with a suitable adjective/noun collocation.

    1 Do you think <u>the civilization of today</u> will change much over the next century?

    2 Should we try to protect the remaining <u>societies that live off the land</u>?

    3 Are <u>populations that live in the towns</u> under threat from increasing violence?

    4 Will the <u>cultures that are stronger than others</u> always be in control?

    5 Are <u>peoples that have lived in certain parts of the world for centuries</u> under threat?

    6 Do <u>the elites that control countries</u> have any idea what the lives of ordinary people are like?

    7 Do <u>communities that are doing well</u> in inner cities have a beneficial impact on society in general?

    8 Does the opinion of the <u>public at large</u> influence governments?

2 Use a collocation dictionary or a thesaurus to find one more adjective that you can use with each noun in the collocations in exercise 1.

Word building

Rewrite sentences **1–8** below by using an adjective made from the <u>underlined</u> noun and then add a reason.

Example:

Flats in the capital city do not have much space.

Flats in the capital city are not very <u>spacious</u>, because there are so many people looking to find a place to live.

1 Electronic dictionaries are not really of much <u>use</u>.

2 In certain south-east Asian countries <u>technology</u> is much more advanced than in the West.

3 This country has many buildings of great <u>beauty</u>.

4 The <u>population</u> of Bangladesh is enormous.

5 Jobs involved in <u>agriculture</u> are very demanding.

6 Living a life of <u>luxury</u> is not open to all of us.

7 Astronauts face many <u>dangers</u> when they go out into space.

8 Skills that follow old <u>traditions</u> are going out of fashion.

Ways of looking at the future

1   For **1–5** below, put the verbs in brackets into the correct future form.

1   I'm leaving for New Zealand on Friday of this week. The plane (leave) at 6 am in the morning, and after several stops I (sit) in a hotel in Auckland sometime on Monday. I think it's going to be an exciting trip.

2   I don't think the human race (land) on other planets in the solar system by the year 2050 as the cost will be astronomical. However, I do think that the moon will be inhabited in the next 20 years or so.

3   I think that putting money into space research is essential, because it (lead), as in fact it has already done, to many new developments in medicine and technology.

4   I am optimistic about the future. I think we are going to have to face challenges in the near future, but people (rise) to them just as they have done in the past. For example, some deadly diseases like malaria certainly (disappear).

5   I'm not really sure, but generally I think the world in the future (be) a better place than it is today. People (live) in a society free of cares and worries, where all of the work (do) by robots and other machines. These machines will be so lifelike that it (be) impossible to tell the difference between them.

2   Which four of the extracts in exercise 1 would you expect as an answer to an IELTS Speaking Part 3 question? Why is the other extract not suitable?

Proof reading

As quickly as you can, find the mistakes in sentences **1–10** below.

1   By the year 2020 the population will increased to nearly 120 million.
2   By 2015 it is predicted that car journeys will decline. Whereas high-speed rail transport will be expanding.
3   The pie chart show the developments in transportation over time.
4   It is forecast that passengers number will increase substantially.
5   Trafic volume on the railways is projected to rise in the coming decades.
6   The number of journeys taken will fall drammatically in the near future.
7   The majority of trips is make up of train journeys.
8   The strike feature is the rise in rail journeys.
9   The number of passenger journeys made by car will fall, by contrast high-speed transport will shoot up.
10   It is predict that the number of people using the system will rise.

6 Fruits and seeds

1 ◯ With a partner, describe what is happening in each of the photographs below.

2 Skim each of the following short texts **a–e** and match them to the four processes shown in the pictures. It is not possible to match one of the texts to a picture. Decide what process it describes.

a When it has flowered, fruit is produced which in turn becomes seeds. These either fall to the ground or are carried by birds or animals to other places, or they are carried along by the wind. When they drop to the ground they wait until the spring of the next year. Then they germinate and grow, and the process repeats itself.

b Once it blooms, the crop is picked by hand or machine. Then it is taken to a factory where the oil is extracted from the plant. It is then distilled to make an essence which is used in perfumes and toiletries.

c It lays its egg on the leaves of plants. When the eggs hatch, the caterpillars eat the leaves. They then form a cocoon from which a new insect emerges.

d The plants produce flowers. When the flowers open, they attract insects which pollinate the plant.

e When the fruit ripens, it is collected by hand or machine and taken to a factory where it is crushed to extract the juice. Once the juice is packaged, it is sent to shops to be sold.

3 Look at each text again. <u>Underline</u> the words that helped you match them to the pictures.

4 <u>Underline</u> the words that helped you decide which process was being explained in the description that did not match any of the pictures.

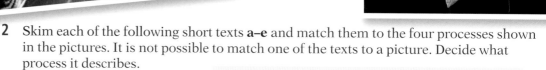

How to go about it

- Look at the picture and the title 'The Life of a Pomegranate'. What kind of information do you think the passage will contain? Decide if the passage is descriptive, factual or argumentative.

READING PASSAGE

You should spend about 20 minutes on **Questions 1–13**, which are based on the reading passage below.

The life of a pomegranate

A Steeped in history and romance and almost in a class by itself, the pomegranate, Punica granatum L, belongs to the family Punicaceae, which includes only one genus and two species, the other one, little-known, being P. protopunica Balf, peculiar to the island of Socotra.

B An attractive shrub or small tree, to 20 or 30 ft (6 or 10 m) high, the pomegranate is much-branched, more or less spiny and extremely long-lived, some specimens at Versailles known to have survived two centuries. It has a strong tendency to sucker from the base. The leaves are evergreen, opposite or in whorls of 5 or 6, short-stemmed, 3/8 to 4 in (1–10 cm) long, leathery. Showy flowers grow on the branch tips singly or as many as 5 in a cluster. They are 1 1/4 in (3 cm) wide and characterized by the thick, tubular, red calyx, having 5 to 8 fleshy, pointed sepals. Nearly round, but crowned at the base by the prominent calyx, the fruit, 2 1/2 to 5 in (6.25–12.5 cm) wide, has a tough, leathery skin or rind, basically yellow, more or less overlaid with light or deep pink or rich red.

C The interior is separated by membranous walls and white spongy tissue (rag) into compartments packed with transparent sacs filled with tart, flavorful, fleshy, juicy, red, pink or whitish pulp (technically the aril). In each sac, there is one white or red, angular, soft or hard seed. The seeds represent about 52% of the weight of the whole fruit.

D The pomegranate tree is native from Iran to the Himalayas in northern India, and has been cultivated since ancient times throughout the Mediterranean region of Asia, Africa and Europe. The fruit was used in many ways as it is today and was featured in Egyptian mythology and art, praised in ancient document and it was carried by desert caravans for the sake of its thirst-quenching juice. It traveled to central and southern India from Iran about the first century A.D. and was reported growing in Indonesia in 1416. It has been widely cultivated throughout India and drier parts of southeast Asia, Malaya, the East Indies and tropical Africa. The most important growing regions are Egypt, China, Afghanistan, Pakistan, Bangladesh, Iran, Iraq, India, Burma and Saudi Arabia.

E It is rather commonly planted and has become naturalized in Bermuda, where it was first recorded in 1621, but only occasionally seen in the Bahamas, West Indies and warm areas of South and Central America. Many people grow it at cool altitudes in the interior of Honduras. In Mexico it is frequently planted.

F The tree was introduced in California by Spanish settlers in 1769. It is grown for its fruit mostly in the dry zones of that state and Arizona. In California, commercial pomegranate cultivation is concentrated in Tulare, Fresno and Kern counties, with small plantings in Imperial and Riverside counties. There were 2,000 acres (810 ha) of fruit-bearing trees in these areas in the 1920's. Production declined from lack of demand in the 1930's, but new plantings were made when demand increased in the 1960's.

G The species is primarily mild-temperate to subtropical and naturally adapted to regions with cool winters and hot summers, but certain types are grown in home dooryards in tropical areas such as various islands of the Bahamas and West Indies. In southern Florida, fruit development is enhanced after a cold winter. Elsewhere in the United States, the pomegranate can be grown outdoors as far north as Washington County, Utah, and Washington D.C., though it doesn't fruit in the latter locations.   It can be severely injured by temperatures below 12° F (-11.11° C). The plant favors a semi-arid climate and is extremely drought-tolerant.

H Rooted cuttings or seedlings are set out in pre-fertilized pits 2 ft (60 cm) deep and wide and are spaced 12 to 18 ft (3.5-5.5 m) apart, depending on the fertility of the soil. Initially, the plants are cut back to 24 to 30 in (60-75 cm) in height and after they branch out the lower branches are pruned to provide a clear main stem. In as much as fruits are borne only at the tips of new growth, it is recommended that for the first 3 years the branches be judiciously shortened annually to encourage the maximum number of new shoots on all sides, prevent straggly development and achieve a strong, well-framed plant. After the 3rd year, only suckers and dead branches are removed.

How to go about it

For questions **9–13**:

- Flow charts usually have a heading so use this to locate the relevant part of the text.
- Treat the flow-chart like a summary. The text may be in note form so pay particular attention to the grammar.
- Sometimes the information in the flow-chart may be in a different order from the reading passage.

Don't forget!

- For questions that require you to complete information, check the number of words required for each blank space.

Questions 1–4

The reading passage has eight paragraphs **A–H**.

Which paragraph contains the following information?

NB You may use any letter more than once.

1 what the inside of the pomegranate looks like

2 domestic cultivation of the pomegranate tree

3 what the pomegranate tree looks like

4 the area where the pomegranate tree originated from

Questions 5–8

Do the following statements agree with the information given in the reading passage?

Write:

TRUE	if the statement agrees with the information
FALSE	if the statement contradicts the information
NOT GIVEN	if there is no information on this

5 The pomegranate tree lives only for a short time.

6 The flowers of the pomegranate are particularly enticing to both bees and birds.

7 The seeds make up a small proportion of the weight of the pomegranate fruit.

8 The pomegranate tree can withstand very dry weather conditions.

Questions 9–13

Complete the flow-chart below.

Choose **ONE WORD ONLY** from the passage for each answer.

The Reproduction of Pomegranates

Cuttings sown in **9** ....

↓

Soil fertility dictates gap between plants

↓

At first plants clipped

↓

To make branchless **10** .... , lower growth is removed

↓

Pomegranate found at the **11** .... of new growth

↓

Branches cut back yearly over 3 years to:

- produce new shoots
- stop untidy **12** ....
- make the plants shapely and sturdy

↓

From the third year onwards only **13** .... and dead branches cut off

Reacting to the text

Is it important for us to know how things like trees, plants, insects and animals grow? Why/Why not?

How common is it for people in your country to grow their own produce? Is it less common now than in the past?

Speaking
IELTS Part 2

1 Work in pairs. Make short notes for one of the Part 2 topics below.

Don't forget!

Write your notes vertically so you can read them easily as you speak.

Expand your notes as you speak.

Describe a park that you like.

You should say:

where the park is

when you first went there

who you go there with

and explain why you like going to this park.

Useful expressions

The park I'd like to describe is (spacious/calm/quiet/relaxing) …

I like going there because it is (an escape from work/a place to meet friends/near my home).

Describe something you have grown.

You should say:

what it is

when you grew it

where you grew it

and explain why you grew it.

Useful expressions

When I was very young, …

Not long ago, …

… in a garden on a small plot of land/ on a terrace/in a window box

… gave me great pleasure/helped me relax

2 Work with a new partner. Take turns talking about the topic, using your notes to guide you. When you have finished, discuss with your partner whether you followed the notes.

3 Improve your notes and take turns talking about the topic again. Before you start look at the checklist on page 210 and choose one or more criteria you would like your partner to check as you speak.

Vocabulary 1: Conservation

1 For sentences **1–8** below, choose a word from **a–e** to complete each of the gaps.

1 Tree _____ is crucial, because trees are the _____ of the planet; we chop them down at our peril.

    a extinction   **b** heart   **c** lungs   **d** preserves   **e** conservation

2 The countryside in my home country needs _____ , because it is being _____ by more and more buildings.

    a spoilt   **b** a guard   **c** protection   **d** defence   **e** broken

3 In the _____ season the countryside is not at all _____ as it is buzzing with activity.

    a plant   **b** tranquil   **c** seed   **d** scenic   **e** planting

4 A huge factory, which is now derelict, _____ the landscape, but the scenery is still _____ with wooded hills and streams.

    a controls   **b** dominates   **c** extravagant   **d** spectacular   **e** rules

5 People come for miles to admire the _____ across the valley, because the area has some breathtaking _____ .

    a scenery   **b** scenic   **c** outlook   **d** observation   **e** view

6 From the mountain top you have a _____ view of the valley, with beaches _____ into the distance.

    a stretching   **b** panoramic   **c** lengthening   **d** panorama   **e** landscape

7 People go to New York to shop and to take in the _____ like the Statue of Liberty, but they also like to visit open _____ like Central Park.

    a sightings   **b** spaces   **c** areas   **d** sights   **e** views

8 I think it is necessary to _____ the environment, because wildlife will _____ if we don't.

    a disappear   **b** depart   **c** safeguard   **d** uphold   **e** offend

2 For sentences **1–6** below, complete the gaps with a word from the **a–e** choices in exercise 1. Make any necessary changes.

1 The coastline has some breathtaking _____ , which attract people from all over.

2 As trees produce oxygen they keep us alive, which is why they are often called the _____ of the planet.

3 The beach _____ for miles with lots of wildlife, but it is a _____ that is in danger of being _____ if we don't conserve it for future generations.

4 Tourists spend a lot of money travelling around trying to take in as many _____ as possible in a city.

5 Wildlife like lions and tigers should not be kept in zoos, but how else can they be protected from extinction and _____ forever?

6 _____ schemes that protect particular _____ of international importance like the Amazon forest are vital to all of us.

3 🔘 Work in groups. Read the sentences in exercise 1 and 2 and discuss the questions below.

1 Do you think it is important to have conservation schemes to protect the environment? Why/Why not?

2 In what ways can people safeguard the countryside?

3 Do you think the landscapes in countries around the world will be destroyed or protected in the future? Give reasons and examples.

Useful expressions

I think … is important/crucial/ vital/essential/necessary, because …

In order to …

If we don't do anything, …

One way is to …

Another possibility is to …

… can/could/should …

for example, …

Language focus: Transitive and intransitive verbs

1   Read explanations **a** and **b** below. Decide which describes a transitive verb and which describes an intransitive verb.

   a   A verb which takes an object and can be used in the passive.

   b   A verb which does not take an object and cannot be used in the passive.

   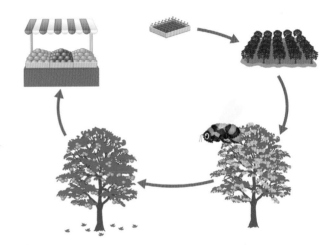 Read more about transitive and intransitive verbs in the Grammar reference on page 222.

2   Look at text **a** in exercise 2 on page 72 and <u>underline</u> the verbs. Then decide which are intransitive and which are transitive.

3   The verbs in the box below can all be used to describe processes and lifecycles. Some verbs can be transitive or intransitive depending on the context in which they are used. Decide whether the verbs in the box are transitive, intransitive or both and write them under the correct heading in the table.

| grow   make   look   produce   decrease |
| weave   happen   smell   collect   rise |
| sow   become   harvest   lay   flow   roast |
| pick   emerge   occur   crush   disappear |
| increase |

Transitive	Intransitive	Both

4   ⬭ Work in pairs. Use your own knowledge to answer questions **1–6** below using suitable singular or plural nouns.

   1   What rises and sets every day?

   2   What is harvested to make bread?

   3   What leaves are picked to make a hot drink from China?

   4   What is white and is woven to make a very light cloth?

   5   What emerges from a cocoon to become a flying insect?

   6   What are colourful, grown in gardens and look and smell very nice?

5   Write a sentence for each question **1–6** in exercise 4. Where possible, replace the verb in the question with one of the verbs in the box below or a verb of your own.

| reap/gather   harvest   come out of   bloom |
| break up   break   produce   plant   cultivate |
| utilize   create   increase   exist   keep in touch |
| go down |

6   <u>Underline</u> the intransitive verbs and verb phrases in the box below.

| plant   pollinate   blossom   harvest   grow tall |
| disperse   become bigger   come out   prune |
| sprout   transplant   grow   ripen   appear |
| open up   cultivate   bear   eat   fall   sow |

7   Work in pairs. Decide which verbs and verb phrases in the box in exercise 6 can be used with each of the nouns in the box below.

| seeds   saplings   branches   tree   buds |
| flowers   fruit |

8   Before you look at the text below, describe the lifecycle of an apple tree in your own words using the diagram below.

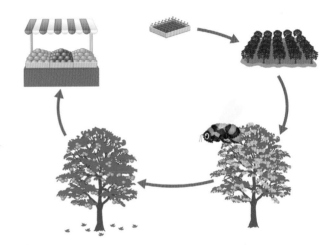

9   Complete the gaps in the text below with the verbs and nouns from exercise 6 and 7. Use the present tense and make any necessary changes to the nouns.

The life of an apple tree

The **1** _____ of the apple tree **2** _____ in trays where they grow until they reach a certain size. Then they are **3** _____ into the fields. When they reach a certain height, the saplings are **4** _____ to increase the production of apples. As the **5** _____ grow taller, the branches **6** _____ , and then the branches sprout **7** _____ . The tree blossoms attract bees that in turn **8** _____ the flowers. In the autumn, the **9** _____ begins to **10** _____ , and then the leaves fall. The fruit is then **11** _____ and the apples are graded, sorted and taken in special refrigerator lorries for storage or distribution to the market.

How to go about it

For questions **14–17**:

- Study the map carefully. Do not assume that 'A' will be the first thing you hear, the description is more likely to start at the Entrance.

- Think of words that are related to sequence, for example, *then, next* etc. as these will indicate steps in the sequence.

- *North* is marked on the map, so think about the four points of the compass.

◉   1.10   **SECTION 2   Questions 11–20**

Questions 11–13

Choose the correct letter, **A**, **B** or **C**.

11 The weekend scheme for teenagers was started up

    A 15 years ago.

    B 2 years ago.

    C 10 years ago.

12 When the teenagers first arrive, they don't like it, because they can't

    A contact people.

    B use the Internet.

    C watch TV.

13 The centre receives most of its money from

    A donations.

    B the nursery.

    C courses.

Questions 14–17

Label the map below.

Write the correct letter, **A–K**, next to the questions 14–17.

Fairbridge Countryside and Woodland Centre

14 Oak Lodge	....	
15 Ash Lodge	....	
16 Picnic Area	....	
17 Plant Nursery	....	

Questions 18–20

Complete the sentences below.

Write **NO MORE THAN TWO WORDS** for each answer.

18 As the centre is high up, there are spectacular .... of the surrounding area.

19 As no trees have been cut down, the .... has not altered for centuries.

20 As people walk through the woodland, people are asked not to remove .... or ....

Vocabulary 2: Describing sequences

1 Decide which one of the follwing linking words or phrases in the box below cannot be used to describe sequences.

initially	first	at last	then	next	as soon as	once	after
before	following that		after that	finally	when	where	

2 Work in pairs. <u>Underline</u> the linking words in **1–7** below and find the first step in the sequence. Then decide what is being described and put the sentences in order.

1 If it is the latter, the broken components are mended

2 and the phone is then sent for sale.

3 Once a device is broken, it is either thrown away or sent for recycling.

4 These are then shipped to a different factory for assembly.

5 First, the various internal components like the chip are manufactured in one place.

6 After that they are dispatched to a central warehouse for distribution.

7 At the same time, the case and the SIM card are produced.

3 Compare this manufacturing process with the natural lifecycle described in the life of an apple tree on page 77. Decide which contains the most transitive verbs.

4 Match **1–6** below with a sentence or part of a sentence **a–f** to complete the sequence.

1 As soon as the wheat is fully grown,

2 Before it is wrapped,

3 Once the mangoes are ripe they are picked,

4 The components are imported and then put together.

5 When the tea bush reaches a certain height, the leaves are picked.

6 Milk production goes through various stages. When the cows are milked, the milk is taken to a dairy where various products are made.

a the chocolate is put into moulds and left to cool.

b It is heated to kill bacteria to make it suitable for drinking, or churned to produce butter.

c and sent to the market for sale, or kept in a cold refrigerator for export.

d it is reaped.

e They are then dried, sorted, blended and wrapped in packets for sale.

f After that the machines are put into boxes and transported to warehouses or to shops.

5 Match each of the words below to a sequence in exercise 4.

storage	delivery	pasteurization	harvesting	assembly	packaging

6 Decide what the verb is for each noun in exercise 5.

Writing:
IELTS Task 1

1 ⬭ Work in groups. Describe the steps in the process below. Try to use the words in the box.

throw away	recycle	crush	buy	rubbish	tip	landfill	collect
transport	separated	colour	crush	recycled	new bottles		

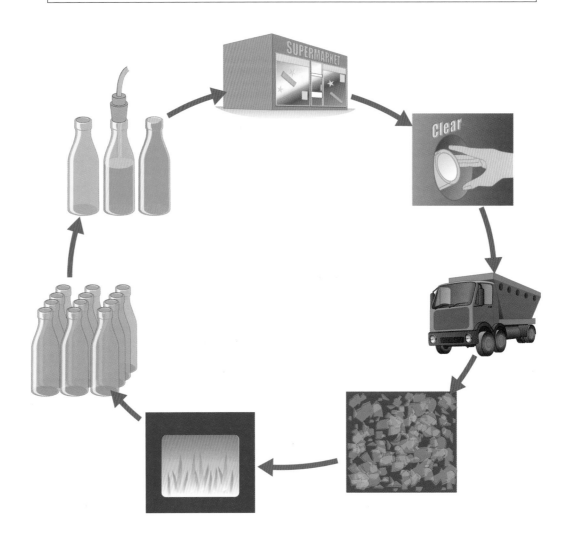

2 Complete the gaps in the text below with suitable linking words from Vocabulary 2 on page 79. Think of as many linking words as you can for each gap.

The fizzy drink is bought in the shop. 1 _____ it is drunk, it is either

thrown away, in which case it is thrown into a rubbish tip, or it is put into a recycling

bin. 2 _____ the recycled bottles are collected and taken to a special

centre, 3 _____ the glass is sorted. After this step, the glass is

crushed and 4 _____ it is used for making new glass. This glass is

5 _____ made into new bottles which are delivered to various bottling

plants, 6 _____ the various drinks are added.

3 Find the word *step* in the text in exercise 2. Which other words can you use instead of *step*?

4 Write an introduction and an overview for the text in exercise 2.

5 Write your own answer for the Task 1 question below. When you have finished, check your answer using the checklist on page 209.

How to go about it

- Write an overview using words to describe sequences such as *stage*, *step* and *phase*.
- Use the correct tense to describe the sequence. As this is a cycle that is repeated, use the present simple.
- Make sure that you use transitive and intransitive verbs correctly.
- Make sure that you use the active and passive correctly.
- Use linking words related to sequence, eg. *first, then, next, after that, subsequently, once, as soon as, when, where … .*

Don't forget!

Make sure you write an introduction which paraphrases the rubric. Do not copy it.

Write a minimum of 150 words.

WRITING TASK 1

You should spend about 20 minutes on this task.

> The diagram below shows the production of a lead pencil.
>
> Summarise the information by selecting and reporting the main features, and make comparisons where relevant.

Write at least 150 words.

The production of a pencil

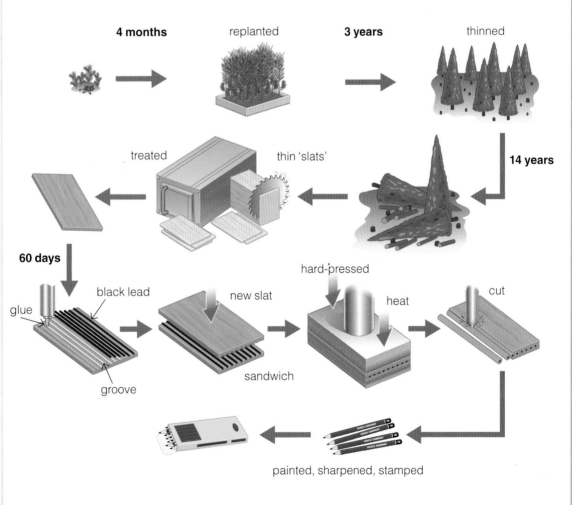

81

6 Review

Vocabulary

Texts **A** and **B** below are short extracts from IELTS Speaking Part 2. Complete the gaps with a suitable form of the word in brackets.

A

The countryside where
I was brought up is completely
1 _____ (spoil). The area is part of a large
2 _____ (conserve) scheme, which aims to protect
the trees from destruction. There are several notable landmarks
which 3 _____ (domination) the landscape, but there are
no factories or large motorways, which means that being there is
very relaxing. The best thing is the spectacular
4 _____ (scene), and the
5 _____ (panorama) views across
the valley.

B

If you go to a city like Paris,
you have to make sure you take in all the
important 6 _____ (sightings) like the Eiffel
Tower. Paris is a city which is famous for its open
7 _____ (spacious) as well as old houses.
It is important that both aspects of the city are
8 _____ (protection), because if they
9 _____ (appear), it will be a loss
for all of us.

Transitive and intransitive verbs

1   In the text below, <u>underline</u> the verbs and decide which are transitive and which are intransitive.

> *When the rain falls to earth, it is absorbed by the soil, from which it is extracted by trees and other plants. Any extra water runs off the land into streams or rivers, which are important for reducing flooding as they carry the water away down to the sea or to lakes. If there is a lot of rain, the water level in rivers rises and flooding occurs. Water is collected in dams to provide drinking water. When it is needed, it is sent to water treatment plants where it is treated and purified.*

2   For **1–6** below, write sentences to describe a step or sequence using the words given. Add conjunctions such as *after* and adverbs such as *then*. Make sure that you use the letter *s* in the correct place.

1   sun/shine
2   rice/harvest/clean/store/sell
3   cotton/grow/make cloth/pick/weave/made into
4   fruit/pick/squeeze/dilute/concentrate/bottle
5   mobile/sell/use/become worn/throw away
6   butterfly/lay/caterpillar/eat/leaves/make cocoon/butterfly/emerge/lay/repeat

Listening

The following sentences take you on a tour through the map below. Follow the line and decide whether the sentences are correct or not. Correct the sentences that are wrong.

1 We start off here at the bottom of Theed Street.
2 The tour takes us past Wren House on the right.
3 We then turn left into Chatham Street.
4 We go past Brompton Palace which is on the north side of the street on our left.
5 Just after the palace we immediately turn right into Manor Way, where we stop and look at the building of the College of Music, which is on our left.
6 We then turn left into Weston Avenue to look at the Old City Hall, which is on the north side of the street.
7 We continue to the end of Weston Avenue where we go south.
8 We then turn left and finish our tour on the north side of the Old City Hall.

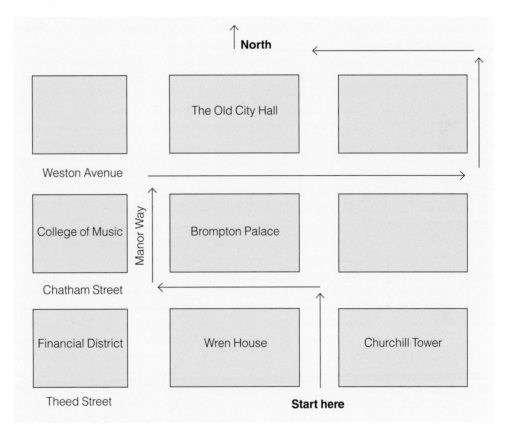

Proof reading

In sentences **1–9** below, there is either a letter *s* missing or there is one too many. Find the mistakes and correct them. Try to complete the exercise in less than two minutes.

1 When the seed germinate, the plant begins to grow.
2 As soon as the wood is burnt, carbon dioxide is released into the atmospheres, which can then cause serious problems.
3 The diagram show how the water is purified.
4 Trees are the lung of the planet as they purify the air we breathe.
5 If the plant produces fruit, it releases the seed which are either carried away by the wind or birds.
6 More conservation projects need to be organized if we are to save the countrysides.
7 Pomegranate are now found in many countries in the world.
8 What are the most common fruits in your parts of the country?
9 It is clear that there are seven step in the process.

Introduction

In the IELTS Academic Reading module there are three passages which are from various sources like books, journals, magazines and newspapers. The passages do not require specialist knowledge for you to understand them. At least one of the three passages contains a detailed logical argument.

The question types used are:

- choosing suitable paragraph headings from a list
- identification of information using 'True/False/Not Given' questions
- identification of writer's views/claims using 'Yes/No/Not Given' questions
- multiple-choice
- short-answer
- sentence completion
- notes/summary/flow-chart/table completion
- labelling a diagram
- classification
- matching

You will have one hour to answer 40 questions, which is about 90 seconds for each question. This means that you need to learn to move around the reading passage and the questions quickly. In the exam there is no time to 'study' the reading passages. In order to be as fast as possible there are three important strategies that you need to learn:

- scanning and skimming – these are reading skills that you need to employ at different times to answer various types of questions

- understanding the different questions types

- understanding when to leave questions you cannot do initially, move on and come back later

Scanning a text

You can use scanning to look for words and paraphrases of words. How you find the words does not matter, and if you scan from left to right it is difficult to stop your brain from reading. Try the following methods, using a pen or pencil to guide your eye.

1 Scan from the bottom up through the text, looking left to right or right to left.

2 Scan in a zigzag from left to right.

3 Scan in a zigzag from right to left.

3   Text Text Text Text Text Text
Text Text Text Text Text Text
Text Text Text Text Text Text

Below is an extract from a reading passage. Scan the paragraphs for the words below.

1 linear   **2** sacred   **3** elite   **4** symbolic   **5** complicated

THE BRONZE AGE: XIA DYNASTY

The Bronze Age in China refers to the period between about 2000 and 771 BC, when bronze was produced on a massive scale for weapons and ritual objects used by the ruling elite. Traditional Chinese histories, written in later centuries, speak of a series of ancient rulers who invented agriculture, writing, and the arts of government. The last of these legendary rulers, Yu, is credited with controlling floods and founding the Xia dynasty. Yu also cast nine sacred bronze vessels that became symbolic of the right to rule, and these were passed on to subsequent dynasties. While the account in the traditional histories is linear, with states following one another in a logical progression, the archaeological record reveals a more complicated picture of Bronze Age China.

Archaeological investigation has confirmed much of the legendary history of the dynasty following the Xia – the Shang – but the existence of Xia itself is still debated. Today Chinese scholars generally identify Xia with the Erlitou culture, but debate continues on whether Erlitou represents an early stage of the Shang dynasty, or whether it is entirely unique. In any event, new prototypes emerged at Erlitou – in architecture, bronze vessels, tomb structures, and weapons – that greatly influenced material culture in the Shang and subsequent Zhou dynasties.

Skimming a text

Skimming involves moving over the text quickly without engaging deeply in order to get a general understanding. Work in pairs. Read alternate sentences in the text above only using the nouns and verbs and see how much you can understand.

Understanding 'True/False/Not Given' statements

'True/False/Not Given' statements are used to check if statements agree with information in the reading passage.

1 Work in pairs. Without looking back at the extract on page 85, underline the words which you think are the most important to help you understand the meaning in the 'True/False/Not Given' sentences **1–10** below. Use the list **a–j** to help you identify the important words.

   a verbs to do with cause and effect, for example, *lead to, bring about*

   b restricting words, for example, *only*

   c quantities, for example, *all, majority, little*

   d adjectives that qualify, for example, *particular, inevitable, mistaken, higher*

   e adverbs that qualify, for example, *largely, slightly*

   f numbers

   g 'negative' verbs, for example, *ignore, fail*

   h verbs/phrases that indicate doubt, for example, *suggest: It is suggested …*

   i comparisons

   j verbs to do with linking, for example, *connect, link*

   1 The Bronze Age in China lasted more than a thousand years.

   2 Bronze was used more for weapons than for ritual objects.

   3 According to later Chinese histories, ancient rulers were only interested in the administrative side of leadership.

   4 Yu is said to have established the Xia dynasty.

   5 Ten sacred vessels were made by Yu.

   6 The sacred vessels were destroyed at the end of each dynasty.

   7 The Chinese Bronze Age was a simpler period than discoveries show.

   8 All of the legendary history of the Xia has been substantiated by archaeology.

   9 The Xia are connected with the Erlitou culture.

   10 The Erlitou culture had an impact on the Zhou.

2 Scan the text to locate the information in statements **1–10** and decide whether they are 'true', 'false' or 'not given'.

Understanding 'Yes/No/Not Given' statements

'Yes/No/Not Given' statements are used to check if statements agree with the claims or views of the writer in the reading passage – i.e. does the writer make a judgement about information in the reading passage?

Checking claims is similar to checking information. Look at the 'True/False/Not Given' statements above. All of the statements can be classed as claims, but only statement **7** could be classed as an opinion or view. For example, statement **1** cannot be an opinion because it is either a statement of fact or a claim. The same applies to statement **2** and so on. You can put *It is a fact that* or *I claim that* in front of all these statements, but you cannot say *I believe that* before the statements, because it is not a matter of opinion. Can you say: *I believe that water boils at 100 degrees centigrade?* It is a claim until it is proven.

1 Work in pairs. Look at the extract and statements **1–9** below. The words <u>underlined</u> highlight the views expressed in the statements. These words can occur in statements checking the views of the writer. Decide what the function of the words underlined is in each sentence.

THROUGH THE LIBRARY DOORS

There are different ways to encourage people, both adults and children, to read. Some adults are clearly intimidated by the environment of libraries and bookshops in a way that children are not. Therefore, making libraries more appealing by creating an inviting environment that is modern and relaxing is likely to appeal to both young people and adults, even those who would not normally use a library. Offering facilities other than books such as a coffee shop, computers, DVD lending facilities and a wide range of magazines and newspapers will also entice people through the library doors. Once in, there is then a chance that some may look at books as people have a tendency to browse just as they might do in a supermarket or other shop. So maybe there is a place for teaching library managers marketing skills. This, however, may be a step too far for some people. Nevertheless, if the aim is to encourage people to read, then any solution is worth a try.

Starting young and using the young to attract the old is the long-term approach. Bookshops and libraries in the UK organize reading groups for young children, discussion groups, lectures and chess clubs, all of which are worthwhile activities for attracting readers. Reading groups for children have the added benefit of attracting adults who may not read themselves, but who may start browsing while they are waiting for their children.

Do the following statements agree with the views of the writer in the extract above?

Write:

YES	if the statement agrees with the views of the writer
NO	if the statement contradicts the views of the writer
NOT GIVEN	if there is impossible to say what the writer thinks of this

1 <u>It is easier</u> for children to go into libraries than some adult members of the public.

2 <u>The best way</u> to attract people into libraries is by making them more welcoming.

3 Libraries <u>should</u> be allowed to sell books and magazines.

4 People <u>tend to</u> browse when they enter any large building.

5 Marketing skills <u>could</u> be taught to those who run libraries.

6 <u>There is a chance</u> that teaching marketing skills to managers will be unpopular.

7 Having reading clubs for children in libraries is an <u>effective</u> measure.

8 Discussion groups are of <u>little</u> use in encouraging people to visit libraries.

9 Reading clubs are <u>better suited</u> to book shops than libraries.

2 Answer questions **1–9**.

READING PASSAGE

You should spend about 20 minutes on questions **1–13**, which are based on the reading passage on page 89.

the reading passage on page 89.

Questions 1–6

The reading passage has eight paragraphs **A–H**.

Choose the correct headings for paragraphs **B** and **D–H** from the list of headings below.

List of Headings

i	Organizations observing coastal change and their specific duties
ii	The importance of geoscientists in coastal management
iii	The link between research and funding
iv	The complexity of making decisions about coastal defences
v	Sites that are of special interest
vi	A contrast between engineered and natural defence techniques
vii	The role played by the Environment Agency in preventing flooding
viii	The methods employed to check coastal change
ix	The need for an integrated approach to coastal management
x	Factors leading to coastal erosion
xi	How management plans for the coastline operate

Example	*Answer*
Paragraph **A**	**x**

1	Paragraph **B**

Example	*Answer*
Paragraph **C**	**iii**

2	Paragraph **D**
3	Paragraph **E**
4	Paragraph **F**
5	Paragraph **G**
6	Paragraph **H**

The Impact of Coastal Erosion

A There is little doubt that rates of coastal change will escalate with enhanced rates of sea level rise and increasing storminess, both of which are associated with global warming. These changes are likely to have a significant impact on coastal populations and infrastructure. Sea levels are expected to rise significantly over the next century, largely as a result of the melting of ice sheets and thermal expansion of the oceans. Global warming will also change ocean currents, world weather patterns, winds, coastal currents, waves and storms. The increase in the frequency and size of the latter, which have an enormous influence on coastal change and near-shore sediment transport, will have a major impact on the form of UK coasts.

B Geological, archaeological and historical records are used to establish the nature of past coastal change. Monitoring of coastal change is also undertaken using a broad range of techniques including airborne laser ranging technology (LIDAR) and digital aerial photogrammetry. These techniques are used to determine coastal topography, coastal erosion, and shoreline position with high accuracy. The bathymetry of offshore areas is determined by several geophysical techniques including side-scan sonar or multi-beam surveys. In the UK geoscientists are widely involved in projects that address past coastal change and monitor how coasts are changing today. The principal aim of many of these studies is to understand the natural processes that govern coastal change in order to predict the patterns and rates of future coastal evolution.

C A broad range of decision-makers, including coastal zone planners, government and authorities require accurate and well-researched information in managing the coastal zone. Much of the impetus and funding for such research is derived from the Department for the Environment, Food and Rural Affairs (DEFRA).

D Some agencies have particular responsibilities for monitoring particular aspects of coastal change. For instance, the Environment Agency has responsibilities for flooding in England and Wales. Three national agencies (English Nature, the Conservancy Council for Scotland and the Countryside Council for Wales) are responsible for preserving flora, fauna and geological features, including those along the coast. The best examples of wildlife habitats, geological features and landforms are designated as Sites of Special Scientific Interest (SSSI: there are about 6500 of these covering about 9% of the UK land area). Many surveys are carried out by the Ordnance Survey, the Hydrographic Office or the British Geological Survey. Other monitoring schemes are run by other government research institutes, universities and local government. Some funding for UK coastal projects is derived from the European Union.

E Much of this research on coastal change forms the basis for integrated coastal zone management on a local, national and international level. In the UK, Shoreline Management Plans (SMPs) are required for coastal management. Each of the SMPs is required to consider coastal change and issues such as sediment transport in the near-shore zone. Most

SMPs consider distinct parts of the coast, such as complete estuaries or sections of coast in which near-shore sediment is largely 'contained' within a coastal cell, or behaves in a consistent manner. SMPs broadly recommend, in scientific and technical terms, where: the process of erosion can be checked; the line can be held; 'managed retreat' of the coastline is the only option. Such evaluation is important given the high costs of coastal defences, which can only escalate in future years.

F Currently about 44% of the English and Welsh coast is protected by some form of coastal defence. Difficult decisions will need to be made to determine how this percentage will change in response to the increased rates of coastal erosion caused by sea-level rise. These decisions cannot be made without widespread consultation and will need to balance the socio-economic needs of developers, landowners and residents with coastal protection and environmental groups. Furthermore, they will need to take aspects of European legislation (e.g. the Habitats Directive) that have been incorporated into British law, into consideration.

G Coastal managers have to consider not only which parts of the coast they should attempt to defend, but also which type of defence is most appropriate.

Locally it will be best to defend coastal areas using traditional constructions, such as sea-walls, dykes, groynes and breakwaters. Such engineered 'hard' structures are expensive and may only result in enhanced coastal erosion on adjacent coasts. The alternative approach is to work with natural processes and create 'soft' engineered solutions, e.g. by encouraging accumulation of sediments in selected areas. For example, sediments accumulating in estuarine salt marshes protect the estuaries and associated human infrastructure from erosion, storm surges and coastal flooding.

H Whatever approach is used, no section of coast should be studied or managed in isolation. The whole picture must be understood, in regard to changes in the past, the present position and how any coastal management scheme will be affected by future changes. The best and most sustainable options probably lie in an integrated coastal zone management approach. These may contain multiple response strategies that can be modified for different socio-economic factors and environmental conditions, working with natural processes rather than against them. Geoscientists have a key role to play in providing the foundations for such management.

Don't forget!

- Read the stem and underline any words that you think will be paraphrased, for example, *accelerate* in question 7. This will help you locate the information in the text.
- Read each alternative as a complete sentence by combining it with the stem.
- Locate the information in the text.

Questions 7–9

Choose the correct letter **A**, **B**, **C** or **D**.

7 Coastal change will accelerate as

    A coastal populations increase.

    B various events in the oceans occur.

    C sea levels gradually fall.

    D the oceans cool down.

8 Methods like LIDAR are employed to

    A confirm the shape of the coastline of the past.

    B halt the spread of coastal erosion to neighbouring areas.

    C provide data on off-shore areas of the coastline.

    D establish the shape of the coastline with great precision.

9 Some national agencies have

    A coastal and inland responsibilities for conservation.

    B only inland preservation responsibilities.

    C charge of designating SSSIs.

    D duty to monitor coastal and inland flooding.

Don't forget!

- Check the instructions carefully. The summary can be of the whole passage or just part of the passage. The instructions for questions 10–13 tell you that the summary only covers paragraphs F–H.
- Always check the word limit.
- Always think about the types of words that are needed, for example, nouns, verbs, adjectives, etc.
- Do not write down any words on the answer sheet that are paraphrased in the summary.

Questions 10–13

Complete the summary of paragraphs **F–H** below.

Choose **NO MORE THAN TWO WORDS** from the passage for each answer.

It will not be easy to decide how much of the coastline will have some form of protection in years to come. Any decision will need to be taken after **10** ...., taking into account the needs of local people and agencies. **11** .... need to look at the parts of the coast which they ought to try and protect and the most suitable defence. Local answers will involve the use of **12** ...., such as breakwaters, but these 'hard' structures are not cheap and may only cause coastal erosion on nearby areas. Alternatively, methods like encouraging the build up of sediments in certain places may be the answer. In any case, no stretch of the coastline should be dealt with in **13** ....

Recognizing and understanding basic text relationships

Work in groups. Learning to recognize the type of texts that are contained in the reading passages can help you to find your way around the text more easily. In your groups, answer questions **1–10**.

1 Look at the heading of the passage on page 89. What does the word 'impact' tell you about the passage?

2 Is the word 'erosion' related to cause or effect?

3 In the headings you have chosen for paragraphs **A–H**, do any of them contain causes, effects or solutions?

4 Are these words for causes, effects and solutions, or synonyms?

5 Look at question **7**. Is the stem the cause or the effect?

6 Look at question **8**. Is the stem the cause or the effect?

7 In the summary (questions **10–13**), find a synonym for the word *solutions*.

8 Is the passage based on cause/effect and problem/solution or is it historical?

9 Is the passage on The Bronze Age: Xia Dynasty on page 85 based on cause/effect and problem/solution or is it historical?

10 What other text types do you know from your own reading?

Speaking
IELTS Part 3

1 ◯ With a partner, look at the photographs below and describe what kind of training is taking place and how it is being conducted.

Don't forget!

- Talk about abstract details and avoid personal examples.
- Make sure you support your answers by giving examples and causes and effects.

2 ◯ Work in pairs. Take turns asking and answering the following Part 3 questions. When your partner has finished speaking, give him/her feedback using the checklist on page 210.

Work and aspirations

Do young people today have the same aspirations as previous generations? Why/Why not?

Do you think it is good to have aims and goals in life?

In what ways can these aims and aspirations be achieved?

How different do you think the world of work and training is for young people today? Do they have more opportunities now compared to the past?

Is the way that students learn nowadays different from the past?

Vocabulary 1: Work

1 Work in pairs. For sentences **1–8** below, <u>underline</u> the correct word in *italics*.

    1 I want to be independent, so I'd like to earn my own *profession/qualifications/livelihood*.

    2 The *job/work/profession* ethic varies from country to country and from one profession to another.

    3 I would really like to have a good *job/work/livelihood,* which allows me to achieve my aims.

    4 It isn't easy holding down a *job/work/livelihood,* especially with children to look after.

    5 Is your idea of a *profession/qualifications/job* based on a 9 to 5 job?

    6 I am a teacher by *career/profession/qualifications*.

    7 In order to improve their *qualifications/job/work* prospects, and thus to climb the *career/ profession/qualifications* ladder, students need to study hard.

    8 Being up-to-date is essential; otherwise, it is possible to miss out on the best *job/work/ livelihood* opportunities.

2 Look at the sentences in exercise 1. Decide if you can use the word *occupation* instead of any of the alternatives.

3 ⬤ Work in pairs. Use the list of skills below and your own ideas to decide which three skills are most important for your work life and your social life. Give examples and reasons for your choices.

    • using the computer

    • writing longhand

    • playing a musical instrument

    • calculating in your head

    • socializing

Reading
IELTS Reading Passage

Don't forget!

• If there is no title, look at the last question and the illustration, then skim the questions and the text.

READING PASSAGE

You should spend about 20 minutes on **Questions 1–13**, which are based on the reading passage below.

Few students taking a Masters in Business Administration (MBA) are there through sheer love of learning. Most want to learn in order to apply their knowledge once the course is over. On the other hand, the MBA is an academic course. How do you take account of these conflicting needs when it comes to assessment? 'In education generally – not just in the MBA world – there is a move away from traditional exams towards people looking for ways to make assessment more relevant,' says Jeannette Purcell, chief executive of the Association of MBAs (AMBA). She says that exams will always exist because so much of an MBA involves acquiring knowledge best tested through a written paper, but 'business schools are developing programmes to become more practical, more applied, using real life situations and assessment has to reflect that change.'

One reason for this is the rise in the executive over the full-time MBA, which means most students are studying while working for a company. Another is a changing approach towards learning. Oliver Westall, Lancaster University Management School's MBA director, says: 'When I began teaching many years ago, there was an attitude that we decided what ought to be taught, because we knew what students needed to know. Now, increasingly, especially when students come to our MBA programme with an average of seven years' experience, sensible faculties realise that students can bring a lot more to the table when they share their experience.'

Business schools therefore now often assess students on their ability to work as part of a team, while some even include an element of peer assessment in which students mark each other's contributions. Dublin City University assesses its MBA students through team presentations, team-written assignments, case study analyses, individual work-based projects, strategic organisational analyses and business plans. Exams account for less than 50 per cent of the total marks awarded, while teamwork accounts for around 30 per cent. Melrona Kirrane, academic director of the MBA programme, says team-based assessment raises issues every year. 'MBA students are enormously competitive and quite aggressive and hostile,' she says. 'They are there for their own purposes and they aren't impressed when other team members don't play their part.' But she says it remains a key part of assessment, because being able to function well in a team is vital in any business organisation.

Teamwork is also tested in consultancies for real companies, which is also playing an increasingly important role in assessment for many institutions. Full-time MBAs at Ashridge complete their written exams within three months of starting the programme, to provide a foundation of knowledge, and the rest of the course focuses on practical work. They can choose to take a consulting project for up to eight weeks or submit a 10,000 word dissertation. For the past two years, Coventry University has allowed students to do a company internship rather than a dissertation in their final semester. Three quarters of their mark in this is based on a report they present to the company, a further 10 per cent on the employer's assessment, and 15 per cent on a piece reflecting on their own learning.

Gareth Griffiths, MBA programme director at Aston University, where students undertake a consultancy project at the end of the course worth a third of the overall mark, says that while employers' opinions are important they have to be treated with caution because they can expect far too much or too little. Sometimes they cannot be objective because they hope to employ the student in future. This struggle to be objective is a common concern when it comes to alternative methods of assessment. 'I think any alternative to assessment by exams is not going to be as rigorous or as accurate,' says Purcell. But she argues that the more these alternative assessment methods are used, the better business schools will get at using them effectively. And there are ways of ensuring rigour, such as benchmarking across different courses and assessors, and making sure that assessments are based on more than one person's opinion, and on fixed criteria.

While AMBA (the Association of MBAs) would expect a course to involve some exams before it gave accreditation, Purcell says, it would be concerned if exams were the only assessment method. Meanwhile, few would suggest that alternative assessment methods are an easy option for the student. Marie Hardie, postgraduate internship manager in Coventry University's business school, says students find they not only have to get used to a company's culture in a few weeks, they often have to persuade them to part with money – 'Not an easy thing to do'. Overseas students can find non-exam assessments particularly stressful. While exams can be challenging for those whose first language isn't English, so can verbal presentations.

Dan Gray, an Ashridge MBA student, says that while he appreciates his course's practical focus, exams are still important, 'After all,' he says, 'exams test your ability to perform under pressure, and that's a critical skill for any senior manager.' But it is not the only skill. 'If you think about what employers want from MBA students, they want well rounded people who have demonstrated skills in all areas and have been assessed in many different ways,' says Purcell. Marco Romero's assessment for consultancy work he carried out for the Birmingham Chamber of Commerce during his MBA was so positive that he is still working for them.

**ow to go
bout it**

questions **1–5**:

Put a box around
the names of the
people in the
passage. This will
help you find the
answers more
quickly.

Underline words
or phrases in the
statements that will
help you match the
statements and the
people.

Some sentences
will be complete
paraphrases of the
text so you need to
be able to recognize
meaning.

r questions **6–12**:

Decide which
types of words are
missing. Try to guess
the meaning of the
missing word and
look for a synonym
in the passage.

Check the word
limit.

Don't write words
on the answer
sheet that are in the
question.

Questions 1–5

Look at the following people (Questions 1–5) and the list of statements below.

Match each person with the correct statement, **A–H**.

1 Jeannette Purcell
2 Oliver Westall
3 Melrona Kirrane
4 Gareth Griffiths
5 Dan Gray

List of Statements

A concedes that practical skills are important, but maintains that exams are a valuable assessment tool

B feels that testing by exams is more thorough and precise than other methods

C says that written exams are becoming more and more critical

D suggests the views of employers are not always impartial

E thinks that MBA students have more practical know-how nowadays

F states that evaluation by peers should be included in any course assessment

G thinks persuading companies to pay for courses is difficult

H believes team-based assessment to be essential in evaluation of MBA students

---

Questions 6–12

Complete the sentences below.

Choose **NO MORE THAN TWO WORDS** from the passage for each answer.

6 Purcell believes that other methods of assessment are replacing ....

7 Business students are now tested on being able to function in a ....

8 At Dublin City University .... still makes up less of the total marks than exams.

9 On full-time MBAs at Ashridge written exams are done early so students can concentrate on ....

10 One way to ensure the thoroughness of testing is not to rely on just one individual's ....

11 To students from outside the UK the testing that is not based on exams is sometimes especially ....

12 One form of assessment that is sometimes demanding for students who are not native speakers of English is ....

Question 13

Choose the correct letter **A**, **B**, **C** or **D**.

13 Which of the following is the most suitable title for the reading passage?

A The end of written exams?

B The importance of MBAs

C Practical assessment in decline?

D Teamwork and written exams compared

⬤ **Reacting to the text**

Do you think that written exams are old-fashioned? Why/Why not?

What kind of tests do you like or dislike. Why?

If you were able to create your ideal course, what would it be like?

Listening
IELTS Section 3

1  Work in pairs. Make a list of points that you need to consider when you are doing a presentation. Then discuss which would be the most important for you and why.

Don't forget!

• Skim the questions to see what the topic is and underline words that will help you listen for the answer.

1.11 **SECTION 3   Questions 21–30**

Questions 21–25

Choose **FIVE** letters, **A–H**.

Which **FIVE** improvements does Olivia suggest?

    A   check the equipment
    B   reduce the pace
    C   include more data
    D   distribute the handouts
    E   make the talk longer
    F   improve the organization
    G   make the talk shorter
    H   check the room layout

Questions 26–28

Complete the sentences below.

Write **NO MORE THAN ONE WORD** for each answer.

    JACK'S FEEDBACK

    26 He thinks that he used an excessive amount of .... in his talk.

    27 He was frightened that they would appear ....

    28 He feels the main thing for him is to control his ....

Questions 29 and 30

Answer the questions below.

Write **ONE WORD ONLY** for each answer.

    29 What did the students and the tutor say the presentation was?

    ....

    30 What is the tutor going to photocopy for them to take away?

    ....

2  Have you ever given a presentation? What kind of presentation was it?

Did you feel it went well? Why/Why not? What would you do differently if you had to do it again?

Language focus: Conditionals 1

1 Look at the statements below from the listening practice on page 96. Identify the tenses and number the boxes as follows:

1 1st conditional

2 2nd conditional

3 3rd conditional

☐ *If we had given ourselves more time, it would have flowed better.*

☐ *… but if I had to do it again, I'd change a few things.*

☐ *If I do it again, I'll spend more time practising to make it run more smoothly.*

🅖 Read more about conditionals in the Grammar reference on page 223.

2 For sentences **1–8** below, put the verbs in brackets into the correct tense.

1 If young people _____ (give) opportunities to prepare for the changes affecting the world, finding a job will prove easier for them in the future.

2 If time and effort _____ (devote) to creating closer economic ties in the past, countries would have come closer together.

3 Unless young people invest time in acquiring new skills, they _____ (find) life harder in the future.

4 I would not have achieved the results unless I _____ (work) hard.

5 Going to university _____ (turn out to be) an enjoyable experience if students balance studying time with making new friends.

6 I think more money needs to be put into education; otherwise, the high standards we have reached _____ (decline).

7 If people pursued their goals, they _____ (succeed) whatever happened.

8 Many people would love to turn the clock back and lead the same life again if they _____ (have) the chance.

3 ⬭ Work in pairs. Each person should choose one of the statements in exercise 2. Discuss each statement by explaining why you agree or disagree with it. Give reasons and examples.

4 Complete sentences **1–6** below with your own words.

1 Were the government to take more responsibility for people's training needs, then …

2 Had I been able to choose …

3 If the change in the pace of life continues at its current rate, …

4 If people are not adaptable and prepared to change jobs, then …

5 It is important for everyone nowadays to aim to have some kind of profession; otherwise, …

6 Unless my parents had been prepared to sacrifice a lot to educate me, …

5 For **1–6** below decide which word is missing in each sentence.

1 The educational process for children is free of unnecessary stress, they won't develop properly.

2 Had there been skills shortages in rich countries, workers from poorer countries would not have moved there.

3 If my father had not migrated to Australia, I have been born in Japan.

4 If people did have qualifications, it would be more difficult to assess their suitability for a job.

5 Some adults had better literacy and numeracy skills, they would access the job market more easily.

6 Had universities permitted to expand faster, there would have been a more skilled workforce now.

6 ⬭ Work in pairs. Take turns asking and answering the following questions. You will need to decide which questions are relevant to your partner.

1 What would happen if you didn't go to university?

2 What would have happened if you hadn't learnt English?

3 What will you do if you get through university?

4 If you had another chance, would you follow a different career path?

5 Were you to go to university, how would it change your life?

7 ⬭ Do you think success as a student and in life in general is a matter of luck or a result of planning? Give reasons and examples.

Vocabulary 2: Collocations

1 Work in pairs. For **1–10** below, <u>underline</u> the word or phase in each list which cannot be used with the noun in *italics*.

1 *benefit*   considerable / enjoy / make / derive / accrue / gain / financial

2 *advantage*   huge / considerable / education / enjoy / gain / outweigh / take

3 *opportunity*   ample / once in a lifetime / silver / career / provide / seize / squander

4 *success*   enormous / large / enjoy / achieve / guarantee / depends on

5 *prospects*   excellent / get / offer / boost / damage / long-term / employment / career

6 *disadvantage*   distinct / obvious / suffer / have / enjoy / offset

7 *failure*   total / complete / achieve / result in / end in / expect

8 *achievement*   outstanding / accrue / impressive / proudest / represent / a lack of

9 *improvement*   huge / massive / show / make / take up / scope / room

10 *chance*   good / deserve / give somebody / throw away / possess / arise / take

2 Complete the gaps in **1–8** below with a word or phrase from exercise 1. There may be more than possible one answer.

1 Achieving _____ in life depends on many factors like qualifications, but it cannot always be _____ by having them.

2 Even if an academic career ends in _____ , it does not mean that someone's _____ career _____ are seriously _____ .

3 Everyone _____ a fair _____ at succeeding in life, but all too often people squander the opportunity.

4 I made a huge _____ in my last years at school, but looking back there was certainly _____ for more.

5 A person who has a vocational education in plumbing or engineering does not suffer any _____ in life. On the contrary, having such an education is a _____ _____ .

6 The financial _____ that _____ from acquiring training and skills means that one can enjoy the fruits of one's labours.

7 Finding my first job _____ the proudest _____ in my life so far.

8 Going to university in my country is a _____ _____ that needs to be _____ once it comes.

3  With a partner, discuss what advantages, opportunities and achievements you have had in your lives so far. Are there any opportunities that you have thrown away?

Speaking
IELTS Part 2

1 Prepare brief notes for one of the following Part 2 task cards. Limit yourself to no more than ten words. Use words and phrases from Vocabulary 2 on page 98.

> Describe a school that you liked.
>
> You should say:
>
> > where the school was
> >
> > when you attended it
> >
> > what it was like
>
> and explain why you liked this school.

> Describe an achievement that you will never forget.
>
> You should say:
>
> > what the achievement is
> >
> > when it happened
> >
> > what it means to you
>
> and explain why you will never forget this achievement.

2 ○ With a partner, take turns talking about the topic. When your partner has finished speaking, give him/her feedback using the checklist on page 210.

Writing:
IELTS Task 2

1 Work in groups. Discuss the structure and content of the answer required for the following Task 2 question, using questions **1–4** below to help you. Before you discuss the question you may want to skim the reading passage on page 93 again and look at Vocabulary 1 on page 93 and Vocabulary 2 on page 98.

WRITING TASK 2

You should spend about 40 minutes on this task.

Write about the following topic:

> *In the modern world there is a movement away from written exams to more practical assessment.*
>
> *Discuss the advantages and disadvantages of this trend.*

Give reasons for your answer and include any relevant examples from your own knowledge and experience.

Write at least 250 words.

---

1 Do you have to write about both the advantages and the disadvantages?

2 Do you have to devote equal space to each?

3 How many advantages/disadvantages do you need to write about?

4 Do you have to use as many connecting devices as possible?

2 Read the model answer below and <u>underline</u> the words from Vocabulary 2 exercise 1 on page 98.

Testing students and workers takes various forms including written, oral and practical assessment. However, although written tests are still the most popular way to check achievement at work and university, a range of alternative methods like problem-solving, role-play, oral presentation and work-based assessment are becoming more common. Both approaches of evaluating student attainment are valid, but each tests different things.

Some people believe that there is considerable benefit to be gained from using written exams compared to more practical testing methods. For example, from an administrative point of view, the former are generally easier to deal with. Moreover, if factual knowledge is being tested, then it is easier to check it on a written paper than in a group problem-solving exercise. However, the obvious disadvantage of written tests is that they do not suit everyone. Take students in Italy where oral exams are used as a means of checking knowledge. Switching to written tests could then be problematic. Conversely, students used only to written tests would be at a distinct disadvantage, if they were asked to take a more practical exam.

Other people feel that written tests are of little benefit, as they do not always assess students or workers fitness for the vast array of opportunities that the real world of work provides. Functioning in the real world involves making quick decisions, working with other people and using different types of intelligence like emotional and social intelligence. Therefore, it makes sense to test in the same way. Those people who will enjoy success in the future will be those who are able to operate efficiently within systems and find their way around, i.e. the ones who can manipulate knowledge and use experience rather than possess knowledge.

3 Find words and phrases in the model answer that have the same meaning as each of the words and phrases in the box below. There may be more than one possible answer.

| assessing/examining   preferred   various means   while   methods |
| enormous   derived   angle   on the other hand   be appropriate for   use |

4 Work in pairs. Find examples of the following in the second paragraph of the model answer. <u>Underline</u> the linking words that identify these functions.

- a result
- a condition
- a contrast
- an example

5 Work in pairs. For sentences **1–5** below, add punctuation to connect the information.

1 Learning skills as opposed to knowledge makes people more practical moreover it gives them greater flexibility as skills are often transferable.

2 Skills are very much in vogue however knowledge is also essential.

3 There are many skills that young people have acquired take texting for example this is sometimes criticized but it teaches language skills in a different way.

4 It is difficult to distinguish knowledge from experience furthermore skills are also linked to both.

5 If skills like manipulating knowledge are learnt then it will benefit both the individual and the economy.

6 ⬭ Work in groups. Discuss the following Task 2 question. Then write your own answer. When you have finished, check your answer using the checklist on page 209.

Don't forget!

- Make a list of any words or ideas that come into your head related to both sides.
- Sometimes writing a full idea might take too long. 1–3 words are enough to remind you.
- As you make your list, do not exclude any ideas.

WRITING TASK 2

You should spend about 40 minutes on this task.

Write about the following topic:

In the modern world, more and more emphasis is being placed on the acquisition of practical skills rather than knowledge from text books or other sources.

Discuss the advantages and disadvantages of this trend.

Give reasons for your answer and include any relevant examples from your own knowledge and experience.

Write at least 250 words.

7 Review

Vocabulary

1 Match each sentence beginning **1–8** with an ending **a–h**.

1	He is a policeman	**a**	work ethic always helps.
2	She earns her	**b**	living working in a chemist shop.
3	I don't really like the idea of	**c**	jobs is difficult if you have a family.
4	Holding down several	**d**	career prospects.
5	I would like to improve my	**e**	by profession.
6	I gained new qualifications to	**f**	climb the career ladder.
7	I wouldn't change my	**g**	occupation.
8	Having a very strong	**h**	a 9 to 5 job.

2 For **1–8** below, unjumble the words to make a sentence and find the unnecessary word.

1 qualifications needed for the job livelihood what are

2 both and work is good for job you physically mentally

3 in wood profession by making earns his carvings he living delicate very

4 as profession a very noble working farmer is qualification a

5 the future profession will have social work I to do be connected the job with in

6 is demanding career an like very occupation teaching but also having rewarding

7 a engineering have possible work career in if I like would to

8 in especially interested banking I'm in a occupation finance career

3 For sentences **1–8** below, replace each of the <u>underlined</u> words with a word of your own.

1 They achieved <u>considerable</u> success in their working lives.

2 I <u>derived real</u> benefit from a university education.

3 My qualifications gave me a <u>huge</u> advantage at the interview.

4 His employment prospects are <u>enhanced</u> by the opening of the new bank.

5 Many opportunities have been <u>wasted</u> here.

6 There is an <u>obvious</u> disadvantage to concentrating on only one learning mechanism.

7 There is always <u>scope</u> for improvement, no matter who you are.

8 It was such an <u>outstanding</u> achievement to come top in the exams.

Conditionals 1

1   For each sentence **1–7** below, complete the first gap with *if, unless* or *otherwise*; some sentences may not require a word. For the second gap, put the verb in brackets into the correct tense.

  1 _____ they had followed the guidelines, they _____ (succeed).

  2 _____ the country is to progress, then new technologies _____ (need) to be embraced with open arms.

  3 _____ they don't put more effort into the scheme, it _____ (not succeed).

  4 _____ the government _____ (encourage) more people to take up training, it would benefit us all.

  5 I think that more houses need to be built; _____ there _____ (be) a crisis.

  6 _____ were we ever to inhabit the moon, I _____ (be) very surprised.

  7 _____ written exams are removed from the education system, it _____ (cause) enormous upset.

2   Rewrite sentences **1–7** in exercise 1 using the words below.

  1 had
  2 otherwise
  3 unless
  4 were
  5 if not
  6 if
  7 otherwise

Proof reading

1   Find and correct the mistakes in the following extract from an IELTS Writing Task 2 answer.

> If people feel that they are not given the same oportunities as their colleagues in the work place, they will then begin to feel disatisfied. That's when the problems set in. For the work environment to be relaxe, people need to work as a team. This can reduce quiet a lot of tension. Morover, by working with people rather than against them, the work enviroment will be much more comfortable ...

2   Look at the following list of words and decide whether the spelling is correct. When you have finished, check your answers with a dictionary.

  1 thoroughness
  2 acheivement
  3 *enhanced*
  4 *improvment*
  5 profession
  6 carier
  7 *qualfications*
  8 flexbility
  9 *conversly*
  10 assessment
  11 memorable
  12 *excesive*

Vocabulary 1: Nouns relating to places

1 ◯ Work in groups. Describe the similarities and the differences between the maps. Then discuss the questions below.

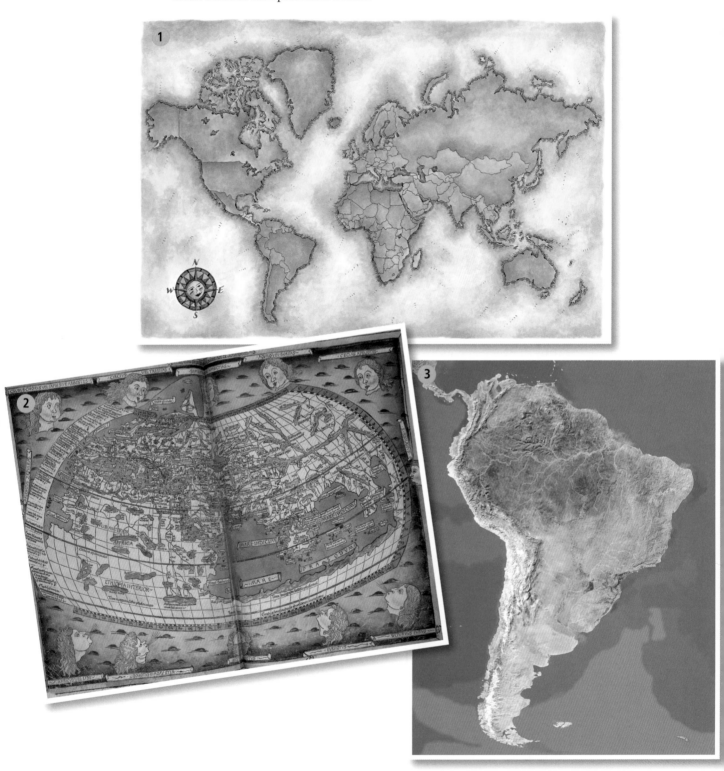

- What do you think the purpose is of each map?
- When was the last time you consulted a map of some kind? Why did you use it?
- How has technology changed the way we prepare maps?
- Do you think satellite maps invade our privacy?

2 For **1–8** below, decide which of the nouns in brackets go in each gap. Some nouns are interchangeable. Make any necessary changes.

1 The poor _____ I grew up in is very different now. It used be a very rough _____ , but now it is a quiet residential street.   (area/neighbourhood)

2 Yes I had a favourite _____ I liked to visit, but it has become a real tourist _____ , so I don't go there anymore.   (place/spot)

3 The park in the business _____ is surrounded by a pedestrian_____ , which makes it a real haven of peace.   (zone/district)

4 My family home is in a magnificent _____ overlooking the sea. It's a _____ famed for its views.   (region/location)

5 The _____ I now live in is quite built-up, but it still has quite a lot of big open _____ .   (area/space)

6 There have been a few burglaries in the _____ recently, but by and large it is a very safe _____ .   (vicinity/neighbourhood)

7 India has some beautiful _____ to visit, especially in the northern _____ of the country, where you can avoid most of the tourist hot _____ . (regions/spots/places)

8 The house was built in a beautiful _____ on a hillside with a stream and surrounded by trees. This whole _____ is spectacular at any time of the year but especially in the autumn.   (region/setting)

3 Work in pairs. You can build up a description of a place by adding phrases after the noun. Decide which phrases **1–10** you associate most with phrases **a–j.** There may be more than possible one answer.

1	on a cliff top	a	surrounded by trees
2	on a hillside	b	overlooking the sea
3	a wooded hillside	c	with no houses, just endless fields
4	an open space	d	covered with trees
5	an empty desert	e	with lots of cars and people
6	a noisy neighbourhood	f	covered with rock and crags
7	a temperate zone	g	fed by a high waterfall and disturbed only by birdsong
8	a sandy beach	h	with huge sand dunes and no people
9	a secluded lake	i	teeming with wildlife
10	a rugged mountain	j	stretching into the distance and pounded by the Pacific Ocean

4 For **1–4** below, put the words in *italics* into the correct order.

1 I live in a block of flats, *small a overlooking garden.* It's in a really beautiful and quiet *old buildings neighbourhood with.* And though it's in the heart of the city, it is a peaceful area, *sound only the odd by the of birds and disturbed car.*

2 My family home is on a beach *seashore miles along the stretching for.* It's an ideal place for sports enthusiasts *opportunity of boating with for lots of plenty and swimming.* The house, though *two built years ago hundred*, is still in good condition.

3 My family come from a village *by mountains beautiful surrounded.* In summer the mountainside, *purple its with flowers,* is a blaze of colour.

4 My dream location for a house would be a secluded lake with a *height falling by trees great waterfall from a surrounded* or even a hillside *with covered views out but with looking trees* over the countryside.

Speaking

IELTS Part 2

1 Work in pairs. Make questions with the phrases below.

a region of your country

the neighbourhood you live in

a place with fond memories

a square you like

a seaside town you like

Useful expressions

Can you describe … ?

Where … ?

When … ?

How often … ?

Why do you … ?

2 ◯ Work with a new partner. Take turns asking and answering the questions you made in exercise 1.

3 Work in pairs. It is important to try to control the rhythm of your speech. Mark the stress in the words in the sentence beginnings **1–5** below. Put *o* above the syllables which have a secondary stress and *0* above the syllables which have the main stress.

Example:

    o   o   o   0 o

We went to a nice place by the sea yesterday.

1 I was living in a small flat when I first came here, but then I …

2 We stayed in a nice hotel overlooking the sea, because …

3 The place is very special to me, because it …

4 The place I'm going to describe for you is …

5 I like the area very much, because it's …

4 ◯ Work in pairs. Practise saying the phrases in exercise 3. First say the words with the stressed syllables (*went nice place sea yesterday*). Then say the sentence (*We went to a nice place by the sea yesterday.*).

5 Work in pairs. Make notes for the following Part 2 task card. Where possible, use words from Vocabulary 1 on page 104 and the sentence beginnings in exercise 3.

Describe a place which is special for you.

You should say:

   where it is

   when you first went there

   what appeals to you about it

and explain why this place is special to you.

6 ◯ Take turns talking about the topic. When your partner has finished speaking, give him/her feedback using the checklist on page 210. Then practise talking about the topic again.

Don't forget!

• Time yourselves. You should speak for up to two minutes

Listening
IELTS Section 4

1   How are lectures usually organized? How can you understand the main ideas in a lecture?

2   Read the notes in questions **31–40** below. Decide what the subject of the lecture you will hear is. Then decide how many major sections there are.

3   Look at each gap in the notes and answer questions **1–6** below.

   1 What kind of information is missing? Is it a noun, adjective, verb, adverb or number?
   2 If it is a noun, is the noun singular or plural?
   3 Which answers relate to time?
   4 Which answers relate to a reason for something?
   5 Which is an idea suggested by the other words in the notes?
   6 Which is a number or a percentage?

2.1   **SECTION 4   Questions 31–40**

Questions 31–40

Complete the notes below.

Write **NO MORE THAN THREE WORDS AND/OR A NUMBER** for each answer.

Migration of early humans

Human migration has occurred throughout history

First significant migration occurred approximately **31** .... years ago

Early pioneers did not survive

Earth experienced changes in **32** .... about 70,000 years ago

New band of modern humans left Africa

Colonization

- China about 50,000 years ago and Europe about **33** .... years ago

- the open steppes of Siberia some 40,000 years ago

- roughly 20,000 years ago arriving in Japan, then linked to the main **34** ....

- Australia was reached across the sea on **35** .... 50,000 years ago

- America via Alaska some time between 15 and 13,000 years ago

Migration within Africa

Bantu occupied around **36** .... of the African continent by 1,000 AD

Stimulus for the Bantu migration was perhaps the farming of the **37** ....

Population expansion led to movement into surrounding areas that were not heavily populated

Iron production introduced from **38** ....

The Bantu used iron tools to fell trees, clear forests and **39** ....

Iron meant they had a **40** .... over their neighbours

---

Language focus: Referring in a text

1 Look at the following extracts from the listening practice on page 107. Decide what the words in **bold** refer to.

*If we look at the first slide here, we can see the route this first group of modern humans took as they made their way across the Red Sea here, which was then a dry bed. Then through Arabia and into what is now the Middle East. But **these early pioneers** soon died out.*

*But at that time, just like today, the earth was subject to shifts in temperature. About 70,000 years ago, **the planet** became warmer and another group ...*

2 Look at sentences **1–3** below. What does the word in **bold** refer to in each sentence?

1 The neighbourhood is very noisy because **it** is full of shops and restaurants.

2 As the region is full of large farms, **it** is very rich.

3 The cost of farming has increased dramatically over the period. **This** (rise) has led to inflation.

3 Why is it not possible to use *this* instead of *it* in sentences **1** and **2**?

4 It is not possible to use *it* instead of *this* in sentence **3**, although you can leave out the word *rise*. Decide why.

(G) Read more about referring in a text in the Grammar reference on page 223.

5 Underline the correct alternative in *italics* in **1–8** below.

1 The poor neighbourhood where I live now was very different a few years ago. *The neighbourhood/It/This* used to be much more pleasant then.

2 The region is full of many places to see. *That/This/It* is what makes *this/it/that* such a fantastic place to live.

3 The location for the new airport has been changed to somewhere completely different. *This new development/ It/They* will cost a lot of money.

4 When I first discovered the woodland *it/this/that* was not known by many people, but now *it/this/that* is visited by dozens of people everyday.

5 The area has been transformed by the building of new factories and a business park. *This/It/That* has unfortunately made the place less attractive.

6 Various industrial sites are for sale at the moment, but *they/it/these* are too expensive. *This/That/It* will stop the area from developing.

7 The neighbourhoods in the north of the city are industrialized, while *these/they/those* in the south are more residential.

8 More people have moved away from the city centre to the suburbs. As a result, *these/they/these areas* are becoming more crowded and expensive.

6 For **1–7** below, remove the repetition in each sentence by using a suitable reference.

1 The price of property in this region is increasing, and the increase in the price of property in this region is set to continue.

2 The neighbourhood was poor once but the neighbourhood is rich now.

3 I like visiting the seaside when nobody is around; visiting the seaside when nobody is around is very relaxing.

4 If people make an effort to clean up after themselves when people visit parks, then parks will be much more inviting for the public in general.

5 He suggested I should go away for a couple of days. The suggestion that I should go away for a few days is okay, but the suggestion that I should go away for a couple of days is an expensive solution.

6 The government should pass laws to protect more areas of great natural beauty. Passing laws to protect more areas of great natural beauty would benefit all of us.

7 Progress cannot be stopped. Progress is inevitable, even if the progress is very slow and the progress stops altogether for a while. But progress stopping altogether for a while is unlikely to happen.

7 ⬤ Work in groups. Discuss the idea in sentence 7 in exercise 6. To what extent do you agree or disagree?

Reading
IELTS Reading Passage

1 Work in pairs. As quickly as you can, find words in the reading passage which have the same meaning as words **1–10** below.

1 intricate
2 intangible
3 representations
4 associations
5 local

6 future
7 non-spiritual
8 man-made objects
9 deep
10 assemble

2 Work in groups. Bring together the information you have about the text so far.

READING PASSAGE

You should spend about 20 minutes on **Questions 1–13**, which are based on the reading passage below.

Cartography

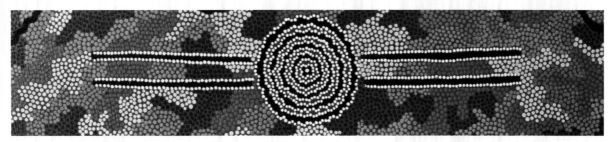

The history and study of cartography or map making shows how maps have influenced human affairs in the past. It necessarily involves not only the technical process used to make maps, but also observes the motives for their making and their role in forming society's views of space and place.

All humans possess a complex spatial knowledge of their environment. This 'cognitive mapping' is created through direct experience and by communication with others. However, the more formal activity of map making usually arises from the social needs of complex, extensive, and often highly bureaucratic societies. For societies in which humans live and communicate within small groups, there is little need to make maps of the terrestrial environment. Thus, it is probable that the function of a few petroglyphs that can broadly be identified as maps from the Upper Palaeolithic period, c. 30,000 BC, was probably magical and cosmographical (perhaps associated with agricultural fertility rites), and most of the images are in abstract as if viewed from above. Important Neolithic examples include a representation of the Anatolian town Çatal Hüyük (in present-day Turkey) from about 6200 BC, and a series of complex topographical images from the foothills of the Italian Alps in Valcamonica dating from around 1500 BC.

The very terms 'map' and 'cartography', with their strong Western overtones, are unsatisfactory for small indigenous local cultures, even though iconic representations of territory that approach the European functions of maps have existed. The form of these spatial expressions may be in an oral or kinaesthetic ritual performance rather than an inscription industrial societies normally regard as a map.

There are several characteristics that indigenous maps share cross-culturally. One is to serve as a record of a creation story or genealogical lineage of a people, as in many Ojibwa migration charts. Here, where migrations, astronomical events, battles, and other events are recorded for posterity, the representation of time and space is conflated in the form of the map, so that events separated by many centuries may appear side by side. In Australia, reconstructions of the legendary tracks of ancestors, the Dreamings, are recorded in bark paintings and other media of Aboriginal art. Sacred and secular uses are often merged, so that a representation of the cardinal directions in the cosmos may be embodied in the plan of a village or house, as in the Dogon peoples of the Sahara.

There are also didactic or mnemonic uses of maps in local indigenous cultures. For example, the stick charts of the people of the Marshall Islands (the only group that made these forms of map) are a training aid for navigators for understanding the location and pattern of ocean swells. In Africa, memory boards are used in initiation rites establishing lineage of kingships and recalling the location of famous events. Among the Apache, notched sticks were used to remember landmarks for expeditions.

Surviving artefacts from the civilizations of Mespotamia show a profound knowledge of astronomy for astrological purposes, as well as a practical knowledge of geometry and surveying in field surveys for taxation and irrigation purposes. These are mainly in the form of hundreds of clay tablets recording cadastral (landownership) information, mostly dating from the 1st millennium BC. Fewer map artefacts survive from ancient Egypt, but there is graphic evidence in wall paintings, inscriptions, and manuscripts of surveying instruments used to survey buildings and re-establish field markers after the annual flooding of the Nile had swept them away. The A'h-mosè or Rhind mathematical papyrus in the British Museum (dating between 1750 and 1580 BC) is an important source of such information.

Different types of maps were made in the European Middle Ages. The first of these are manuscript sea charts, mainly of the Mediterranean (the so-called portolan charts), originating from the 13th century. From the earliest known chart, the Carte Pisane (c 1275), to charts of the 17th century, the method of construction appears to have been the same: they seem to have been compiled from bearings and rough distances gleaned from repeated voyages, written itineraries, or other charts. The radiating lines of constant direction commonly found on these charts appear to have been used for navigation purposes rather than in their compilation, for they are usually added later, and are rarely found in the same place on two charts. The mention of the magnetic compass on board ship in the 13th century has led some to associate it with these lines.

How to go about it

For questions **1–5**:

- First read the sentence beginnings and then the endings.
- Check for beginnings and endings that don't fit together.
- Scan the reading passage for words or paraphrases of words in the sentence beginnings. Put a box around the words in the text to help you refer to them.
- Match the endings to the words you have located in the text.

Complete each sentence with the correct ending, **A–G**, below.

1 The analysis of a map

2 Awareness of one's surroundings

3 A land map

4 A Neolithic example

5 The term cartography

> **A** teaches us about the trade and commerce.
>
> **B** indicates the main settlements in antiquity.
>
> **C** reveals its impact on human development.
>
> **D** conjures up images that are related to developed, as opposed to traditional societies.
>
> **E** develops through practice and contact with different people.
>
> **F** serves very little purpose for isolated communities.
>
> **G** contains an image of a town.

Questions 6–11

Complete the table below.

Choose **NO MORE THAN TWO WORDS** from the passage for each answer.

The ways different groups used maps

People	Use
Ojibwa	employed maps where 6.................... and .... were brought together
Australian Aborigines	recorded information on various materials including 7 ....
Dogon	combined bearings in the 8 .... with the 9 .... of their living spaces

Apache	marked sticks as a memory aid for **10** ....
Mesopotamians	used geometry and surveying for various reasons with details recorded on **11** ....

Questions 12 and 13

Choose **TWO** letters, **A–E**.

Which **TWO** features of the creating of manuscript sea charts are mentioned by the writer in the passage?

    A The lines on the maps were drawn as the maps were made.

    B The lines on the maps seem to be used for map reading at sea.

    C The lines are always located in the same place on sea charts.

    D Other charts were not used in the creation of sea charts.

    E The process of making the maps is apparently identical in each case.

◯ Reacting to the text

Is modern technology like satnavs lessening our ability to interact with the environment first-hand and reducing spatial awareness in people?

Vocabulary 2: Verbs relating to changes in maps

1   Work in pairs. Match each sentence beginning **1–7** with an ending **a–g**. There may be more than one possible answer

1 The centre of the town	**a** replaced the old hospital.
2 Several old buildings	**b** were knocked down to make way for a new supermarket.
3 A new school	**c** were pulled down, with a new multi-storey car park taking their place.
4 The old houses	**d** were demolished to create a large open space which was turned into a park.
5 Some old derelict factories	**e** was chopped down to widen the road.
6 A line of old trees	**f** was converted into a restaurant and the cinema was torn down.
7 The bank	**g** was completely transformed over the ten year period.

2   Underline the most suitable verb in *italics* in sentences **1–8** below. Then put it into the correct tense.

    1 The railway *extend/expand* to the centre of town, and three new stations were built.

    2 As the town *extend/expand*, all the open spaces were used up for housing.

    3 An airport *construct/become* on a greenfield site on the edge of the town.

    4 The neighbourhood completely *change/demolish* with the building of new apartments.

    5 The area around the town *turn into/become* more built-up.

    6 A number of dramatic developments *take place/convert*, which *alter/expand* the character of the town completely.

    7 The area *turn into/become* less rural and leafy with the building of new offices.

    8 The empty space near the university *develop/become* into a park.

3 Work in pairs. Decide which verbs in exercise 2 can be turned into nouns with the endings below.

-ation   -ition   -sion   -tion   -ment

4 For **1–8** in exercise 2, decide if it is possible to rewrite the sentences using a noun and adding the verbs below. Rewrite the sentences where possible.

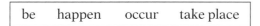

be   happen   occur   take place

5 In the following sentence, <u>underline</u> the phrase which would give a good overview.

The area *underwent a complete transformation/became different/turned into something new* over the period.

Writing:
IELTS Task 1

1 Work in pairs. <u>Underline</u> the adverbs in each sentence **1–5** below which relate to the map on page 206 and decide if they are in the correct position. If they need to be moved, decide if you need to make any other changes to the sentence.

1 A residential area is located in the north-west of the town.
2 In the north and east of the residential area there are several derelict warehouses.
3 South of the warehouses in the north are located some offices.
4 West of the river and south of the residential area is situated the Arts Centre.
5 The university is sited in the north-east, west of the woodland.

2 Work in pairs. Write sentences to describe where the remaining places **6–11** are on the map.

3 ⬤ Work in pairs.

Student A: Look at the map of the town of Sandring in the year 2009 on page 206, which has the names of places **1–11** missing. Listen to Student B's description and write down the name of each place.

Student B: Look at the map of the town of Sandring in the year 2009 on page 208, which has the names of the places marked. Describe to Student A where each place is located. When you have finished, show Student A your map to check their answers.

> **Useful expressions**
>
> *in the north/south/east/west of …*
> *north/south/east/west of …*
> *to the north/south/east/west of …*
> *there is … ,*
> *… lies, is situated, is sited, is located, stands, runs/flows*

4 Look at the map of the town of Sandring in 2000 on page 206 and the Student B map of Sandring in 2009. Decide if sentences **1–10** below about Sandring in 2009 are true or false.

1 The hospital in the west of the town was converted into a hotel.
2 Where the park stands there used to be a university.
3 The public gardens in the south-east of the town were destroyed to make way for an entertainment area.
4 The school was still in the same place in the west of the town.
5 In place of the park there is an industrial wasteland.
6 The fields on the south-west border of the town have become an industrial zone.

7 The quarry just south of the centre of the town has been transformed into a lake.

8 The coach station in the centre of the town was converted into a railway station.

9 A shopping centre was built in the north of the town, replacing part of the residential area.

10 Overall, the town has become much less rural with more buildings being constructed.

5 Words and phrases **1–10** below can all be used to describe change. Rewrite each sentence **1–10** in exercise 4 using the words below. There may be more than one possible answer.

1 build in place of	**5** turn into	**9** replace/build
2 give way to	**6** give over to	**10** urban transformation
3 build on the site of	**7** become	
4 not change	**8** reconstruct to become	

6 Write an answer for the Task 1 question below. When you have finished, check your answer using the checklist on page 209.

Don't forget!

You need to write an overview.

Avoid listing the information.

You cannot summarize trends, but you can summarize overall changes.

WRITING TASK 1

You should spend about 20 minutes on this task.

> The maps below show the changes experienced by the town of Lakeside at the beginning of the 21st Century.
>
> Summarise the information by selecting and reporting the main features, and make comparisons where necessary.

Write at least 150 words.

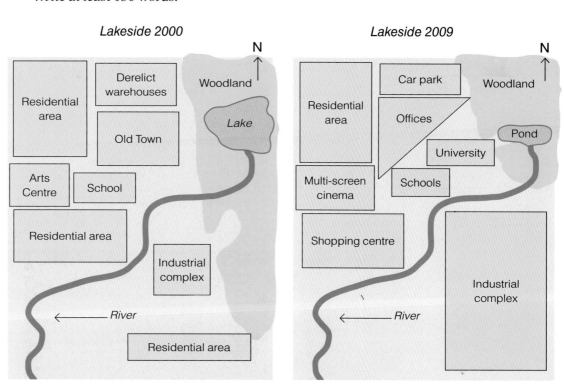

Lakeside 2000   Lakeside 2009

Vocabulary

Some of the <u>underlined</u> nouns in sentences **1–8** below have been moved between the sentences. Decide which sentences are correct.

1 The world is a wonderful <u>region</u> teeming with life of all kinds.

2 The mountainside provided a perfect <u>location</u> for the end of the film.

3 This animal is only found in the southern <u>place</u> of Africa and nowhere else.

4 The world is divided into different climate <u>spaces</u>.

5 There are very few open <u>zones</u> in the centres of major cities.

6 This is the exact <u>spot</u> on the river where I first learnt to swim.

7 There are very few empty houses in the <u>district</u> as there is a shortage of housing.

8 The financial <u>vicinity</u> of the city stretches along the river bank for miles.

Speaking

1 In the extract from IELTS Speaking Part 2, the candidate is describing a special place. Complete gaps **1–5** with a phrase **a–e.**

  a If I remember rightly, the first time

  b What I particularly like about it is the

  c And why do I like it so much?

  d it would have to be

  e breathtaking setting of any place

> I think
> **1** _____ a sandy beach near where I was born. It has the most **2** _____ I have seen in the world. I don't believe it can be beaten. **3** _____ I laid eyes on it I was about 15 years of age. **4** _____ sand seems to stretch as far as the eye can see. On the other side of the bay there are mountains sweeping gently down to the sea. **5** _____ .
> Well, it's . . . .

2 In the extract below the candidate is talking about the same topic. There are seven words which should not be there. <u>Underline</u> the extra words.

> And why it is this place so special for me? Well, I think it's because it is really peaceful over there. I can sit for hours without seeing anyone, just gazing into the distance space; it is so relaxing. There are no any noisy streets with the car radios and people, only a peaceful riverbank surrounded by trees and flowers with the only sounds be those of the birds and the river flowing down through the wood. I am often wonder how long it will stay like that.

3 Mark the stress in the words in phrases **1–5** below. When you have finished, practise saying the phrases. First read the words with the stressed syllable. Then practise saying the whole phrase.

1 The place I'd like to describe is a hillside covered …
2 A place that's special for me is a mountain with …
3 The place I like the best is a park stretching …
4 It has to be a forest teeming …
5 I'd like to tell you about a valley surrounded …

4 Complete the sentence beginnings **1–5** in exercise 4.

Referring in a text

For **1–6** below, complete the gaps with *it*, *this*, *that* or *these*.

1 My neighbourhood is improving gradually. _____ is now a safer place to walk around at night.
2 The map was created by craftsmen of the highest standard. It is clear _____ were highly trained.
3 The Bantu migrated through huge areas of central and southern Africa. _____ led to the spread of the language from its origins in West Africa.
4 The government should try to improve facilities for people in your area, as _____ would surely help reduce crime.
5 And what can be done about the problem of the rubbish in scenic areas? _____ can be cleared away, but _____ is not the best solution to the problem. _____ needs more drastic measures. _____ can take the form of fines for people who dump their waste wherever they want rather than taking _____ to special rubbish dumps.
6 It is surely the government's responsibility to protect animals in the wild. _____ could be done by making the smuggling of endangered species from one region of the world to another more difficult by increasing checks on animal imports. _____ in turn would make …

Proof reading

As quickly as you can, <u>underline</u> the ten mistakes in the following model answer for an IELTS Writing Task 1 question.

The maps illustrates how the town of Marsden underwent a total tranformation in the twenty years between 1988 and 2008, changing from a small to a large town.

First, it lost the park in the north of the town, which was substituted by a supermarket. The hospital was chopped down and instead a five-star hotel was built surrounding by trees and a huge car park. The centre of the town also saw a number of change. Moreover, several skyscrapers erected on the site of the old factories and the university halls of residence were turned offices. The territory is also less green than it used to be with the main park east of the shopping complex being converted into a car park.

As the population increase there was a greater demand for housing. So the fields on the edge of the town were given over to housing estates, further increasing the urbanization of the area.

9 What is beauty?

Vocabulary: Beauty

1 ⬤ Work in groups. Describe the buildings in each of the photographs. Name them if you can. Then discuss the questions below.

- What is your reaction to the buildings in the photographs? Do you think they are beautiful? Why/Why not?
- What is your favourite building or monument?
- Is it important to live in beautiful surroundings? Why/Why not?

2 ⬤ In your groups, evaluate each of the buildings in the photographs in exercise 1. Rank the buildings according to how beautiful you think they are: 1 = the most beautiful, 5 = the least beautiful. Give reasons.

3 For **1–6** below, complete the gaps with a building from exercise 1 so that the statement is true for you. Then complete the statement using your own ideas.

Example:

I think building _____ is breathtaking, as …

I think building 1 is breathtaking, as it combines the old and the new and fits perfectly into the space it is in.

1 I find building _____ very old-fashioned, because …

2 Building _____ says nothing to me at all, because …

3 Building _____ is not as beautiful as Petra, because …

4 I find structures like building _____ very depressing, as they …

5 Building _____ is very charming, but building _____ is very alluring; it makes me want to …

6 When I look at the photograph of building _____ it makes me feel nostalgic, because …

4 Work in pairs. When you evaluate a building you can: **A** describe it physically; **B** say what effect it has on you. Look at the adjectives in the box below and decide which category they fit in, **A** or **B**.

evocative	overawed	tall	melancholic	thoughtful	ancient
spacious	dazzling	humbling	beautiful	magnificent	impressive
overwhelmed	emotional	ecstatic	high	overjoyed	stone
nostalgic	majestic				

5 Complete the gaps in **1–6** below with a word made from an adjective in exercise 4.

Example:

When I saw the Taj Mahal for the first time it made a huge _impression_ *on me.*

1 They tried to _____ the town centre by putting flowers in baskets and painting and renovating the buildings, but it didn't work.

2 Standing next to the Sphinx made me feel very _____ .

3 I was filled with _____ at the sight of the Himalayas. I was taken aback by their majesty.

4 Thinking of places that I love sometimes fills me with _____ , but this is not a negative feeling.

5 When I look at photographs of my home country they _____ so many memories and usually make me feel homesick.

6 The sight of the old people wandering through the ruins made me _____ about life and how things can change very suddenly.

6 Work in groups. Transform at least three sentences from exercise 5 by changing the noun to a verb or an adjective where possible.

Example:

When I saw the Taj Mahal for the first time it made a huge impression on me.

When I saw the Taj Mahal for the first time it impressed me enormously.

7 ⬤ Work in pairs. Choose at least three monuments that you think represent important times in your country's development or are symbolic of your country. Describe each structure to your partner and explain why it is of importance. Try to use the vocabulary from this section.

Listening
IELTS Section 3

1 You are going to listen to a conversation between a tutor and a student about a film project. Look at questions **21–30** below and decide what the project is about.

2 Work in pairs. You will hear words **1–10** below during the conversation. Check the meaning of the words. Use a dictionary to check the meaning of any words you don't know.

1 perception	**3** take in	**5** digital stills	**7** access	**9** fade
2 collage	**4** grandeur	**6** narrow down	**8** discipline	**10** click

Don't forget!

- Underline the words in the questions that warn you that the answer is coming soon.

🔘 2.2 **SECTION 3   Questions 21–30**

Questions 21–25

Choose the correct letter **A**, **B** or **C**.

21 Malcolm thinks the subject of his project may not be

  A concrete enough.

  B interesting enough.

  C very academic.

22 Malcolm's reaction to India was one of

  A indifference.

  B dislike.

  C awe.

23 Malcolm feels the pictures he took of the Ganges etc. are

  A breathtaking.

  B interesting.

  C uninspiring.

24 The tutor suggests Malcolm should

  A concentrate on photos of buildings only.

  B reduce the number of photographic stills to ten.

  C use only photos of famous places.

25 Malcolm intends to make a film that is similar to a

  A movie preview.

  B TV advert.

  C music video.

Questions 26–30

Complete the sentences below.

Write **NO MORE THAN TWO WORDS AND/OR A NUMBER** for each answer.

26 Malcolm's tutor thinks it would be a useful discipline to stick to a ....

27 The tutor reminds Malcolm about the shortness of people's ....

28 The details about submitting the project can be found on the ....

29 The submission form needs to contain details about the ....

30 With the submission form, ... copies of the DVD need to be handed in.

3 🔘 Would you like to make a film about a place you have visited? Which place would you choose? Why?

Word building: Prefixes *under-* and *over-*

When Malcolm is describing the buildings in New Delhi during the conversation with his tutor he says: 'I think they are really *underrated*'. You can add the prefixes *under-* and *over-* to change the meaning of words.

1 Complete the gaps in sentences **1–10** below using a word made from a verb in the box by adding the prefix *under* or *over*.

> fund   value   ~~price~~   run   state   come   estimate   awe   rate (x 2)   take

Example:

However stunning the tourist attraction is, the entrance fee is definitely <u>overpriced</u> .

1 Many scientists have _____ the importance of early archaeological discoveries. They are much more significant than was once thought.

2 The monuments were totally _____ by tourists. I couldn't take any pictures.

3 The museum is really _____ . It's a very boring building.

4 Artefacts from a long time ago are frequently _____ . At auctions they may only sell for a fraction of the price of modern art.

5 Some people are completely _____ with emotion when they visit Florence. It's a syndrome called the Stendhal effect.

6 The museum _____ the theme park as the most popular attraction last year.

7 Many buildings and monuments of international significance are crumbling, because government repair schemes are _____ .

8 The ruins of Greater Zimbabwe are seriously _____ . I think they are more important than they are thought to be.

9 The architecture of the building is very _____ . It is this simplicity which makes it magnificent.

10 I was completely _____ by the carvings. I've never seen anything like them.

2 Write a sentence about each of the following:

- a place, country, monument or film etc. which you think is important, but which other people do not value

- a place, country, monument or film etc. which you do not rate highly, but which other people do

119

Speaking
IELTS Part 2

1 You can emphasize your own opinion by contrasting it using linking words such as *but*, *though*, *although*, *however*, *nevertheless*, *even so*, *even though*, etc.

Even though it leaves some people cold, I have a sentimental attachment to it.

Write sentences about buildings that are important, or have been important, in your life. Use at least five of the words and phrases **1–6** below and the linking words above.

Example:

Even though the building where I went to secondary school leaves some people cold, I have a sentimental attachment to it.

1 leave me cold
2 bring back memories
3 bleak but my home
4 ugly/unattractive/unsightly/unpleasant
5 in a rundown area
6 beautiful to see/to look at/to visit

2 Choose one of the sentences you have written and practise the rhythm by reading it out loud. Read the secondary stresses first and then the whole sentence. Then, decide which syllable has the main stress in each clause.

o   o   o   o   o   o   o   0
Even though the building where I went to secondary school leaves some people cold, I have

0   o
a sentimental attachment to it.

3 Think of at least two buildings that have had an impact on you or reflect your life or personality. With a partner, explain the effect these buildings have had on you. Use the sentences in exercise 1.

> **Useful expressions**
>
> *What made (the building) important to me is …*
> *The reason I chose (the building) is …*
> *(The building) makes me …*
> *When I see (the building) or photographs of (the building), it makes me feel …*
> *(The building) is underrated, but …*

4 Look at the following Part 2 task card. Choose ten verbs and or adjectives from this unit so far, which will help you explain why the building is important to you. Write a note for each heading on the task card. Then narrow your verbs and adjectives down to three or four. Use the useful expressions in the box to help organize your answer.

> Describe your favourite building.
>
> You should say:
>
>   what the building is
>
>   where it is
>
>   what it is like
>
> and explain why it is your favourite building.

Don't forget!

• In the exam you will only have one minute to prepare.

5 Work in pairs. Take turns talking about the topic. Use your notes to guide you. You should speak for up to two minutes; time each other using a stopwatch. When you have finished, give each other feedback using the checklist on page 210.

Speaking
IELTS Part 3

Don't forget!

- Use adjectives to evaluate. Then give reasons and examples.
- Use linking words like *but, although, however* etc.
- Keep your ideas abstract.

Work in pairs. Discuss the following questions. Try to include the verbs and adjectives that you have used in this unit so far.

Beautiful surroundings

Do people need to have beautiful surroundings? Why?

What is the effect of living and working in attractive buildings?

Which is more important, the design or the function of a building? Why?
Is it important to try to make cities pleasing to the eye?

Concepts of beauty

What does beauty mean? Does it mean the same for everyone?

Do you think the desire to acquire beautiful objects drives consumerism? How?

Are there differences in the concepts of beauty and taste between cultures? What are they?

Reading
IELTS Reading Passage

1 Work in groups. Look quickly at the title of the reading passage and skim the passage and the questions. Close your books and share as much information about the passage as possible.

2 In your groups, make a list of three or four things that you would expect to read in a passage about an architect.

3 Scan the passage and find words and phrases that have the opposite meaning to **1–7** below.

1 separated	**3** hated	**5** revealing	**7** unoriginal
2 alien/strange	**4** attacked	**6** talentless	

How to go about it

- As some of the questions relate to dates, put boxes around the dates in the passage.

READING PASSAGE

You should spend about 20 minutes on **Questions 1–13,** which are based on the reading passage below.

Giles Gilbert Scott Architect (1880–1960)

A bastion of the architectural establishment in early 20th century Britain, Giles Gilbert Scott (1880–1960) fused tradition with modernity by applying historic styles to industrial structures in his designs from the Battersea and Bankside power stations in London, to Liverpool Anglican Cathedral, and to the K2 telephone kiosk.

At the top of the splendid Portland stone tomb of the 19th century architect John Soane and his wife and son, in St Pancras Old Church Gardens, north London, is a dome in a surprisingly familiar shape. Designed by Soane in 1815 as a monument to his beloved wife, the tomb is one of his most romantic designs, ornate in form and decorated by stone carvings of snakes and pineapples. It is familiar not because of its association with Soane's family tomb, but because of its influence on the design of the red K2 telephone kiosks, which were once a common sight throughout Britain.

The architect who designed the K2, Giles Gilbert Scott, admired Soane's work and had recently become a trustee of the Sir John Soane Museum in London when invited in 1924 to enter a competition to design a public telephone kiosk. The shape of his design was inspired by the central domed structure of Soane's tomb. By rooting his design in Britain's architectural heritage, Scott transformed the telephone kiosk from what was then seen as an intimidating symbol of modernity into something that seemed reassuringly familiar. When the wooden models of the competing designs were exhibited outside the National Gallery, Giles Gilbert Scott's was chosen as the winner.

Scott continued to package modernity in British traditionalism throughout his career. In his inaugural address as president of the Royal Institute of British Architects in 1933, when Britain was finally succumbing to modernism and the architectural profession was split by battling 'trads v. rads', he advocated a 'middle line' of both embracing technological progress and the human qualities of architecture. The 'middle line' was illustrated by Scott's best known London buildings, the power stations at Battersea (1929–1935) and Bankside (1947–1960), where he disguised their industrial purpose behind Gothic facades. Battersea, in particular, became a popular London landmark. Yet in an age when progressive architects such as Le Corbusier and Jean Prouvé romanticised technology, Scott's attempts to popularise industrial buildings by obfuscating their function seemed, at best, conservative.

It is not surprising that Giles Gilbert Scott appeared unable to escape Britain's architectural tradition as he was born into it. His grandfather George Gilbert Scott (1811–1878) was the eminent High Victorian Gothic architect of the Albert Memorial, the Foreign Office and the Midland Railways Terminus Hotel at St Pancras station. His uncle John Oldrid Scott was also an architect, as was his father, the second George Gilbert Scott, who was nicknamed Scott Jnr. A gifted yet tragic figure, Scott Jnr showed youthful promise by designing a series of churches in London and Yorkshire that bridged Victorian gothic and the arts and crafts movement, only to succumb to alcoholism and, eventually, to be committed to a mental asylum.

In 1923, Giles Gilbert Scott was commissioned to design Memorial Court, a hall of residence at Clare College, Cambridge (begun in 1923), which he completed in a Georgian-inspired style. The following year he won the telephone kiosk competition. Traditional though his kiosk was in style, functionally it was very advanced. An ingenious ventilation system was installed using perforations in the dome, and the glass was divided into small panels for speedy replacement in case of breakages. Scott's original proposal was for a mild steel structure, but the Post Office insisted on changing it to cast iron. It also insisted on painting the kiosks bright red for maximum visibility in emergencies rather than Scott's suggested shade of duck egg blue. Following protests in rural areas, where people complained that the bright red kiosks looked overbearing in the open countryside, the Post Office agreed to repaint them in green.

Despite the rural complaints, the K2 kiosk was a popular success, and Scott was invited by the Post Office to modify his design in 1930 for the concrete K3, intended principally for country use. He was recalled again to design the K6 in 1935 to commemorate King George V's silver jubilee. This became the most widely used version of the kiosk with thousands being installed.

As well as these landmark commissions, Scott designed dozens of churches throughout his career, as well as more modest public projects such as monuments and extensions to existing buildings. One of his most conspicuous commissions was as a consultant, rather than an architect, to Battersea Power Station in south London. Charged with making the enormous electricity generating station more appealing, Scott suggested brick as the main material for the central structure and turned the four chimneys – one on each corner – into reassuringly familiar neo-classical columns. The result is surprisingly engaging for such a vast structure, but with the showiness of the Art Deco cinemas then being constructed across Britain.

His most significant post-war commission came in 1947 when Scott was invited to design a second London power station at Bankside beside the Thames in Southwark. More austere in style than Battersea, Bankside did not match its popularity until its conversion in 2000 by the Swiss architects Herzog and De Meuron into the Tate Modern museum. Yet formally and functionally it is the more sophisticated of the two buildings, not least as Scott combined all of Bankside's chimneys into a single central tower.

Questions 1–6

Complete the sentences below.

Choose **NO MORE THAN TWO WORDS** from the passage for each answer.

1 Scott combined the old with the new in the .... he designed.

2 Scott's design for the K2 phone box was based on the .... of Britain.

3 Scott's desire to make industrial buildings more appealing to the public appeared ....

4 Despite not being innovative style-wise, from a practical point of view Scott's telephone box was ....

5 When people in the countryside complained about the colour of the telephone boxes, the colour was changed to ....

6 Although people objected to the K2 phone boxes, they were generally a ....

Questions 7–11

Classify the following events as occurring in Scott's life

    A between 1920 and 1930
    B between 1930 and 1940
    C after 1940

7 a modification in telephone design to mark a special occasion

8 a request to design a power station

9 success in the contest to design a telephone box

10 an invitation to design accommodation for students

11 Scott's support for architectural progress with a human face

Questions 12 and 13

Choose **TWO** letters, **A–E**.

Which **TWO** features of Bankside Power Station make it different from Battersea Power Station?

    A It was a more severe structure.
    B It was more popular.
    C It was much bigger.
    D It had only one chimney.
    E It is a less complex building.

Reacting to the text

Do architects have more influence on our lives than we realize? Should there be more or less control over the work of architects? Give reasons and examples.

Language focus: Modal verbs for evaluating

In addition to using adjectives and verbs to give evaluations, we can also use modal verbs. Look at the following statement from the listening practice on page 118.

I should have been halfway through by now.

Malcolm is criticizing himself for something he did. He is reflecting on and evaluating his own actions.

Read more about using modal verbs for evaluating in the Grammar reference on page 224.

1 Work in pairs. Think of three things that you did recently which you shouldn't have done, or you should have done but didn't. Tell your partner about the events.

2 For **1–9** below, underline the correct word in *italics*.

1 They *should/shouldn't* have knocked that building down ages ago; it was rather hideous.

2 The government *could have/could* dealt with this more diplomatically.

3 He *might have/should* have told me; I'm not sure.

4 She *might/couldn't* have told me! I really wish she had.

5 Something *must/should* have happened, because suddenly everyone seems happier.

6 Fines *could be/must have been* imposed on those who make the environment ugly.

7 With the involvement of UNESCO, more and more places of great natural beauty *should be/shouldn't have been* protected in future.

8 The government definitely *ought to/might* control advertising on TV to stop people becoming addicted to buying consumer goods.

9 The car *could/must* be incredibly expensive, because it's stunning to look at.

3 Which of the sentences **1–9** in exercise 2 show that something 'didn't happen' in the past?

4 Which of the sentences **1–9** in exercise 2 express the following:

- a conclusion
- a criticism
- a regret
- an expectation
- a suggestion
- a possibility/ weak suggestion

5 Work in groups. You have been asked by the local council to come up with ways to make the city or town you live or study in more attractive for the general public. Make a list of the following things in order to improve the area. Use other modal verbs where appropriate and the words from the Vocabulary and Wordbuilding sections in this unit.

Things that should not have been done.

Things that should have been done.

Things that should be done.

Writing:

IELTS Task 2

1 You can use particular words and phrases to show the effects or consequences of something, for example, *affect, make, produce, lead to, have an effect/impact on, result in.* To describe effects and consequences you can also use adjectives from previous units, for example, *exciting, exhilarating, interesting.*

Work in pairs. For **1–6** below, separate each list of letters **a** and **b** into words. Then decide the order of **a** and **b** so that they make sense.

1 a andsoneighbourhoodsinmanycitieswherepeoplelivearebeingmademoreappealing

b everythinginthephysicalworldaroundusmakesanimpressiononusdirectlyorindirectly

2 a peopleareabletoseeandappreciatedifferentcitiesallaroundtheworld

b thankstocheaptravelandtheInternet

3 a somecountriesarenowbecomingricherthaninthepast

b leadingtoprideintheirnationalstanding

4 a forexampleaparkwasopenedandtreeswereplanted

b andthensuddenlythehealthofthepeopleinthatdistrictofthecityimproved

5 a thelackofspacehassavedmanyoldbuildings

b withplannersturningtorenovationratherthanerectingnewbuildings

6 a peoplearehappierandarenowmoreproductive

b asaresultofturningoldruinsintogardens

2 For **1–6** in exercise 1:

    a decide which part of the text, **a** or **b**, describes the 'cause', and which describes the 'effect'

    b underline the words and phrases which indicate 'cause'. Then underline the words and phrases which indicate 'effect'

    c decide if there any sentences where no linking words are used to indicate a cause or effect

    d decide if any of the linking words can be removed without affecting the connection

3 Work in pairs. For **1–5** below, complete the gaps with one phrase from box **A** and one phrase from box **B**. There may be more than one possible answer. Each phrase can be used more than once.

> **A** with   as a result, there are   which in turn   thanks to

> **B** has a positive effect   shouldn't have relaxed   are focusing on
>   now lighten up   should be attractive

    1 For example, the government _____ the restrictions on building in green spaces in the city. _____ very few places for people to relax.

    2 The built environment in modern cities _____ to the people that live there, but often it is overwhelming and ugly _____ skyscrapers, which shut out the light.

    3 _____ new construction techniques and materials, modern buildings _____ cities and make them attractive.

    4 It is obvious that beauty _____ on people's well-being, _____ increases their happiness and productivity.

    5 _____ awareness of the impact that healthy environments have on employees, more and more architects _____ design and not just function.

4 Work in pairs. Make notes for the Task 2 question below. Make a list of ideas about the built environment and the natural environment. If necessary, use the ideas in the box on page 208. When you have finished, change partners and explain your ideas.

WRITING TASK 2

You should spend about 40 minutes on this task.

Write about the following topic:

> *At school greater emphasis should be placed on an appreciation of the built as well as the natural environment.*
>
> *To what extent do you agree or disagree?*

Give reasons for your answer and include any relevant examples from your own knowledge or experience.

Write at least 250 words.

---

5 Write your own answer for the question. When you have finished, check your answer using the checklist on page 209.

9 Review

Vocabulary

1 For **1–4** below, complete the gaps with an extract **a–e**.

1 How do buildings affect people?

> _____ , depending on the mood of the person and the attractiveness of the buildings. For example, some people might find buildings like the Louvre museum in Paris formal and boring, _____ might think it is dazzling.

2 Are you ready to start?

> My favourite photograph is one that I took of old ruins near where I was brought up. They are really magnificent. _____ I didn't have a camera, but the next I made sure I had one with me.

3 What sort of buildings do you like?

> Old buildings say nothing to me. _____ the Guggenheim Museum in Bilbao more appealing. So I am rarely impressed by old palaces or houses; I find them depressing.

4 What are the buildings like in your home city?

> Most of them are _____ are allowed to be constructed in order to protect the area. So it means that we have lots of tourists.

   a They can make them sad or happy

   b very old and evocative, because no new buildings

   c I find modern architecture like

   d The first time I saw it

   e but other people

2 For **1–4** in exercise 1, decide whether each is taken from Part 1, 2 or 3 of IELTS Speaking and why.

3 For **1–8** below, complete the gaps with a word made from the word in brackets.

1 When they cleaned up the monument, they made it very _____ (beautify), which is why it is my favourite structure.

2 The sight of my old school after so many years made me very _____ (think).

3 The old town was _____ (evoke) of a bygone age. It is important that such places exist to remind people of their culture.

4 I was overcome with waves of _____ (nostalgic) when I looked at the photographs.

5 Being among the ruins of Angkor Wat was a very _____ (humility) experience.

6 I found the building very _____ (melancholy) at first, but then I realized it was very relaxing to be here and my attitude changed.

7 The city of Tokyo made a huge _____ (impressive) on me the first time I visited it.

8 Architecture such as that found in Florence has the power to affect people in different ways. Although some of the palaces and houses there are quite austere, they have the power to fill people with _____ (ecstatic).

4 Rewrite sentences **1–8** in exercise 3 using the words in brackets. For verbs you may need to change the form of the word. Some of the words will need to be changed.

Example:

1 *When they cleaned up the monument they beautified it, which is why it is my favourite structure.*

Word building

1 In **1–7** below, decide which two words need to change places.

1 The last time I visited the overrun city of Pompeii it left me cold. It was so magnificent by tourists.

2 The photographs of my home town brought back lots of emotion. I was really overcome by memories.

3 The countryside around where I was brought up is very overawed, but I am still bleak by it each time I go home.

4 The vast open spaces of the Steppes are underestimated. Their beauty is so beautiful, perhaps because it is so difficult to get there.

5 The architecture of the railway station is not plain; it is just understated and subtle. That is why it is appealing.

6 The preservation of the architecture of former times reflects the traditions and values of a nation. When such precious national items are underfunded by people generally, it unfortunately leads to them being undervalued or not supported financially at all.

7 If tourist attractions are cheaper, it puts people off visiting them. So the main way to attract tourists and increase revenue is to make the cost of travel to and from the attractions overpriced and reduce the entrance fees.

2 Sentences **6** and **7** in exercise 1 are taken from an IELTS Writing Task 2 answer, but they need examples to make them clearer to understand. Add examples using the following:

- *like* + noun
- *for example* + sentence

- *for example*
- *if* + two clauses

Modal verbs for evaluating

1 <u>Underline</u> the modal verbs in the following extract from an IELTS Writing Task 2 answer.

> When they are constructing new buildings in the centre of old cities like London and Paris, Damascus or Rome, planners should be sensitive to the existing architecture. Many old buildings in London, for example, shouldn't have been demolished. Instead, they ought to have been preserved in some way. For example, they could have erected buildings in the same style as existing buildings, or blended the old with the new to stunning effect, as has happened recently in central London, where parts of the facades of old buildings have been kept with new features added on. This should now make the city more attractive. Of course, they might have started doing this sooner! But better late than never.

2 Match the verbs you have underlined to **1–4** below. You may use each one more than once.

1 a criticism
2 an expectation

3 a weak suggestion
4 a recommendation

Introduction

The IELTS Academic Writing module lasts one hour and there are two tasks. You are advised to spend 20 minutes on Task 1 and asked to write at least 150 words. For Task 2 you are advised to spend 40 minutes and asked to write at least 250 words.

In both tasks, you are assessed on your ability to write in a style that is suitable for the task.

Task 1

In Task 1 you are asked to describe data, presented as a graph, chart or table, or a diagram such as a map or process, using your own words.

Assessment for Task 1 is based on your ability to:

- summarize, organize and compare data where possible
- describe the stages of a process
- describe an object or event or explain how something works
- write accurately and coherently
- use a range of vocabulary
- use a range of grammatical structures

Describing a graph

1   Work in pairs. Look at the following list of words and phrases **1–20** and the graph in the Task 1 question on the opposite page. Decide which you can use to write about the graph.

1	trends vary	**11**	overtake
2	an upward trend	**12**	contrasted with the steady recovery
3	hit a low	**13**	the dramatic decrease
4	latter part of the period	**14**	peak at
5	soar	**15**	proportion
6	follow different patterns	**16**	reach a high
7	a gradual fall	**17**	overall
8	reach a plateau	**18**	outnumber
9	a sharp drop	**19**	generally speaking
10	surpass	**20**	similarly

WRITING TASK 1

You should spend about 20 minutes on this task.

> The graph shows children by age group as a percentage of the population in the United Kingdom between 1990 and 2001.
>
> Summarise the information by selecting and reporting the main features, and make comparisons where relevant.

Write at least 150 words.

Percentages of children aged under 20 years by age group in the United Kingdom

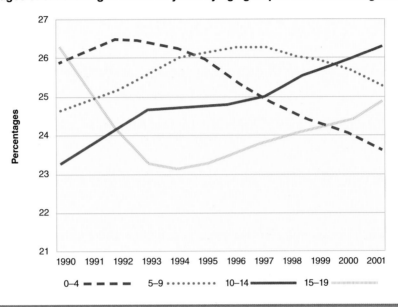

2 Read the following sample answer and <u>underline</u> the words from the list in exercise 1.

> The graph shows the proportions of children in four age groups, namely 0–4, 5–9, 10–14 and 15–19 in the UK between 1990 and 2001.
>
> Generally speaking, despite the two contrasting trends (downwards for the children of 0–4 and 15–19; and upwards for those aged 5–9 and 10–14), the decline in the birth rate was the most striking point. In the youngest age group, there was an increase during the two first years from just below 26% in 1990 to about 26.6% in 1992 followed by a gradual fall to 23.6%, the lowest percentage, in 2001. Regarding the 15–19 age group, the dramatic decrease from approximately 26.3% in 1990 to just over 23% in 1994 can be contrasted with a steady recovery over the latter part of the period up to nearly 24.9% in 2001.
>
> By contrast, an upward trend was noticed in the categories of children aged 5–9 and 10–14. Looking at the former group, the percentage peaked at approximately 26.3% in 1997, but the final proportion (about 25.3%) remained greater than the initial (nearly 24.6%). As regards the latter, the percentage of the children in this category not only increased over the period but also was the greatest in 2001, approximately 26.3%.

3 Work in pairs. Turn to page 207 and answer questions **1–8**.

4 Write your own answer for the task. When you have finished, check your answer using the checklist on page 209.

Describing a bar chart

1 Work in pairs. Look at the Task 1 question in exercise 2 below. To help you practise paraphrasing descriptions of data in your introduction, rewrite the following sentence using the words in brackets or your own words.

The chart reveals the results of a Labour Force Survey on occupations of males and females in the United Kingdom in 2007.

(employment in the United Kingdom/provide a breakdown by gender and occupation/ranging from … to …)

2 Work in pairs. Decide which of the following three overviews for the chart in the question below is most suitable. Give reasons.

1 *As can be seen from the chart, there are more males than females in certain occupations.*

2 *It is clear that while women account for the largest proportion of workers in the lower level jobs, men fill most of the posts in the higher managerial level and in skilled trades.*

3 *Overall, women have as many jobs as men at the top.*

WRITING TASK 1

You should spend about 20 minutes on this task.

> *The chart shows the results of a Labour Force Survey in the United Kingdom in 2007.*
>
> *Summarise the information by selecting and reporting the main features, and make comparisons where necessary.*

Write at least 150 words.

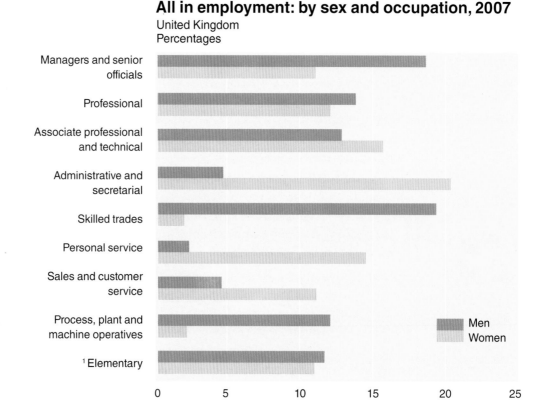

All in employment: by sex and occupation, 2007
United Kingdom
Percentages

¹ Such as catering assistants, bar staff and shelf fillers

3 Work in groups. Look at the list of phrases below and decide which occupation on the chart they can be used to describe. Write the number of the phrase next to the occupation. Each phrase may apply to more than one occupation.

1 the only occupation ... almost equal
2 account for less/fewer than ...
3 far outstripped/exceeded
4 was approximately four times as many ... as ...
5 slightly less than ...
6 not as many as ...
7 the reverse was true
8 a different pattern
9 about a third more
10 considerably more men made up
11 almost ten times as many
12 almost double/almost half as many
13 were more than ...

4 Write your own answer for the task. When you have finished, check your answer using the checklist on page 209.

Describing a table

1 Work in groups. Look at the Task 1 question below and the sample answer on page 132. The teacher asked the student not to describe certain rows and columns in the table as there was too much information. Decide which rows and columns the student was asked to ignore.

WRITING TASK 1

You should spend about 20 minutes on this task.

The table shows world demographic indicators for various regions of the world in 2005.

Summarise the information by selecting and reporting the main features, and make comparisons where necessary.

Write at least 150 words.

World demographic indicators, 2005

	Population (millions)	Population density (sq km)	Infant mortality rate	Total fertility rate	Life expectancy at birth (years)	
					Males	Females
Asia	3,938	124	48.6	2.47	65.8	69.4
Africa	922	30	93.2	4.98	50.3	52.8
Europe	731	32	8.8	1.41	69.6	78.0
Latin America & Caribbean	558	27	25.4	2.52	68.8	75.3
North America	322	15	6.7	1.99	74.9	80.3
Oceania	33	4	28.6	2.37	71.6	77.3
World	6,515	48	53.9	2.65	63.9	68.3

The table compare various population markers in various areas, namely Europe, Latin America and the Caribbean, North America and Oceania, to the world features in 2005.

On the whole, Europe, despite having the lowest total fertility rate per 1,000 live births (1.41), was the most populated area among those studied. The features shows that 731 million people (about 11% of the world population) were living in Europe in 2005 with a life expectant at birth standing at 69.6 years for men and 78.0 years for women, above the world average of 63.9 for men and 68.3 for women. By contrast, Latin America and the Caribbean, with a higher total fertility rate of 2.52, was second on the table as regard the size of the population (558 million). People's life expectancy (68.8 years for males and 75.3 years for women) was lower than that in Europe, but higher than the international average.

Turning North America where the life expectancy at birth was the highest on the table with females likely to live longer than males (80.3 years as against 74.9), the total fertility rate was 1.99, while the population stoods at 322 million. About only 0.5% of the world population (33 million) lived in Oceania, where the fertility rate of 2.37 surpassed the other regions except North American and the Caribbean, but was less than the world average of 2.65. Likewise, life expectancy exceeded the world average (71.6 years against 63.9 years for men and 77.3 years against 68.3 years for women).

2 Find seven mistakes in the sample answer.

3 Work in pairs. Read the sample answer again and find synonyms for the words and phrases below.

1	being	**5**	came second
2	of the countries analyzed	**6**	outstripped
3	while it had	**7**	which had a greater total fertility rate of
4	regarding		

4 Write your own answer for the task. Use the overview in the sample answer as a guide. When you have finished, check your answer using the checklist on page 209.

Describing a process

1 Work in groups. Look at the Task 1 question on the opposite page and answer questions **1–10** below.

1 Where can you start the description: at the cold water feed or the solar panel?
2 Do the four orange arrows represent heat or the sun's rays?
3 How does the cold water begin to move through the system?
4 What happens when the cold water passes through the solar collector? How do you know from the diagram?
5 What does the Controller do?
6 What happens to the water after it passes through the solar collector?
7 Does the hot water in the tank also heat the boiler which supplies the heating?
8 Does the same water go round inside the pipes from the boiler and the pipes that go through the solar collector or are they two separate systems?
9 Is the water that comes out through the taps the same as the water that flows through the boiler system?
10 Does the pipe heated by the solar collector work like heating elements in an electric kettle?

WRITING TASK 1

You should spend about 20 minutes on this task.

> *The diagram illustrates how solar energy is used to provide hot water for domestic use.*
>
> *Summarise the information by selecting and reporting the main features, and make comparisons where necessary.*

Write at least 150 words.

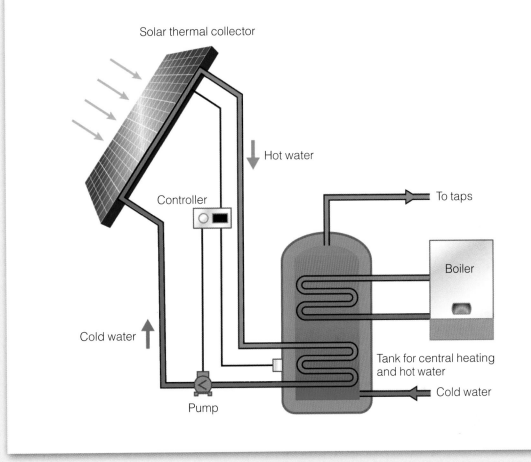

2 Make a list of verbs that you can use to describe the process.

heat up _____

3 Make a list of linking devices you can use when you are describing the process.

first _____

4 Complete the introduction below.

The diagram shows how _____

5 Complete the overview below.

The _____ involves a series of _____ from

_____ to _____ .

6 Write your own answer for the task. When you have finished, check your answer using the checklist on page 209.

Describing a map

1 Work in groups. Look at the Task 1 question below. Describe the differences between the two maps using the verbs and nouns below to help you.

Verbs:

turned into
had been replaced
took place
were demolished
became

Nouns:
relocation
development
changes
expansion
construction
conversion
urbanization

WRITING TASK 1

You should spend about 20 minutes on this task.

> *The maps show the transformation of the village of Eastminster over a ten year period.*
>
> *Summarise the information by selecting and reporting the main features, and make comparisons where relevant.*

Write at least 150 words.

1999 Eastminster

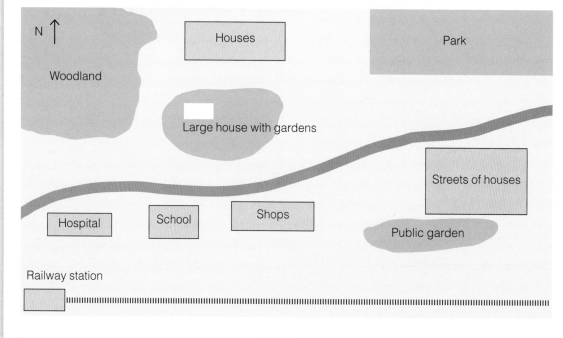

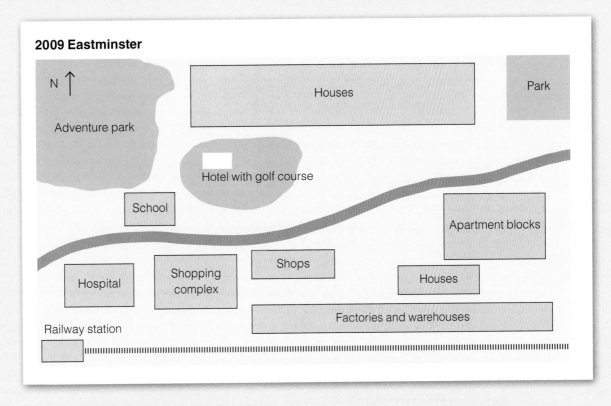

2009 Eastminster

2   Complete the model text below using the verbs and nouns in exercise 1.

The maps show the **1**_____ that **2**_____ in the town of Eastminster between the years 1999 and 2009.

It is clear that Eastminster **3**_____ more urbanized with less open spaces over the decade. North of the river, which divides the town, the woodland in the northwest was **4**_____ an adventure park. Moreover, by 2009 the large house with gardens **5**_____ with a hotel and a golf course. More houses were also built encroaching on the park in the northeast. The other main **6**_____ north of the river was the **7**_____ of the school from the south bank of the river.

The area south of the river experienced greater **8**_____. To the east, the streets of houses **9**_____ to make way for blocks of flats. By 2009, where a public garden stood south of the old streets of houses, there were more houses. Further developments that occurred were the **10**_____ of factories and warehouses along the railway line together with the **11**_____ of the school on the river into a new shopping complex. The final transformation was the **12**_____ of the hospital west of the old school situated on the river.

3   Write your own answer for the task. When you have finished, check your answer using the checklist on page 209.

Task 2

In Task 2 you are given a point of view, argument or problem.

Assessment for Task 2 is based on your ability to:
- present and support your opinion
- compare and contrast evidence and opinions
- write a solution to a problem
- evaluate and challenge ideas, evidence or arguments
- write in an appropriate style

The instructions in the questions follow these patterns:
Discuss the advantages and disadvantages of ...
Discuss both these views and give your own opinion.
To what extent do you agree or disagree?

Or you may be asked a specific question such as:
Which do you consider to be the major influence?
What do you think are the causes of this problem, and what solutions can you suggest?

1   ◯   Work in groups. Discuss the Task 2 question below.

WRITING TASK 2

You should spend about 40 minutes on this task.

Write about the following topic:

> *Some people think it is better to give donations to local charitable organizations, while others choose to give to national or international bodies.*
>
> *Discuss both views and give your own opinion.*

Give reasons for your answer and include any relevant examples from your own knowledge and experience.

Write at least 250 words.

---

2   Classify the ideas below according to the two sides of the argument. Note that some ideas will fit on both sides. Add your own ideas and opinions. Then explain one or more of the ideas giving reasons and examples, purposes and results and expressing any doubts or reservations.

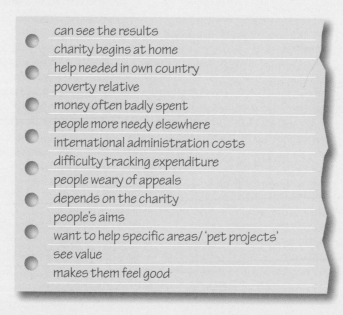

- can see the results
- charity begins at home
- help needed in own country
- poverty relative
- money often badly spent
- people more needy elsewhere
- international administration costs
- difficulty tracking expenditure
- people weary of appeals
- depends on the charity
- people's aims
- want to help specific areas/ 'pet projects'
- see value
- makes them feel good

3 Work in groups. Choose one of the following Task 2 questions and brainstorm ideas. Then compare your ideas with a group that has chosen the same task and select the three best ideas.

Don't forget!

* As you brainstorm, do not exclude ideas. Write down any ideas that come into your head. Exclude unsuitable ideas only when you come to the selection stage.

1

WRITING TASK 2

You should spend about 40 minutes on this task.

Write about the following topic:

Employers should ensure that there are equal numbers of males and females in managerial posts in companies.

To what extent do you agree or disagree?

Give reasons for your answer and include any relevant examples from your own knowledge and experience.

Write at least 250 words.

2

WRITING TASK 2

You should spend about 40 minutes on this task.

Write about the following topic:

In some families there is more than one television in the home, with each family member even having their own TV.

Discuss the advantages and disadvantages of having more than one TV set per home.

Give reasons for your answer and include any relevant examples from your own knowledge and experience.

Write at least 250 words.

3

WRITING TASK 2

You should spend about 40 minutes on this task.

Write about the following topic:

Research has shown that technology is having more influence on people's lifestyles than any other factors in our lives.

What do you consider to be the major influence?

Give reasons for your answer and include any relevant examples from your own knowledge and experience.

Write at least 250 words.

4   Work in pairs. Add punctuation, including capital letters, to the first two paragraphs of the sample answer below.

nowadays there are demands on both parents to work and look after their children at the same time for this reason I think that children should be sent to school early but during the first years priority should be given to play rather than to formal study

Play is crucial because it develops children's coordination communication and social interaction skills for example if children are throwing a ball to each other the physical and mental skills required are sophisticated as eye to hand coordination is involved furthermore children develop a sense of communication and socialize with each other the mental and physical development brought about by these games must also be taken into account and what is more while playing children compete with each other and learn to lose which is as essential as learning to succeed in life children fully engaged in play activities from an early age under their parents supervision gain various skills that they will need in their adulthood.

However, in modern society both parents need to work in order to afford the increasing cost of living, and to ensure a bright future for their families. Therefore, they no longer have enough time to dedicate to their children and are forced to send them to school earlier than before. Instead of starting to teach these young children to write, schools should focus more on play to compensate for the lack of play experience they may miss at home. Teachers in nursery and reception classes, and even in the first years of primary school, should take on the role of parents by supervising play activities . They can then gradually insert some educative games into the curriculum in order to prepare children for formal teaching.

In conclusion, despite various social and financial pressures that modern society exerts on parents forcing them to send their children to school earlier, play cannot be neglected. The traditional role of parents should be played by teachers in the early years, and steps taken to ensure that all children participate in play to gain the precious skills that they will need for their adulthood.

5 Read the rest of the sample answer. Decide which of the following two questions it answers.

    1 Some people think that children should be encouraged to play in the early years rather than being sent to school.

    To what extent do you agree or disagree?

    2 Formal education is essential if children are to be prepared for the modern world.

    To what extent do you agree or disagree?

6 For **1–7** below, write a number next to the relevant part of the sample answer.

    1 The writer's opinion

    2 Reasons

    3 A complex sentence with a condition and an example

    4 Additional information

    5 A contrast

    6 A purpose

    7 Recommendations

7 Write your own answer for the Task 2 question below. When you have finished, use the checklist on page 209 to check your answer.

Don't forget!

- Develop your ideas by giving reasons, examples, results etc. and writing complex sentences.

WRITING TASK 2

You should spend about 40 minutes on this task.

Write about the following topic.

> *Some people think that health care is a basic human necessity that should not be provided by the private companies, but should be provided by the state.*
>
> *Discuss the advantages and disadvantages of health care being provided by the private sector.*

Give reasons for your answers and include any relevant examples from your own knowledge and experience.

Write at least 250 words.

10 Is it art?

1 ○ Work in groups. Decide what art form is represented in each photograph and share your opinions about each of them.

Don't forget!

- Develop your ideas by giving examples and reasons.
- Use abstract not personal examples.
- Focus on breathing and maintaining the rhythm of sentences.

2 ○ In your groups, discuss one or more of the Part 3 questions below. Choose someone to write down the ideas as you discuss them. When you have finished, look at the notes and summarize what has been discussed.

The Arts

What are the advantages of the arts to society?

How do you think the arts should be funded – by the tax payer or by fees?

Do you think the arts have an educational role to play in society? Should young people be encouraged to be involved in the arts? Should an arts component be made compulsory for all students at university, even for scientists?

3 Work in groups of three. Take turns performing the following roles using the questions in exercise 2:

- the candidate
- the examiner
- the monitor (make notes about the candidate's performance using the checklist on page 210 and gives feedback when he/she has finished speaking)

Listening

IELTS Section 2

1 ⬭ What would you expect to see at an art exhibition?

What kind of opinions might people have about an art exhibition?

2 Look at questions **11–20** below and underline the words that warn you that the answer is coming soon.

◉ 2.3 **SECTION 2 Questions 11–20**

Question 11

Answer the question below.

Write **NO MORE THAN TWO WORDS** for your answer.

11 What has the opening of the new art exhibition created?

....

Questions 12–14

Choose **THREE** letters, **A–G**.

Which **THREE** of the following criticisms of the Street Art exhibition are mentioned?

A misuse of public funds

B size of the exhibition

C high cost of entrance fee

D inspiration for vandalism

E overcrowding at the gallery

F no support for local artists

G increased hospital admissions

Questions 15–17

Choose the correct letter, **A**, **B** or **C**.

15 The public didn't go to the art galleries and museums, because of the

A cost.

B crowds.

C time.

16 The email survey showed approximately

A 70% backed Mrs Cook.

B 70% were against Mrs Cook.

C 70% were not sure.

17 According to Mrs Cook, people in the art world are concerned about the

A timing of the introduction of support.

B level of financial support from the state.

C loss of jobs in the sector.

Questions 18–20

Complete the sentences below.

Write **NO MORE THAN TWO WORDS AND/OR A NUMBER** for each answer.

18 The radio show will have two .... on the street.

19 The purpose of the walk-about is to .... public opinion.

20 The second reporter will be outside the .... in the shopping centre.

Vocabulary: Art

1 Work in pairs. For **1–10** below, write as many people you associate with each word as you can.

   1 play _____

   2 orchestra _____

   3 novel _____

   4 book _____

   5 newspaper _____

   6 sculpture _____

   7 song _____

   8 symphony _____

   9 ballet _____

  10 film _____

2 Work in pairs. In each bubble **1–3** below, circle the words that go together.

1

draw   play

direct   artist

sketch   illustrate

3

sculptor   musician

soap opera

symphony   compose

conduct

2

fiction   stories

composer   novels

actor

3 For texts **1–4** below, <u>underline</u> the correct words in *italics*.

1 I studied *drama/plays/acts* at school. We had a theatre with all the props and *scenes/scenery/backgrounds* and a really great drama teacher, who *showed/produced/composed* at least one *theatre/play/stage* or musical a year. Sometimes he also produced a dance routine. It wasn't very *highbrow/lowbrow* art, but it was very good experience for us.

2 I don't think this is graffiti but a real *working/work/bit* of art. It is obvious that the person who *drew/wrote/put up* this is a real artist and not a vandal or hooligan as some people say. *Figure/Extract/Abstract* art like this with boxes and colours can be very difficult for people to understand but *classical/established/orthodox* paintings are just as difficult. Few people, for instance, now understand the *illusions/delusions/allusions* in, say, Renaissance paintings.

3 Many people attack *today/modern/these days* art, mainly, I think, because they don't *appreciate/see/realize* it. If people look at it a little more closely, they will be less *unfavourable/critical/approving* of it.

4 Dickens wrote very long *novels/narrations/fictions* about social issues, mainly set in or around London in the mid 19th century. They were often serialized and were eagerly awaited by the reading public. His books are considered *masterstories/big pieces/masterpieces,* and the *tales/dramas/pieces* that they *say/write/tell* are as pertinent today as they were 150 years ago. For the modern world the language is a bit dense and heavy, but they were the *visual/popular/sacred* art of their day just as *soap operas/soap plays/opera plays* are today.

4 For **1–7** below, complete the gaps with a form of the words in the box below.

exhibit	sculpt	scene	criticize (x2)	vision	collect

1 The _____ cost a lot of money to visit and was a waste of time; it was full of avant-garde work I couldn't understand.

2 The bronze _____ were displayed in the garden and the galleries.

3 My _____ is purely subjective I know, but I think the paintings were not just childlike but childish.

4 The new extension where the sculptures are on show is more stunning than the _____ itself.

5 His works have been hailed as masterpieces by _____ , but I honestly can't see anything in them.

6 The _____ in the play was a work of art in itself. The artist who painted the panels must be a genius.

7 I think I prefer the performing arts to the _____ arts; I just find paintings tiring to look at.

5 ⬤ Work in pairs. Discuss the area of the arts you like the best: performing, visual, literature, etc.

Describe something you have seen that you would never want to see again and something you never tire of seeing or thinking about. Use as many words as you can from the exercises above.

Language focus: Defining and non-defining clauses

Defining clauses provide information which cannot be left out, as it identifies what is being referred to. They do not have commas at the beginning and end of the clause.

The water colour that she painted in her teens has just sold for a record sum.

You can leave out the relative pronoun only if it is the object of the clause and only in defining clauses.

The sculpture (that) I made at school was stolen.

Non-defining clauses provide additional information, which can be left out. They have commas at the beginning and the end.

A building nearby, which I like very much, has just been demolished and caused a huge mess.

🔊 Read more about defining and non-defining relative clauses in the Grammar reference on page 224.

1 Work in pairs. For each pair of sentences **1–6** below, decide what the difference in meaning is between **a** and **b**.

   1 **a** A new play by Shakespeare, which the playwright wrote when he was young, has just been discovered.

   b The play that he wrote at the age of 21 has just won a major prize.

   2 **a** The music in the film, which is taken from Beethoven's 9th symphony, is very well known.

   b An anthem that I heard on the car radio yesterday was very familiar.

   3 **a** That is the director that I was talking about.

   b The director, who has just left, won't be here again till the end of the week.

   4 **a** That exhibition which you recommended was brilliant.

   b The exhibition, which incidentally was very good, finishes on Friday.

   5 **a** Was he the same architect who built the Sydney Opera House?

   b Mr Renne, who was an unknown architect for years, designed the bridge.

   6 **a** The singer who sang the anthem at the beginning of the performance was out of key.

   b One singer, who sang the anthem at the beginning of the performance, was out of key.

2 Work in pairs. For **1–8** below, complete each gap with a suitable relative pronoun where necessary. Leave the gap blank where it is not necessary to use a relative pronoun.

   1 The book _____ he gave me as a present was really superb.

   2 An actor, _____ name I have forgotten now, was in the shop this morning.

   3 My art class, _____ started last week, has been cancelled.

   4 I think literature, _____ was not my favourite subject at school, should have more time devoted to it in the school curriculum.

   5 The painting _____ he bought for $50 000 was a fake, the other one was genuine.

   6 The sister _____ is the dancer got married, not the singer.

   7 I see the show _____ we went to last week has had very good reviews.

   8 This is the friend _____ I was talking to you about yesterday.

3 For **1–7** below, complete the gaps with a clause **a–g**. Add any necessary punctuation.

   1 My uncle's flat _____ is empty for the next two weeks, so I'm staying there.

   2 The friend _____ got me into the film preview.

   3 One of my sculptures _____ has just won an art prize.

   4 The film _____ starts in a few minutes.

   5 I like literature _____ .

   6 Is that the folk concert _____ ?

   7 The culture tour _____ was dazzling.

   a that you were praising last night because of the quality of the singer

   b which I made when I started the art course

   c which overlooks the opera house

   d whose father is the film director

   e which was incredibly expensive for the length of the trip

   f which has some breathtaking locations

   g that is not dumbed down or simplified in any way

4 Complete one or more of sentences **1–6** below so that they are true for you. Then explain your sentences to a partner, giving reasons and examples.

   1 I like literature (which/that) I …

   2 I don't like films (which/that) I …

   3 I'm really mad about music (which/that) I …

   4 I want to go to an exhibition (which/that) I …

   5 I dislike (operas/rock concerts) most of all, which I have never liked, …

   6 I have seen loads of films, which is a hobby of mine, …

Writing:

IELTS Task 2

1 ◯ Work in groups and discuss the Task 2 question below. Decide whether you are going to write your answer using advantages, purposes or reasons. Make a list of three or four positive ideas and three or four negative ideas relating to involvement in the arts.

WRITING TASK 2

You should spend about 40 minutes on this task.

Write about the following topic:

> *Being involved in the arts makes people feel better.*
>
> *To what extent do you agree or disagree?*

Give reasons for your answer and include any relevant examples from your own knowledge or experience.

Write at least 250 words.

---

2 The text below is part of an answer to the Task 2 question above. For **1–10**, complete the gaps with a suitable word. The first letter of each word is given.

It is not possible for many of us to achieve greatness in the **1 a_____** like painting or literature, but it does not mean that we should not be involved in some kind of **2 a_____** activity, even if it only means visiting art **3 g_____** or attending lectures on the arts to gain more knowledge.

There are, of course, different advantages, which benefit the individual and the nation as a whole, to be derived from children and adults **4 p_____** in some way in the arts. **5 T_____** dancing, for example. Dance, which requires a lot of physical activity, is obviously very good for **6 p_____** health as it helps the body to fight disease and also improves **7 c_____** , provided that is that one doesn't overdo it. **8 L_____** , painting and pottery help coordination, which is a skill that is missing in a lot of education today as children focus on learning through computers.

For some, the purpose of involvement in the arts is to help them relax, even if it is only going to see an **9 e_____** at an art **10 g_____** .

3 Find **1–5** below in the text in exercise 2.

   1 the writer's opinion

   2 examples of non-defining relative clauses, if they exist

   3 examples of defining relative clauses, if they exist

   4 an example of a purpose

   5 an example

4 Complete the final paragraph of the text in exercise 2. In this part of the answer you should write about the various reasons why people get involved in artistic activities.

1 ⬭ Work in groups. Discuss statements 1 and 2 below.

1 'Graffiti is a legitimate art form.'

2 'Street artists should be made to clean up the damage they cause rather than sending them to prison.'

2 Work in groups. The following words and phrases **1–10** all appear in the reading passage below. Without looking at the passage, decide if the meanings on the right are correct.

1	*on the face of it*	superficially
2	*wielding*	carrying
3	*polarised*	driven apart
4	*facade*	outside surface
5	*crew*	people working on a ship
6	*pop*	jump up and down
7	*retrospective*	forward-looking
8	*spawned*	created
9	*upstanding*	not sitting
10	*draconian*	severe

3 Scan the reading passage and find the incorrect words from exercise 2 to check the correct meaning.

READING PASSAGE

You should spend about 20 minutes on **Questions 1–13**, which are based on the reading passage below.

Graffiti: Street art or crime

those who spray and those who remove the paint. Great British institutions have been polarised. Last week the might of English law delivered its verdict at Southwark Crown Court in London where five members of the DPM Graffiti Crew were jailed – one, Andrew Gillman, for two years – after admitting conspiracy to cause criminal damage, costing the taxpayer at least £1m.

On the face of it, as a society, we seem to be a little mixed-up when it comes to 'graffiti', as you call it if you work in the local council's cleansing department, or 'street art' as you say if you're the man – and they do mainly seem to be male – wielding the spray can.

But the confusion now runs deeper than

By contrast, just down the road from the Court, the riverside facade of Tate Modern had been covered in giant murals by six urban artists with international reputations, including Blu from Bologna, Faile from New York, and Sixeart from Barcelona, in the first display of street art at a major museum.

The courtroom and the museum were so close that supporters of the men on trial popped down to the Tate to do a bit of retouching during one lunchtime break at the court. 'There is a huge irony in the juxtaposition of the two events,' said one of the artists.

The man to credit for bringing street art into established gallery spaces is Banksy. A few years ago he was sneaking his work into galleries such as the Louvre and Tate Britain. Now Tate Modern is selling his book in its gift shop. His works sell for hundreds of thousands of pounds and he was recently featured in a retrospective exhibition alongside Andy Warhol. He, more than anyone else, has legitimised the genre and spawned a new generation of young imitators – much to the displeasure of those who want to clean up behind them.

Bob has been involved in graffiti since 1982 when he was a punk. He now works, by day, for a London art gallery and describes himself as an upstanding taxpayer. 'London is to street art, at the start of the 21st century, what Paris was for Impressionism at the start of the 20th,' he says with genuine immodesty. 'And yet we hate graffiti more than anywhere else in the world. England is by far and away the most draconian for punishments for what are only economic crimes.'

A gallery in New York in the United States launches an exhibition next week based on the work of those convicted at Southwark. 'DPM – Exhibit A', at the Anonymous Gallery Project in Soho, will display large photographs of the convicts' work alongside copies of their charge sheets to ask whether the men are criminals or artists.

It is a question which prompts different answers in different parts of the world, says Cedar Lewinsohn, the curator of the exhibition at Tate Modern. 'Brazil for instance is more relaxed about it,' he says. 'In parts of Australia, they are like the UK and people really hate graffiti and tags on vans and trains, but in Melbourne drivers compete with each other as to whose van is more decorated.'

They have similarly schizophrenic responses in other nations too. In Toronto, police have just hired a street artist to paint walls to help find the man who murdered the street artist's brother. Elsewhere in Canada, a court has ruled that, after a police crackdown on graffiti artists, a 28-year-old man is only allowed to venture into town if he is accompanied by his mother. One internet blogger wrote: 'In their twenties and still vandalising other people's property – shouldn't they have moved on to drug dealing, or perhaps become real estate agents by that age?'

Street art, you see, is a highly polarising phenomenon. On the one hand there are those like the American artist Elura Emerald, who is also involved in next week's New York exhibition, who insist that 'artists who paint on the street are merely expressing themselves, not hurting anyone' and should not be punished 'but appreciated and celebrated'. Then there are those like Judge Christopher Hardy who, in court in Southwark, described the activities of the DPM Crew as 'a wholesale self-indulgent campaign to damage property on an industrial scale'.

How is such a dichotomy to be resolved? How, The Independent asked the street artist Bob, can artistic expression be reconciled with the fear and loathing that graffiti inspires in many citizens who see it as a symbol of lawlessness and the deterioration of their neighbourhood? 'Well, not by sending them to jail,' he says.

Greenwich and Tower Hamlets councils in London agree. They commissioned members of the DPM to lead summer workshops as street art tutors for young and vulnerable people. The two councils sent references to court vouching that the DPM men were 'positive' and 'inspirational' in working with 'young people who aren't able to do reading or writing'. But it was not enough to save them from prison.

Questions 1–9

Complete the summary using the list of words, **A–Q**, below.

The debate as to whether graffiti constitutes art is **1** .... the establishment in Great Britain. While one group of 'graffiti artists' were being sent to prison, in an art gallery not far from the court the work of several major street artists was being **2** .... on the side of the gallery facing the river. The street artist Bansky is responsible for **3** .... street art, leading to his being **4** .... by a new band of imitators, to the **5** .... of some people. London has been described as the centre of street art in the world, but ironically at the same time the **6** .... there are greater. Whether graffiti artists are considered **7** .... to be imprisoned or not depends on which country you are in. So the question is whether street artists should be **8** .... as wrongdoers or **9** .... as artists.

A cleaned	**B** uniting	**C** criticizing
D dividing	**E** destroying	**F** punished
G exhibited	**H** penalties	**I** annoyance
J criminals	**K** pleasure	**L** promoting
M avoided	**N** painters	**O** rewards
P copied	**Q** appreciated	

Questions 10–13

Look at the following countries (Questions 10–13 below) and the list of statements below.

Match each country with the correct statement, **A–F**.

10 the USA
11 Brazil
12 Australia
13 Canada

List of Statements

A vehicle adornment is a form of competition

B a street artist has been employed by the police

C it causes street disturbances

D imprisonment for two years is mandatory

E people are easygoing about street art

F it is exhibiting work of the artists imprisoned in the UK

○ **Reacting to the text**

Do you think that graffiti is a genuine art form? Why/Why not?

Does graffiti brighten up dull areas in cities or do people find it threatening?

Why do you think people spray graffiti around cities? Will it ever be stopped?

Speaking
IELTS Part 2

1 Work in pairs for exercises 1–4. Read the extract below in which the candidate is responding to the Part 2 task card below. As you will see, each point in the answer needs to be expanded to make it long enough for the exam.

I'm going to describe a piece of art, which I think is a work of great craftsmanship and the most beautiful object in the world for me. It is David by Michelangelo, who is a great Italian sculptor. The first time I saw it was when I went from Rome to Florence to see my aunt … One day she took me there to visit the statue of David. I didn't want to go as I hated art galleries and museums … I thought they were boring and old-fashioned … But I was completely overawed, because it is such a breathtaking sculpture … As for its appearance, it is very tall and it is made of marble. The statue is looking off into the distance as if he is looking into the future … Because Michaelangelo's David changed the way I looked at art galleries, I shall always be very fond of it.

Describe your favourite work of art.

You should say:

    what the work of art is

    when you first saw it

    what it looks like

and explain why you like this work of art.

2 Number the parts of the topic **1–4** on the task card and add the numbers to the relevant sections of the extract.

3 <u>Underline</u> any words or phrases in the extract that you think the candidate included in their notes.

4 Add sentences and clauses to the extract to make it longer. Remember you should speak for one to two minutes.

5 When you are speaking in the exam it is important to try to speak fluently. This does not mean you need to speak fast but at natural speed. One way to help you is to try to control your breathing. A simple technique is to learn where there are natural breaks and take a shallow breath. Look at the first sentence from the extract in exercise 1.

I'm going to describe a piece of art, which I think is a work of great craftsmanship and the most beautiful object in the world for to me.

You can take a shallow breath after the words *art, craftmanship* and *object* and your voice can go up. At the last word in the sentence your voice goes down and you can take a slightly longer breath.

With a partner, go through the text and mark in pencil where you think the natural breaks are. Then read the text to each other.

6 Make notes to prepare your answer for the topic in exercise 1. Try to use some of the words and structures from this unit.

7 ◯ With a partner, take turns talking about the topic, using your notes to guide you. When your partner has finished speaking, give him/her feedback using the checklist on page 210.

10 Review

Vocabulary

1   In **1–8** below, there is one word missing. Decide which word is missing in each sentence.

   1 Actors and actresses act in plays or films. Sometimes some of them become famous because they star in soap.

   2 He the symphony and conducted the orchestra at the performance.

   3 She has written many fantasy novels but people still do not think that she is a great, but there are many children and adults who would disagree.

   4 As a playwright, he wrote many and even directed some of his works in well-known theatres, appearing from time to time on the stage himself.

   5 Is a newspaper journalist an? Many would like to think they have artistic qualities.

   6 He was a great and painter, having carved many famous statues and painted many of the world's greatest paintings.

   7 The producer got on well with the actors and in the film, but he didn't always like the way the director directed it.

   8 The choreographer arranged the ballet very carefully, but some of the found it very difficult to perform.

2   For texts **1–3** below, <u>underline</u> the correct word in *italics*.

1
Studying *drama/play* at secondary school is a very good way to be introduced to acting. Many schools have their own *stages/theatres* at the front of the gym with *scenery/background*. *Drama/Actor* teachers are in great demand to *produce/compose theatres/plays* each year. It isn't very *highbrow/drama*, but everyone enjoys it so I think it's good for drama to be taught at school.

2
For some people I think graffiti can cause problems, because it can make urban areas seem quite threatening. But is it an act of vandalism? I personally don't think so. It is in many ways like primitive art. The problem, I think, is that *extract/abstract* art, like a lot of graffiti, isn't easy for people to understand, but then how much do people these days understand about paintings by *classical/orthodox* artists? Who for instance can unravel the *allusions/illusions/delusions* in early works of art. And I think there are places where graffiti can be a work of *art/artists*.

3
Yes. It's far from easy for people to be able to *appreciate/see/realize* modern art. But if they look at it in greater depth, they will see it in a more *favourable/critical/approving* way.

3   Match the following questions from IELTS Speaking Part 3 with the three texts **1–3** in exercise 2.

   a Do you think it is easy for people to understand modern art?

   b In your opinion is graffiti an act of vandalism?

   c What is the benefit of teaching drama at secondary school?

Defining and non-defining clauses

1 For **1–10** below, link the two sentences together with a relative pronoun or zero relative where necessary. Make any necessary changes. There may be more than one possible answer.

   1 I saw the film. You recommended it to me last week.
   2 That is the house. I bought it last year.
   3 Literature is popular in my country. It is compulsory in the school curriculum.
   4 The gallery had its main piece of art stolen. The gallery is at the end of the street.
   5 Some children are very advanced at school. Some children's parents take them to museums.
   6 The film was attacked by the critics. It was four hours long.
   7 Many books are published each year in the UK. The books do not sell many copies.
   8 My favourite work of art is not a huge tourist attraction. It is a building in Ireland.
   9 Some types of music are very popular in my country. They are not well-known elsewhere.
   10 The man is wearing a red hat. He is the director of the film.

2 Complete the following sentences with a relative pronoun where necessary. There may be more than one possible answer.

   1 One of my sisters, _____ is a dancer, got married yesterday.
   2 Music, _____ they say is good for the soul, is certainly very uplifting.
   3 The antique car _____ we saw in the showroom has been stolen.
   4 Modern dance, _____ many young people are attracted to, is good exercise as well as being an art form.
   5 A famous footballer, _____ name you know, was at the party last night.
   6 Exhibitions, _____ can be outdoors as well as indoors, are good for children to visit.
   7 The type of science _____ I liked most at school was physics.
   8 The musical _____ was very boring has attracted huge audiences.

Proof reading

As quickly as you can, find the mistakes in sentences **1–7** below.

   1 Art exhibition can sometimes be criticized for being elitist as they are very expensive.
   2 Bronze scultures appear to be very old-fashioned nowadays.
   3 The performing arts are much more relaxed to engage with that art exhibits.
   4 Street art as an art form is changing the way young people interact with their enviroment.
   5 Literature, which is more than 100 years old, is not really relevant to the modern world.
   6 Artists are valuable to any society because they push boundries and challenge established thinking.
   7 The vision arts, which includes paintings, etc. are much more engaging than the performing arts.

11 Psychology and sociology

Vocabulary: The family

1 ⬤ Work in groups. Describe the relationships between the people in the photographs below.

2 Work in pairs. Answer questions **1–14** below.

1 What is the collective word for mother and father?
2 What is the collective word for grandmother and grandfather?
3 What is the collective word for brothers and sisters?
4 What is the name for a diagram showing the organization of a family, including ancestors?
5 What is a widow?
6 What is a widower?
7 What is a godparent?
8 What is the word for people you have blood relations with?
9 What is the name for a person in your family who lived before you?
10 What is the name for you in relation to your mother or father's brother or sister?
11 What is the name for the group consisting of parents and children?
12 What is the name for people who live together in one dwelling?
13 What is another word for children?
14 What is the name for a child whose parents have died?

3 Work in pairs. Match a sentence beginning **1–7** with an ending **a–g**.

1 I am an only child,	**a** only me, my brother and my parents.
2 Both my parents come from large families,	**b** so I have no siblings.
3 I have no idea who my ancestors are	**c** but I am sure it was no different in the past.
4 There are not many people in our household;	**d** all four are in their eighties.
5 People often criticize today's young generation,	**e** so I have loads of relatives.
6 My grandparents are really old;	**f** as I have never done a family tree to find out.
7 Our family tree can be traced to the last century,	**g** so I know the names of my ancestors going back four generations.

4 ⬭ Work in pairs. Write at least two sentences about yourself using the ideas in exercise 3. Then write three questions you would like your partner to ask you relating to the sentences. Take turns asking questions and explaining the sentences you have written.

> **Useful expressions**
>
> *Tell me about your (siblings/grandparents).*
> *Can you describe your (household/family/relatives)?*
> *What do you know about your (family history)?*

Word building: Suffixes *-hood* and *-ship*

The suffixes *-ship* and *-hood* are used express the following:

1 a state *membership*

2 an office or position *professorship*

3 a skill *draughtsmanship*

4 a period of time *adulthood*

5 a group *brotherhood*

1 Work in pairs. For sentences **1–9** below, replace the words underlined with a noun with a suffix *-hood* or *-ship*. If necessary, use the nouns in the box below the sentences to help you. Make any necessary changes to the word order.

Example:

Being an adult is certainly fun, but it means one has greater responsibilities.

Adulthood is certainly fun, but it means one has greater responsibilities.

1 He faced a period of great difficulty in his early life, so it is inspiring to see him being so successful now.

2 When the former colony finally achieved the state of being an independent nation, there was widespread celebration.

3 He had qualities that showed he would make a good leader, and therefore he received enormous backing from the public.

4 The problems that occur in the mutual dealings between the two countries were quickly overcome.

5 I have such happy memories of my life as a child in New Zealand.

6 Being a mother or father does not suit some people at all.

7 Various businesses and individuals set up a scheme to provide money to enable young people visit other countries.

8 Bringing up children demands a lot of skill and hard work from women.

9 The aim of the organization is to encourage friendly relations between nations.

hard	sponsor	parent	nation	mother
leader	friend	relation	child	

2 Work in pairs. For sentences **1–7**, complete the gaps with a noun that you made in exercise 1 and a verb from the box below. Make any necessary changes to the verb.

> withdraw   reach   cultivate   face
> maintain   spend   show

1 Over the years, the prime minister _____ a deep _____ with neighbouring countries, but it was suddenly wrecked by unforeseen circumstances.

2 The government _____ _____ from the social programme, but the organizers managed to attract funds from alternative sources.

3 Despite _____ appalling _____ during the journey, the explorers survived.

4 He _____ such a happy _____ with his grandparents, of whom he has fond memories.

5 _____ was only _____ after a long but peaceful political struggle.

6 He _____ outstanding _____ during the crisis.

7 Throughout life they _____ a harmonious _____ .

3 Work in pairs. In sentences **1–10** below, the word in *italics* does not collocate with the word *relationship*. Replace the words in *italics* with the correct collocation.

1 It is said that Britain has a *specialist* relationship with America.

2 Some people think it is important to develop *profession* relationships in the business world that do not involve kinship ties.

3 They have a relationship *long-lasting* many years.

4 In an extended family very *closed* relationships are the norm.

5 *Familiar* relationships are of great importance in most societies.

6 The *parenthood-children* relationship is socially and psychologically complex.

7 It can take a long time for countries to *fabricate* strong relationships with each other.

8 Relations between both countries broke down because they had a *breakable* relationship.

9 They had relationship *troubles* going back many years.

10 He has built up a *net* of relationships that have helped him build his business.

4 ⬭ The words below can be used when describing the different stages in a person's life. Choose two or more of the stages that are relevant to your life and think of a relationship that was important to you in each of them. Tell a partner which relationship you have chosen and why it was important in this period.

childhood   *adolescence*   *adulthood*   *father/motherhood*

Reading
IELTS Reading Passage

1 Work in pairs. Find the words below in the first paragraph of the reading passage on the opposite page and decide what you think it will be about.

socialize   *relatives*   *kinship*   *networks*

2 Skim the passage and underline the main words and phrases in each paragraph that show you what the paragraph is about.

READING PASSAGE

You should spend about 20 minutes on **Questions 1–13**, which are based on the reading passage below.

It takes a village to raise a child

A It takes an African village to bring up and socialize the child into the community. Nothing illustrates this more than the fact that children are sometimes allowed to spend holidays with relatives such as aunts, uncles or grandparents who live far away from home. The children are shown in a practical way the nature of kinship and the extent of familial and kinship relations.

They get to know that they are part of a wide network of relatives, who are as important as the immediate family of father, mother and siblings. Such networks are useful in case of calamities when a child loses one or both parents and is forced to relocate to live with relatives who will be responsible for his or her upbringing. The parents exhibit less of the possessiveness over children that characterizes Western society.

B That adolescence brings with it challenges that ought to be handled carefully is appreciated by the society. Indeed, the initiation ceremonies that mark the transition from childhood to adulthood are primarily meant to address some of these challenges. Instructions during initiation focus on conduct and behaviour as well as duties and responsibilities on the part of the initiate for his/her own good and for the interests of the entire community.

C Kinship and family interests take precedence over individual interests. Young people who go through the process of initiation from childhood to adulthood are taught that life is worth living because the society is there for them in good and bad times. They bond together as members of the same age-grade. They have come of age as a group, been taught the historical information about the cultural group and its rituals, and been united by the rite that they have all gone through. In due course, they are supposed to marry and start raising a family. With the passage of time they in turn will become elders taking over from the generation that preceded them in the initiation ceremony. Kinship networks are still a significant factor in the contemporary economy and politics. Waged employments are heavily influenced by familial and kinship ties.

D Seniority in age is respected and admired because old age is associated with wisdom. Senior citizens therefore are accorded due respect in the light of the fact that they are custodians of societal values. Their counsel is usually sought during times of crisis. They should not be argued with because their curse could ruin one's future. However, the respect and admiration also comes with certain responsibilities.

As an elder an individual is supposed to be unemotional, sober and focused during a crisis or stressful times. As an arbiter an elder has to be candid and sincere in providing counsel. Also, as either father and grandfather, or mother and grandmother, the elder is supposed to be above partisan differences for his word and counsel to be accorded due respect and recognition. He is not supposed to engage in gossip. Thus while in general seniority is synonymous with honour, respect, admiration and wisdom, it is one's ability to manifest these qualities in old age that gives an individual elevated status in society.

E Families strive to take good care of senior citizens because it sets a good example for young children. By treating their elders well parents send a message to their children that they too would like to be accorded that honour, respect and good treatment in old age. Indeed, one of the important reasons for procreation in traditional society was to have somebody to look after you in old age. Children brought up well were considered an asset. It was considered rude for a young man to sit down while an old person was standing. The young person was supposed to give up a seat for the old person as a sign of respect. The parents themselves must set a good example by respecting and taking care of their own parents. When children see that their grandparents are treated well, they learn by example that they too are expected to take care of their parents in old age.

F The elder is the pillar of both the nuclear and the extended family. Being the eldest living male descendant of the eldest son of the founder of the lineage, he is the link between the living and ancestors. He is supposed to unite the family so that the unity survives his death. He reinforces kinship ideology, maintains peace and presides over family gatherings, during which period he keeps members within bounds by insisting on customs, laws and traditional observances. He helps to socialize members of the family, immediate and extended, into the ways of the group. He represents the family whenever there are communal lineage meetings. In this way elders unite family and kinship members. In their oral will, in the presence of other elders, they provide guidance on how land will be parcelled out among family members, appeal for unity among family and kinship members and pass the baton of leadership to the next patriarch of the family. Thus, all members of the society take socialization seriously. That role transcends age and gender. This is because socialization contributes to cohesion.

Don't forget!

For questions **1–6**:
- Read the rubric to check if you can use letters **A–F** more than once.
- Underline words and phrases that will help you look for paraphrases in the passage.
- Look for the plural nouns in phrases **1–6**. They tell you several items are mentioned.

For questions **7–10**:
- Check the word limit.
- Don't write words on the answer sheet that are in the question.

Questions 1–6

The reading passage has six paragraphs, **A–F**.

Which paragraph contains the following information?

NB You may use any letter more than once.

1 steps detailing how the individual learns kinship through life

2 the part played by all family members in a child's development

3 a motive for having children

4 the desire to have a well-raised child

5 how becoming an adult is celebrated

6 a list of the roles of the elder in large and small families

Questions 7–10

Complete the sentences below.

Choose **NO MORE THAN TWO WORDS** from the passage for each answer.

7 African parents are not as overprotective of their children as those in ....

8 Familial and kinship connections come before personal ....

9 Despite the many positive associations connected with old age, it has particular .... attached to it.

10 In African society, an elderly person's .... depends on a capacity to use certain attributes.

Questions 11–13

Choose **THREE** letters, **A–H**.

Which **THREE** of the following statements are true of the elder of the family?

A He advises family members on career choices.

B He is responsible for increasing the wealth of the family.

C He hands over control to the next head of the family.

D He is in charge of distributing land among family members.

E He preserves the bonds between the past and the present.

F He has a duty to preserve unity even at the expense of customs.

G He trains family members in the ways of the society.

H He assigns roles to the various family members according to ability.

Reacting to the text

Does what is described in the passage reflect the family and the society you come from? Give reasons and examples.

Do you think that attitudes to the family are undergoing change in many societies around the world? Is this change an inevitable part of human progress or the result of globalization?

Speaking
IELTS Part 2

1 Look at the Part 2 task cards **A–D** below. Choose one topic that you would like to speak about and make notes.

A

Describe an important friendship that you had when you were younger.
You should say:
> who the friendship was with
> when you first met your friend
> what you did together
and explain why this friendship was important to you.

B

Describe a colleague from your work that you like.
You should say:
> what the work relationship is with this person
> what this person looks like
> what kind of person your colleague is
and explain why you like this person.

C

Describe the period of your life that you have enjoyed the most so far.
You should say:
> when it was
> what happened during this period
> who were the most important people in your life in this period
and explain why you enjoyed it.

D

Describe a family relationship which is important to you.
You should say:
> how this person is related to you
> what this person looks like
> what this person's personality is like
and explain why you like this person.

2 Work in pairs. Choose at least two points from the speaking checklist on page 210 that you would like your partner to check as you speak. Take turns talking about the topic, using your notes to guide you. When your partner has finished speaking, give him/her feedback on the points they chose from the checklist.

3 Compare the notes you made for the topic with your partner's. Discuss what differences and similarities there are.

4 Read the following extract from a model answer to one of the topics in exercise 1. Decide which topic the candidate is talking about. Then underline the parts of the answer that address each point on the task card.

'I'd like to talk about a friendship that I had when I was in my early teens. It was with my best friend at that time, whom I met when I first went to secondary school. I remember very well the first day we ran into each other. I think we knew immediately that we were going to become good friends. We were in the same class at school, and we would sit next to each other, play the same games together – we were just like sisters … The friendship was very important to me. Firstly, because we gave each other support at a time when we were both nervous about being in a new place. And secondly, where I grew up we didn't face any hardship, but I didn't have any siblings, so it was nice to have the companionship of someone at school … And I suppose I felt that I was leaving childhood behind, and it was the first friendship of my adolescence.

5 Work in groups. Add more details to the answer in exercise 4 to make it about 50–100 words longer. When you have finished, check what you have written with the checklist on page 210.

6 Look at the beginning of the answer in exercise 4 again. Decide which ten words you think the candidate wrote in his/her notes.

7 Work in pairs. Choose another topic from the task cards in exercise 1 and repeat exercises 2 and 3.

Listening
IELTS Section 1

1   Work in pairs. You will hear a conversation between a school secretary and a parent about a school trip. Look at questions **1–10** below and make a list of things you think they will talk about.

Don't forget!

Skim the questions and check the following:
- the type of word (noun, verb etc.) that is required
- the maximum number of words you need to write
- if there are any questions where the answer may be a number
- if any answers are likely to be plural

👁 2.4   **SECTION 1   Questions 1–10**

Complete the notes below.

Write **NO MORE THAN TWO WORDS/AND OR A NUMBER** for each answer.

School Trip Information

Example	*Answer*
Name of club:	**International Friendship Club**

Trip to:

Country – **1** ....

Accommodation arrangements:

Students will not be by themselves – students stay with families **2** ....

Cost: *£495*

Duration: **3** .... *days*

Price excluding presents for the host family and **4** ....

Takes place during *spring* **5** ....

Advert released on **6** ....

After application is received **7** .... *necessary*

Number of students on trip: **8** ....

Total no of adults: *six*

Including: **9** .... *parents*

Deposit: **10** *£* ....

---

2   👁   When you were at school did you go on school trips? Where to? For how long? What do you think students learn from school trips?

Language focus: Conditionals 2

1 Look at the following examples of conditional sentences from the listening practice on page 158.

Last year, if it were not for the school fund, it would have been a lot more.

… that's not a problem, provided you make a deposit of £100 …

What tenses are used in each of the clauses in the two sentences? Can you use the simple future to replace any of the tenses? If yes, does this change the meaning?

G Read more about conditionals in the Grammar reference on page 224.

2 For **1–8** below, decide if text **b** is a paraphrase of text **a**. Re-write sentence **b** so that it is a paraphrase where necessary.

1 a Even if the social relationships course is expensive, I'll pay for it.

   b Whatever the price of the social relationships course is, I'll pay for it.

2 a I'll do the psychology option on the course, unless all the places are taken.

   b I won't do the psychology option on the course, even if there are free places.

3 a If the government should happen to address social issues like crime and poverty, we'll see a change in society.

   b There's a possibility the government will address social issues like crime and poverty.

4 a Supposing future generations are even more highly trained than they are now, will their lives be better?

   b Future generations will be even more highly trained than they are now, but will their lives be better?

5 a People need to be psychologically well adapted to the changing face of the workplace; otherwise, they'll find the changing world difficult to operate in.

   b If people are psychologically well adapted to the changing face of the workplace, they'll find the changing world difficult to operate in.

6 a If it were not for improved education opportunities, the world would be worse off.

   b The world's present situation is due to improved education opportunities.

7 a If the government hadn't wasted billions on weapons, more money would be available for social projects like community groups.

   b The government wasted billions on weapons, and so less money is now available for social projects like community groups.

8 a If only I had studied psychotherapy, I would have found it easier to get a job.

   b I did study psychotherapy and I now regret it.

3 Work in pairs. For **1–6** below, underline the correct word or phrase in *italics*.

1 *Unless/If/Otherwise* socialization takes place at home and at school, society will face the consequences.

2 *If only/Provided/Even if* I had met you sooner, we could have had a better time.

3 *Unless/If/Even if* communities are disrupted by the high incidence of crime, they always triumph in the end.

4 *Unless/If only/Provided* you are prepared psychologically for the interview, you'll get the job.

5 *Unless/If only/If* the company hadn't planned for the future properly, they would be in trouble now.

6 *Unless/Supposing/Provided* you were offered a very well paid job abroad, would you take it?

4 Work in pairs. Decide which conditional clauses in exercise 3 describe actions or situations that have already happened.

5 For **1–6** below, make one sentence from the two sentences given using the word in brackets. Make any necessary changes.

Example:

Children will grow up to be unruly adults. Parents need to take an interest in social behaviour.   (unless)

Unless parents take an interest in social behaviour, children will grow up to be unruly adults.

1 Families can help to make society a better place. The government needs to give them support.   (provided)

2 The government may fund more community centres. This will provide a place for people to meet.   (if/would)

3 Globalization occurred. Now there are social and cultural problems around the world.   (hadn't/would be fewer)

4 Volunteer workers helped people deal with the psychological aspect of change. Without them the situation would have been worse.   (if not for)

5 Social interaction between different cultures is increasing. Still more contact is necessary.   (even though)

6 Social intelligence isn't taught in schools. If it were, would it be beneficial?   (supposing)

6 With a partner, discuss your past, present and future, and the things you have done, haven't done and have yet to do. Before you start, spend two or three minutes making notes.

1   Work in groups. Choose one the following Task 2 questions. Then decide what the two sides of the topic are and make a list of ideas for both sides.

1

WRITING TASK 2

You should spend about 40 minutes on this task.

Write about the following topic:

> *Some people think that the world is now one large village and we are all responsible for each other. Others, however, argue that people in other countries should look after their own people and not be concerned with other countries.*
>
> *Discuss both views and give your own opinion.*

Give reasons for your answer and include any relevant examples from your own knowledge and experience.

Write at least 250 words.

2

WRITING TASK 2

You should spend about 40 minutes on this task.

Write about the following topic:

> *Education is the only means to improve the social and psychological well-being of people.*
>
> *To what extent do you agree or disagree?*

Give reasons for your answer and include any relevant examples from your own knowledge and experience.

Write at least 250 words.

3

WRITING TASK 2

You should spend about 40 minutes on this task.

Write about the following topic:

> *Teaching children and young people how to behave is the responsibility of parents, not schools or the government.*
>
> *To what extent do you agree or disagree?*

Give reasons for your answer and include any relevant examples from your own knowledge and experience.

Write at least 250 words.

2 Work in pairs. Look at the extracts below from answers to the Task 2 questions in exercise 1. Decide which question, **1**, **2**, or **3**, each extract answers.

Extract 1

To me the logical answer is a mixture of both sides, and not necessarily equally at all times. It is natural human instinct for people to help each other, so this characteristic should be harnessed for the betterment of mankind. In times of hardship and natural calamities like earthquakes and floods, people from different parts of the world pull together. Shopping is a good example here of people helping the elderly. Unfortunately, it sometimes takes something bad to happen before people act together. Nowadays it is important for different countries to live and work together as the world becomes smaller and smaller. Moreover, as the world is more and more integrated with the Internet and the speed of communication networks, it makes sense that we should all work together ...

Extract 2

Let's say someone is well-educated but has not made even one or two friends in their life. Their life would be affected. For example, someone who has concentrated on their education at the expense of everything around them will not be as happy as someone who forms and maintains deep relationships with family, friends and possibly work colleagues. Important as these relationships are in themselves, such close family ties on their own without education are not enough to help support people in their journey through life. Learning a skill like pottery can help make people's lives relevant and help them relax ...

3 In the extracts in exercise 2, <u>underline</u> the text you can replace with the conditional sentences below.

If the basic human desire to help others were exploited, the human condition could be improved.

Even if someone had a sound education and had not over their lifetime cultivated at least one or two close friendships, then the quality of their life would be affected.

4 In each extract in exercise 2, <u>underline</u> one piece of irrelevant information.

5 Make notes for the topic below, using the checklist on page 209 to help you. Then write an answer for the question. When you have finished, check your answer using the checklist.

> ### WRITING TASK 2
>
> You should spend about 40 minutes on this task.
>
> Write about the following topic:
>
> > *Some people think that managerial posts in private companies and in government are more suitable for men. Others think that given the opportunity women can be successful managers.*
> >
> > *Discuss both views and give your own opinion.*
>
> Give reasons for your answer and include any relevant examples from your own knowledge or experience.
>
> Write at least 250 words.

Vocabulary

Complete each gap with a suitable word. One answer requires two words.

I tried to trace my **1**_____ not long ago to see if I could find out who my
2 _____were, but I found it difficult to go back beyond my grandparents. My
grandmother has been a **3** _____ now for two years since my grandfather
passed away. My grandfather claimed he was a **4** _____ of someone famous,
but I never got round to asking him about it. I have no **5** _____ but I have many
6 _____ as both my parents come from large families. The present young
7_____ seems not to care much about family history, but that may only be age.

Word building

1 Make sentences by choosing one sentence part from each column **A**, **B** and **C**. There
   may be more than one possible answer.

A	B	C
1 I spent a very happy	**a** considerable hardship as	**i** various business people.
2 We celebrate	**b** several very strong friendships with	**ii** my parents in the countryside.
3 He faced	**c** childhood with	**iii** every year without fail.
4 He developed	**d** the day we achieved nationhood	**iv** by having a huge party.
5 He maintained	**e** reaching adulthood	**v** during the turmoil.
6 The government withdrew	**f** his leadership	**vi** the problems began.
7 He showed	**g** their sponsorship when	**vii** the company.
8 He celebrated	**h** a very good working relationship with	**viii** a child.

2 The extract below is from an answer for an IELTS Writing Task 2 question about social
   problems. For **1–8**, underline the correct word in **bold**.

In the world today, there are many social issues like crime, hooliganism, illiteracy
and poverty. Many people blame these social ills on a breakdown in family
1 relationships/relatives, but it is not as simple as that. There may be some
2 flats/households where the **3 relationships/relatives** are very fragile, but by and
large family relationships are very strong. In many cases, it may be a **4 sibling/
generational** difference as the older generation responds to the changes brought
about by the young.

One social ill that could be easily eradicated is poverty. Politicians make grand
statements about getting rid of poverty within a generation. The **5 hardship/
friendship** suffered by many people even in richer countries is difficult for wealthy
people to appreciate. Strong **6 leadership/sponsorship** is needed in this area in all
countries and the hand of **7 friendship/leadership** must be extended from rich
to poor countries; otherwise, **8 childhood/childship** for many will continue to be a
period of great difficulty ...

Speaking

Put boxes **A–K** into the correct order so that they form part of a response to an IELTS Speaking Part 2 topic. Then decide what the candidate was asked to describe.

A	*I have maintained a number of strong*
B	*a very deep friendship. I think*
C	*restaurant where I work*
D	*relationships with people who were my childhood friends, but the friendship I*
E	*would like to describe is one that began only early last year with a friend from the*
F	*we have very similar interests. So I think what really makes the friendship work*
G	*but we still managed to help each other out. Since that day we have developed*
H	*part-time. We first met when we were working on an evening shift. It was very busy,*
I	*the main reason why we get on is because*
J	*doing the same sports, and we rarely disagree on anything.*
K	*is that both of us like reading and*

Conditionals 2

Rewrite sentences **1–4** using the prompts given.

1 Whatever the cost, I shall try to keep the whole family together.
  Even if …
2 I'll attend the seminar on kinship, only if the one on culture and the family is full.
  Unless …
3 If it were not for the community centre, families would have nowhere to meet up.
  … depend on …
4 If they hadn't kept the family together, they wouldn't be in such a strong position now.
  … and so …

Proof reading

In the following extract from an IELTS Writing Task 2 answers, the letter *s* has been removed in some cases and added in others. Find the mistakes as quickly as you can.

Some people believe the sole responsibility in society for bringing up children lies with the parents, while other think it's more the duty of the government. The logical answer, however, is that raising childrens is the responsibility of everyone not just the parent.

If we take social skill, for example, these can in part be taught by the parents and the family, but school as agencies of the government also have a role to play. Obviously, parents can teach childrens to form deep and warm relationship with friends and family and schools can show children how to make relationships outside the home with their peer, while at the same time picking up knowledge and informations. If we as adult had not been introduced to the social norms of society, we would not know how to behave ourselves. Nor would we know how to pass on these skill to our children.

12 Travelling around the world

Listening
IELTS Section 2

1 ⬭ With a partner, describe each of the photographs. Then discuss the questions below.

- Are these the sorts of places that you would like to visit? Which one appeals to you the most/least? Give reasons.
- Have you ever visited anywhere that you would classify as exotic? Where?
- Do you think our desire to visit exotic places is actually destroying them? In what ways?

2 Work in pairs. Decide what preparations you would make if you were going away on a trip to somewhere very hot or very cold. Make a checklist of the most important items to take with you.

Underline the words in the questions that warn you that the answer is coming soon.

 2.5 **SECTION 2**   Questions 11–20

Questions 11–15

Choose the correct letter, **A**, **B** or **C**.

11 The speaker advises people to use a checklist if they

    A   dislike things being chaotic.

    B   don't have much time.

    C   can't easily remember things.

12 Further information may be obtained

    A   by post.

    B   from the website.

    C   from the local chemist.

13 To protect oneself from the sun, the best thing for people to do is

    A   carry an umbrella.

    B   avoid direct sunlight.

    C   wear a hat.

14 Good walking shoes are necessary to

    A   support the feet.

    B   keep out the rain.

    C   protect against injury.

15 An awareness of customs is advisable in order to

    A   enjoy festivals.

    B   mix with people.

    C   avoid trouble.

Questions 16–20

Complete the summary below.

Write **ONE WORD ONLY** for each answer.

> *Extra tips*
>
> Maintain family contact so they don't feel any **16** .... , or even misuse any **17** ....
>
> Take a light waterproof cover and a first aid kit with **18** .... and antiseptic **19** ....
>
> Always keep expensive items like **20** .... safe.

3 ⬯ What anxieties do people face when they travel abroad?

If you have travelled to another country, what were you most anxious about before you went?

Vocabulary: Adjectives with multiple meanings

1   Look at the following sentence from the listening practice on page 165. What does *novel* mean in this sentence? What other meanings does it have?

Remember to enjoy yourselves. Look out for novel experiences, and open your minds to the strange and the new!

2   For **1–10** below, <u>underline</u> the word or phrase in the box that does not have the same meaning.

Example:

alien	strange	<u>native</u>	extraterrestrial		

1 foreign	from another country	unfamiliar	relevant		
2 curious	apathetic	inquisitive	unusual		
3 novel	book	original	film		
4 unique	treasured	only happening in one place	unlike anything else		
5 pristine	new and untouched	morally good	different		
6 odd	unusual	irregular	different types	new	
7 fresh	new and different	cold and windy	odd	recently made	
8 new	recently arrived	extra	inexperienced	replacing something	
9 different	dissimilar	several	diverse	unusual	similar
10 strange	unexpected	unfamiliar	uncomfortable	odd	

3   For **1–10** below, complete the gaps with an adjective from exercise 2 that makes sense in sentence **a** and **b**. Then decide what the noun is for each adjective.

1 a I had quite a _____ experience as I was travelling home today.
   b I think I would rather read a _____ than a travelogue.
2 a I would like to live in a _____ area to where I am now.
   b Having _____ types of houses gives character to an area.
3 a The area was really _____ to me at first, but I soon got used to it.
   b I had this really _____ feeling when I entered the house.
4 a Everyone's fingerprints are _____ and can't be copied.
   b My holiday was full of _____ experiences.
5 a The building had these _____ carvings all over it.
   b He was _____ to know what the town looked like.
6 a Being in a _____ country is not as easy or glamorous as it sounds.
   b Their ideas were totally _____ to me. I couldn't agree with them.
7 a It was mainly sunny, but we did have the _____ rain shower.
   b I had this really _____ experience last weekend when I visited the museum.
8 a I was _____ to the job and didn't really know anything.
   b I bought a _____ set of clothes for the interview.
9 a The sandwiches we bought were very _____ .
   b I wanted to make a _____ start when I went to another town.
10 a I found myself in the middle of an _____ landscape.
   b His ideas were completely _____ to mine.

4   ⬭   Tell your partner about a new experience you had recently, or an interesting event that occurred recently. Use the adjectives and nouns from exercises 1–3.

1 Work in pairs. Decide whether the following statements are true or false.

1 World heritage sites around the world are designated by UNESCO.

2 The Grand Canyon is in the United States of America.

3 The Great Barrier Reef is off the coast of New Zealand.

4 The Aztec ruins are in South America.

5 The Parthenon is in Rome in Italy.

6 The Giant Stelae of Aksum are in West Africa.

7 Mount Fuji is in Japan.

8 The Terracotta Army is in China.

9 The Hermitage museum is in Moscow.

10 The ruins of Persepolis are in Afghanistan.

2 ⬤ Work in groups. Look at the title of the reading passage on page 168. What facts do you already know about this topic? Share your information with the rest of your group.

3 Each of the following words from the reading passage has two different meanings. Look at the words and their meanings and decide which is more likely in this passage. Use a dictionary to check any meanings you don't know.

1 *shelf*	ledge	sill
2 *maturity*	adulthood	fully-developed
3 *system*	scheme	organism
4 *range*	variety	scale
5 *list*	catalogue	slant
6 *vulnerable*	weak	in danger
7 *breed*	reproduce	farm
8 *colony*	collection	settlement
9 *historic*	ancient	momentous
10 *sanctuary*	asylum	place of safety

4 Read the passage to check that you chose the correct meaning.

READING PASSAGE

You should spend about 20 minutes on **Questions 1–13**, which are based on the reading passage below.

The Great Barrier Reef

The Great Barrier Reef was one of Australia's first World Heritage Areas and is the world's largest World Heritage Area. The Great Barrier Reef was inscribed on the World Heritage List in 1981 and was one of 15 World Heritage places included in the National Heritage List on 21 May 2007.

The Great Barrier Reef is the world's largest World Heritage property extending over 2,000 kilometres and covering 348,000 km^2 on the north-east continental shelf of Australia. Larger than Italy, it is one of the best known marine protected areas. The Great Barrier Reef's diversity reflects the maturity of the ecosystem which has evolved over many thousands of years. It is the world's most extensive coral-reef and has some of the richest biological diversity found anywhere.

The Great Barrier Reef contains extensive areas of seagrass, mangrove, sandy and muddy seabed communities, inter-reefal areas, deep oceanic waters and island communities.

Contrary to popular belief, the Great Barrier Reef is not a continuous barrier, but a broken maze of around 2,900 individual reefs, of which 760 are fringing reefs along the mainland or around islands.

Some have coral cays. The reefs range in size from less than one hectare to over 1,000 km2, and in shape from flat platform reefs to elongated ribbon reefs.

The Great Barrier Reef provides habitat for many diverse forms of marine life. There are an estimated 1,500 species of fish and over 360 species of hard, reef-building corals. More than 4,000 mollusc species and over 1,500 species of sponges have been identified.

Other well-represented animal groups include anemones, marine worms, crustaceans and echinoderms.

The extensive seagrass beds are an important feeding ground for the dugong, a mammal species internationally listed as vulnerable. The reef also supports a variety of fleshy algae that are heavily grazed by turtles, fish, sea urchins and molluscs.

The reef contains nesting grounds of world significance for the endangered loggerhead turtle, and for green, hawksbill and flatback turtles, which are all listed as vulnerable. It is also a breeding area for humpback whales that come from the Antarctic to give birth in the warm waters.

The islands and cays support around 215 bird species, many of which have breeding colonies there. Reef herons, osprey, pelicans, frigate birds, sea eagles and shearwaters are among the seabirds that have been recorded.

The Great Barrier Reef is also of cultural importance, containing many archaeological sites of Aboriginal or Torres Strait Islander origin, including fish traps, middens, rock quarries, story sites and rock art. Some notable examples occur on Lizard and Hinchinbrook Islands, and on Stanley, Cliff and Clack Islands where there are spectacular galleries of rock paintings. There are over 30 historic shipwrecks in the area, and on the islands are ruins, operating lighthouses and other sites that are of cultural and historical significance.

About 99.3 per cent of the World Heritage property is within the Great Barrier Reef Marine Park, with the remainder in Queensland waters and islands. Because of its status, many people think the entire Great Barrier Reef is a marine sanctuary or national park, and therefore protected equally throughout. However, the Great Barrier Reef Marine Park is a multiple-use area in which a wide range of activities and uses are allowed, including extractive industries.

This has been achieved using a comprehensive, multiple-use zoning system. Impacts and conflicts are minimized by providing high levels of protection for specific areas. A variety of other activities are allowed to continue in a managed way in certain zones (such as shipping, dredging, research, commercial fishing and recreational fishing).

A new Zoning Plan for the entire Marine Park came into effect on 1 July 2004. The proportion of the Marine Park protected by no-take zones was increased from less than five per cent to over 33 per cent, and now protects representative examples of each of the 70 broad habitat types across the entire Marine Park. Two authorities are now responsible for the Great Barrier Reef: the Queensland Government and the Australian Government.

The majority of the World Heritage property is still relatively pristine when compared with coral reef ecosystems elsewhere in the world. Guided by the principle of balancing conservation and sustainable use, the regulatory framework significantly enhances the resilience of the Great Barrier Reef.

The Australian and Queensland Governments have a cooperative and integrated approach to managing the Great Barrier Reef. The Great Barrier Reef Marine Park Authority (GBRMPA) is the Australian Government agency responsible for overall management, and the Queensland Government, particularly the Queensland Environmental Protection Agency, provides day-to-day management of the marine park for the Authority.

Questions 1–6

Complete the summary below.

Choose **NO MORE THAN TWO WORDS** from the passage for each answer.

The location of the Great Barrier Reef

The Great Barrier Reef, the largest World Heritage property there is, was one of Australia's first sites to become a World Heritage area. Situated on the **1** .... [CONTINENTAL SHELF] off the north-eastern coast of Australia, the Great Barrier Reef is among the world's most famous oceanic **2** .... [PROTECTED AREAS]. The **3** .... [DIVERSITY] of the Great Barrier Reef is a result of the evolution of the **4** .... [ECOSYSTEM] over a very long time. Being the biggest **5** .... [CORAL REEF] of its kind on earth, the Great Barrier Reef is, from the **6** .... [BIOLOGICAL] point of view, very varied.

Questions 7–10

Do the following statements agree with the information given in the reading passage?

Write:

TRUE	if the statement agrees with the information
FALSE	if the statement contradicts the information
NOT GIVEN	if there is no information on this

7 The Great Barrier Reef consists of one large reef. [F]

8 There are more types of molluscs and sponges found in the reef than in any other site in the world. [NG]

9 The loggerhead turtle is under threat of extinction. [T]

10 There are plans to raise some of the sunken ships on the reef. [NG]

Questions 11–13

Answer the questions below.

Choose **NO MORE THAN THREE WORDS** from the passage for each answer.

11 What were enlarged considerably to safeguard sections of all the different marine habitats? [MULTIPLE-USE ZONING SYSTEM]

12 What has a major impact on the Great Barrier Reef's capacity to flourish? [THE REGULATORY FRAMEWORK]

13 What is the Great Barrier Reef Marine Park Authority accountable for in respect of the reef? [OVERALL MANAGEMENT]

Reacting to the text

Provided money were no option, would you like to visit the Great Barrier Reef? What aspect of the reef would appeal to you? Why?
Would you be concerned that carbon produced by travelling there could contribute to the destruction of the reef?

Word building: Words related to memory

1 When people travel, they often bring back something to remind them of their trip. What is this something called? With a partner, use a dictionary to find words with the root *mem* – that are related to *memory*.

2 Work in pairs. For **1–10** below, complete the gaps with a word made from the word *memory*. Make any necessary changes to the form of the word.

   1 I have many happy _____ from my time in the Caribbean. I can still picture the beaches and the surf.

   2 Do you _____ the last time you had a long holiday?

   3 She's writing her _____ now that she is no longer President. They should be interesting reading.

   4 Collecting cinema _____ is not particularly exciting. I'd rather collect holiday posters.

   5 We tried to _____ the route on the map so we would know it perfectly, but when we were going along the road through the forest we got lost.

   6 Would you say that your trip to Japan was a _____ experience or not?

   7 We visited various _____ to a wide range of historic events.

   8 I left him a brief _____ on his desk, because I know he rarely reads his emails.

   9 It's always nice to have even a small _____ of a trip, even if it's only a card.

   10 I lost my _____ for a while, but then it all came back to me. I was so relieved.

3 In the paragraph below the words in *italics* are in the wrong place. Decide the correct position **1–8** for each of the words.

I have really vivid **1** *memorabilia* of my holidays in Mexico last summer. I had a digital camera which takes excellent photographs. And as I am the sort of person who collects **2** *memories* of any kind, like concert tickets or theatre programmes, I came back with loads of **3** *memoirs* like little statues and trinkets. If I ever write my **4** *mementos*, I shall have lots of material to draw on. We visited a beautiful village, and I even bought a replica of a **5** *memorable* to a famous heroine whom I don't really know, but the monument to her was very moving, which is what made it so **6** *memorial*. Unfortunately, I am not sure I'd **7** *memorize* how to get there again as I didn't take much notice of the map. I didn't **8** *remember* the name of the town.

4 ⬤ Work in pairs. Write at least three questions each containing the words made from the word *memory* in exercise 2. Take turns asking and answering the questions.

> **Useful expressions**
>
> *Do you find it easy to memorize …*
> *Are you the sort of person who collects … memorabilia?*
> *What is your (most treasured/fond/vivid) memory … ?*
> *What details do you remember about … ?*
> *What was your most memorable … ?*

Speaking
IELTS Part 1

1 Look at the Part 1 questions below about transport where you live. Decide which two of the following are suitable ways to begin your answer to question 1.

People they travel by car …

More and more people use …

Most travellers …

Commuters get around …

> **The transport where you live**
>
> 1 How do people travel around where you live?
> 2 What problems do people face when they travel?
> 3 How do transport problems affect you?
> 4 How would you improve the transport in your country?

2 Work in pairs. Think of at least two suitable ways to begin your answer to questions **2–4**.

3 Take turns asking and answering the questions in exercise 1. Before you start choose two points from the checklist on page 209 that you would like your partner to give you feedback on.

Speaking
IELTS Part 2

1 Work in groups. Look at the following Part 2 task card and then answer questions **1–6** below.

> Describe a memorable journey you have made.
>
> You should say:
>
> where this journey was to
>
> when it was
>
> what you did on this journey
>
> and explain why this journey was memorable.

1 What synonyms do you know for the word *journey*?
2 Write a list of any words that you associate with the word *journey*.
3 Write a list of adjectives that you associate with the word *journey*.
4 Write a list of verbs that you associate with the word *journey*.
5 Write a list of places that you associate with the word *journey*.
6 Write a list of reasons you associate with going on a journey.

2 Use the words in the lists to help you make notes for the topic above.

> **Don't forget!**
> * You only have one minute to make notes.
> * The words in your notes should be prompts only.
> * Don't be afraid to glance at your notes as you speak.
> * You have to speak for one to two minutes.

3 With a partner, take turns talking about the topic. Before you start, choose two points from the checklist on page 209 that you would like your partner to give you feedback on.

Language focus: Articles

1 In the extract below from the reading passage on page 168, <u>underline</u> examples of the following:

1 the definite article
2 the zero article
3 the indefinite article

Contrary to popular belief, the Great Barrier Reef is not a continuous barrier, but a broken maze of around 2,900 individual reefs, of which 760 are fringing reefs along the mainland or around islands.

Read more about articles in the Grammar reference on page 225.

2 Work in pairs. Answer questions **1–10** below. Pay attention to the articles in your answers.

1 What gives us light during the day?
2 What objects do you see far away in the sky on a clear night?
3 Is the sun a star or a planet?
4 When is the sun a star?
5 Are there different solar systems?
6 What is the highest mountain in the world?
7 Which mountain range is it in?
8 What is the name of the capital of Japan?
9 Is London a capital of the UK?
10 Are there different oceans on our planet? Can you name three?

3 Work in pairs. For sentence **a** and **b** in **1–8** below, decide which sentence requires an article and which does not. Explain why.

1 a I spent the day visiting _____ old monuments.
  b _____ monuments I visited were old.
2 a I like _____ climbing mountains.
  b I'd like to go climbing in _____ Himalayas.
3 a You shouldn't look at _____ sun directly.
  b _____ stars twinkle because they are far away.
4 a The Amazon flows through _____ various countries.
  b Rivers like _____ Nile bring life to desert regions.
5 a _____ capital city of Mexico is enormous.
  b _____ Mexico City is particularly big.
6 a _____ United Kingdom is usually just called the UK.
  b _____ kingdoms are ruled by monarchs.
7 a _____ prime minister runs the country.
  b _____ prime ministers are appointed by heads of state or parties.
8 a _____ heart sends blood around the body.
  b The body has _____ various organs.

4 In the following extract from IELTS Speaking Part 2, <u>underline</u> the articles that should not be there.

A trip I would like to describe is a journey I went on to the Brazil a few years back. I went with my family, two brothers but no the sisters, five people in all. We flew to the Rio de Janeiro which is an amazing city with many people and lots of entertainment. What I really like about the city is that it has the beaches and, of course, it's famous for its nightlife. We all had lots of the fun there with a sightseeing and parties, which we went to nearly every night. The cost of the living is cheap there and a meal in a restaurant is a real treat as everyone is very lively. I recommend Brazil as a place for the holidays and relaxing …

Writing

IELTS Task 2

1 Look at the following Task 2 question. Decide which of the ideas **1–7** below you think is most relevant to the question. Then add your own ideas to the list.

WRITING TASK 2

You should spend about 40 minutes on this task.

Write about the following topic:

> *Some people think that children should be encouraged to travel more while at school to broaden their experience. Others think that not enough time is spent in the classroom learning the basics of a good education.*
>
> *Discuss both these views and give your own opinion.*

Give reasons for your answer and include any relevant examples from your own knowledge and experience.

Write at least 250 words.

---

1 opens them up to new experiences

2 need to learn basics first

3 learn more while travelling

4 travelling is expensive

5 waste of time when away from the classroom

6 too tiring

7 always learning dull facts

2 It is important to be able to develop your ideas in IELTS Writing. For **1–6** below, decide whether the text in *italics* is relevant. Rewrite the text that is not relevant.

1 Cheap air travel enabled people to travel longer distances than before. *A whole family, for example, could fly from India to Europe at less expense than a decade before.*

2 Trains go in and out of fashion in all countries, as they often depend on the support of politicians. *At the moment, more people are travelling by coach.*

3 Tourism can have a negative impact on local culture, *so people should avoid watching TV.*

4 Precious ecosytems around the world are being destroyed by the very tourists who most want to protect them, *so access to such sites needs to be restricted.*

5 Older people find it more difficult to rough it while on holiday compared to the younger generation. *This is surely because young people don't often stay in hotels.*

6 World heritage sites like the Great Barrier Reef are under constant threat of destruction. *For example, even subtle changes in the temperature of the open sea can affect the reef.*

3 Work in groups. Discuss the following Task 2 question. List three main ideas for each point of view and think of an example.

WRITING TASK 2

You should spend about 40 minutes on this task.

Write about the following topic:

> *Today more people than ever are travelling around the world. Some people believe that such travelling helps to broaden people's minds, while others think it just confirms their prejudices.*
>
> *Discuss both these views and give your own opinion.*

Give reasons for your answer and include any relevant examples from your own knowledge or experience.

Write at least 250 words.

---

4 Write an answer for the question. When you have finished, check your answer using the checklist on page 209. Use the articles checklist on page 207 to check your answer for any mistakes relating to articles.

12 Review

Vocabulary

For **1–7** in the following dialogue from IELTS Speaking Part 3, <u>underline</u> the correct word in *italics*.

Examiner: Is it important for young people to travel?

Candidate: Yes. I think travelling to a **1** *foreign/unique/alien* country is essential for young people as it helps to broaden their minds. For example, it can open their minds to **2** *alien/fresh/odd* and **3** *novel/pristine/alien* experiences first hand, instead of just reading about them in books or on the Internet.

Examiner: What kind of **4** *new/odd/alien* experiences?

Candidate: Well, for example, if children go to, say, Canada for the first time from, say, Russia, then they will hopefully be **5** *odd/curious/fresh* not just about the language but about the way of life, especially the **6** *differences/alienation/curiosity* and the similarities.

Examiner: With the growing influence of globalization, how do you think countries are **7** *different/fresh/new* these days?

Candidate: It's difficult to find things that are **8** *strange/foreign/alien* and perhaps unique as things around the world become very similar and less strange because of TV and the Internet.

Word building

1 Before you look at the next exercise, write down as many words as possible that can be made from the word *memory*.

2 Match a question beginning **1–7** with a question ending **a–g**.

1 Do you have		**a**	knowledge?
2 Why do you think people write		**b**	a memorable film you have seen?
3 Is it a good thing to memorize		**c**	memorials to famous people?
4 Are you the sort of person who collects		**d**	a good memory?
5 Can you describe		**e**	people's names easily?
6 Do you remember		**f**	their memoirs?
7 Do you think we should build		**g**	memorabilia about things like the theatre?

3 Complete the sentences below with a word from exercise 1.

   1 The most _____ occasion in my life was my last birthday party.

   2 Collecting _____ relating to the cinema or trains is one way of preserving our heritage.

   3 Being able to _____ words is a useful skill for learning languages.

   4 _____ can be very exciting to read, but they don't appeal to everyone.

   5 If I _____ rightly, there is a film called *Australia*.

   6 Some professions like medicine and architecture require a very good _____ for detail.

Articles

1 For **1–7** below, add *a/an/the* where necessary.

    1 I visited many monuments in Thailand, but monument I remember most was temple in north whose name I don't remember.

    2 I don't think I'd like to go climbing in the Alps as I don't like heights.

    3 I like travelling, especially to exotic places, but trip I had recently was awful.

    4 Education is supposed to broaden mind, but education some people receive does opposite.

    5 I'm afraid of water, so I can't go swimming even in swimming pools.

    6 Information on website may not be correct. I download information every day, and I'm not sure if it's correct.

    7 Quality of hotels varies from resort to resort.

2 Look at the graph and the IELTS Writing Task 1 answer. <u>Underline</u> the six unnecessary definite articles in the text.

Regional coral reef area, classified by degree of risk, 1998

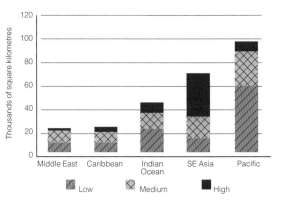

Globally, it is clear that more than half (58 per cent) of the world's reefs are at risk from the human activities.

The significant regional differences exist regarding the degree of risk that coral reefs face. The reefs of the Southeast Asia, which are the most species-diverse in the world, are also the most threatened, with more than 80 per cent at risk, including the approximately 60,000 square kilometres at high or very high risk. By contrast, the reefs in the Pacific region, which contains more reef area than any other region, face comparatively less risk. Forty-one per cent of Pacific reefs were classified as threatened with approximately 10 per cent (10,000 square kilometres) facing a high risk. As regards the Caribbean and the Middle East, where the reefs cover approximately the same area (20,000 square kilometres), the proportion at the higher risk is greater in the former (approximately 5,000 square kilometres).

3 Does the text need an introduction? If yes, write one.

4 Which information is not included in the text?

Introduction

The IELTS Speaking module lasts between eleven and 14 minutes and has three parts. The exam is recorded.

The examiner assesses your ability to communicate effectively in English and specifically assesses:

- fluency and coherence: how well you speak without hesitating and the organization of your answers
- lexical resource: the range of vocabulary you use
- grammatical range and accuracy: the range of grammar you use, for example, the range of structures and complex sentences using connecting words like *because, for instance, and so, but*, etc.
- pronunciation: how clear and intelligible you are when you speak

Part 1

Part 1 takes between four to five minutes. You will be asked general questions about a variety of familiar topics such as your family, your job/studies or your interests. You will be assessed on your ability to give opinions and information on these topics.

1 ⬭ Work in pairs. Look at the two sets of Part 1 questions **A** and **B** and decide how you would answer each question. Then choose a set each and ask each other the questions.

> **A**
>
> Do you prefer to go out with one friend or a group of friends? Why?
>
> What do you do when you go out?
>
> Do you think it's important to keep in contact with friends you make at work or on courses? Why/Why not?
>
> Why do some people stay friends for a long time?

B

What is your favourite form of art (e.g. painting, sculpture, music, drama)? Why?

Do you think art is important in our lives? Why?

Tell me about a traditional form of art from your country.

Do you think art will be popular in the future? Why/Why not?

2   Look at the following beginnings to possible answers to the four questions in set A. Decide which one is not suitable and why.

   1 I like friends.

   2 We tend to go to the cinema or the theatre, because ...

   3 Yes, sometimes, because ...

   4 There are many reasons, but perhaps the most important is ...

3   Using the correct sentence rhythm and stress helps your intelligibility, and good pronunciation leads to a higher score. You can help yourself relax as you speak by developing a rhythm and breathing properly. Look at sentence 2 above. You can create a rhythm by stressing the important words like verbs and nouns:

   *We **tend** to **go** to the **cinema** or **theatre**, **because** ...*

   Say these words and then read the sentence beginning. Take a shallow breath at the comma before the word *because*. Decide which words you should stress in sentence 4.

4   Work in pairs. To help you understand the examiner better, decide which nouns and verbs the examiner will stress in the questions in set A. Then do the same with the questions in set B.

5   Think of your own sentence beginnings for set B. Then decide which words to stress and practise saying the nouns and verbs as in exercise 3.

6   ⬤   Take turns asking and answering the questions again, using a different set from the one you chose in exercise 1.

177

Part 2

In Part 2 the examiner will give you a task card with a topic. You will be given one minute to think about the topic and make notes before you speak. You should speak for one to two minutes. When you have finished speaking, the examiner will ask one or two questions to round off the topic. You will be assessed on your ability to speak at length about a topic, organize your ideas and use appropriate language.

1 Work in pairs. Decide which task cards **1–6** the candidate notes **a–f** relate to.

1

Describe a place where you like to study.

You should say:

where this place is

when you first visited this place

what this place is like

and explain why you enjoy studying there.

2

Describe a charitable organization you admire.

You should say:

how you first became aware of this organization

what this organization does

where this organization operates

and explain why you admire the work of this charitable organization.

3

Describe a skill that you would like to learn.

You should say:

what the skill is

when you would like to learn this skill

where you would like to learn this skill

and explain why you would like to learn it.

4

Describe a meeting with someone that changed your life.

You should say:

who this meeting was with

when this meeting happened

where this meeting happened

and explain why this meeting changed your life.

5

Describe an advertisement that you like.

You should say:

> what this advertisement promotes
>
> where you saw this advertisement
>
> what the main features of this advertisement are

and explain why you like this advertisement.

6

Describe a website that you like.

You should say:

> what this website is
>
> how often you visit this website
>
> what special features this website has

and explain why you like this website.

a

maps

once a week

detailed maps

see world

learn

have fun

b

coffee

TV recently

story

funny

clever

thought provoking

memorable

c

friend

5 years ago

bus stop

funny/laugh

d

cafe

near college

month ago

cheerful

relaxing

friendly

great view

e

musical instrument

soon

privately - class annoying

relaxing

healthy

helps concentration

f

Oxfam

television appeals

relieves poverty

sickness

famine

everywhere

saves lives

2 Work in pairs. Decide how the words in the notes for the first two topics relate to each part of the topic.

3 Look at the shortened version of a possible answer for the topic in task card 3. <u>Underline</u> the synonyms the speaker uses for the notes that he prepared.

> *The skill that I'd like to talk about is playing a musical instrument like the piano, and I'd like to learn it in the coming year. I know it's possible to go to a class to learn to play the piano, but I know I'd find that irritating. Learning to play the piano is one of those skills that'd be better to learn to acquire by paying for one-to-one tuition. I realize that it might be expensive, but it'd be very rewarding in other ways.*
>
> *The reason I'd like to be able to take up the piano is because it's very soothing to play and to listen to. It's a wonderful feeling to lose yourself in the music as you are playing. I've got several friends who're very keen on music and I've listened to them many times. As well as helping to calm people down, playing an instrument like the piano is very good for the brain as it keeps it active. And it's good for your health, because it helps take away part of the stress of modern living. Friends have also told me that it improves their ability to focus, and so they play before they study or do any work, which I think would help me too.*

4 ⬭ Work in pairs. Each choose a card for your partner. Make your own notes or use the notes above. Then take turns talking about the topic on your cards. When you have finished speaking, give each other feedback using the checklist on page 210.

Part 3

In Part 3 you will have a discussion with the examiner, which will last between four to five minutes. The discussion will be linked to the topic in Part 2, but it is more abstract so you cannot talk about personal experiences. You will be assessed on your ability to communicate and justify views and discuss and analyze issues.

1 ⬭ Work in groups. Look at the following Part 3 questions and discuss what you might include in your answers.

Advertising on the web

How useful do you think websites are for bringing information to people? What about training or advertising?

In what ways can websites be of advantage to small businesses?

In business terms, are people more influenced by what they see nowadays on the web than on television? In what ways?

Distance learning

How can the web be used for distance learning?

Should the training that is available on the web be regulated more?

How do people in your country feel about awarding degrees and diplomas based solely on learning over the Internet?

2 ⬭ Work in groups of three. Take turns asking and answering the questions in exercise 1. The third student should use the checklist on page 210 and give feedback on criteria agreed by the student being examined.

> **Don't forget!**
> • Avoid talking about yourself.
> • Explain your answer by giving reasons, examples, results, comparisons, recommendations, etc.

3 ◉ 2.6 Listen to an example of a candidate being examined in Parts 2 and 3.

4 ◉ 2.7 Listen again to Part 2. Look at exercise 3 in Part 2 on page 179. There are seven differences in words and phrases in the text and two extra pieces of information. Identify the differences and make notes about the additional information.

5 ◉ 2.8 Listen to Part 3. Number the examiner's questions **1–6** below in the order that they are asked.

1 How essential do you think it'll be for workforces in the future to be proficient technologically?
2 Do you think it's important to keep acquiring new skills throughout one's life?
3 Should preparation of children and young people for work focus on computing skills at the expense of practical skills?
4 Do you think people will have to work longer in the future?
5 How can people ensure that work does not control their lives?
6 In what way do you think learning only computing skills can be a disadvantage in life?

6 ⬭ Work in pairs. Take turns asking and answering questions **1–6** in exercise 5. When you have finished, give each other feedback using the checklist on page 210.

Vocabulary: Nouns related to systems

1 ⬭ Work in groups. Describe the photographs below and decide what aspects of urban infrastructure you can see in each. Then discuss the question below.

- Do these systems help or hinder people? In what ways?

2 Work in pairs. Look at the questionnaire on page 208 and think of an example of each item **1–10**. Add another system for 'other' and think of an example.

3 Complete the questionnaire on page 208 by interviewing at least two people. Put a tick (✓) next to each system they have used.

4 Work in groups. Compare your findings by answering the following questions:

- Were any systems used by everyone? Which one(s)?
- Were any systems not used by anyone? Which one(s)?
- Which system was used most/least often?

5 Work in pairs. For nouns **1–8** below, look at the words in *italics* on the right that are all related to it in some way. Decide what system each relates to. If necessary, look at the words in the box below to help you.

1 industry	*field wells refineries slick exploration*	
2 infrastructure	*lines bridges tunnels viaducts*	
3 network	*mobile fibre-optic browse satellite*	
4 system	*receiver dish communications channel weather*	
5 web	*host access server directory connection computer*	
6 supply	*tap treatment pressure filter purification*	
7 grid	*national generators cables pylons*	
8 supply	*pipelines industry fields appliance works*	

electricity	gas	telephone	oil
satellite	water	Internet	railway

6 Work in pairs. Choose two of the nouns **1–8** in exercise 4 and describe how each of the words in *italics* relates to it.

Example:

1 industry   *field   wells   refineries   slick   exploration*

'Field' is where the oil is found.

'Well' is the apparatus that brings the oil to the surface.

...

7 Work in pairs. For sentences **1–7**, complete each gap with a word from exercise 5.

1 _____ is produced on wind farms, which then feed into the national _____ .

2 The _____ is sent via _____ from _____ in remote areas and then piped to people's homes.

3 The safety of the _____ _____ is taken for granted in many countries, but without the process of _____ the water many people are drinking is putting their lives at risk.

4 The transport of _____ from the _____ to the _____ can cause pollution, as we have seen with spillages at sea.

5 A _____ can be used to connect people in remote areas of the world that don't have landlines, but it can also be used to collect data on the _____ .

6 The revival of interest in the train as an efficient means of transport has led to investment in _____ like new _____ connecting various towns.

7 If you have a wireless _____ to the _____ , you can browse and download information anywhere, but you have to make sure the _____ is secure.

8 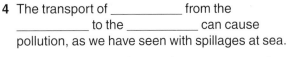 Work in pairs. Think of an incident where a system or part of a system did not work. Describe to your partner what happened and how you reacted.

1 ○ The reading passage below is about tolls on roads. What are they? Are they common in your country? Are they popular?

2 Spend two minutes scanning the passage to find words and phrases relating to the word *road*. Compare your list with a partner and then with the rest of the class.

READING PASSAGE

You should spend about 20 minutes on **Questions 1–13**, which are based on the reading passage below.

E-ZPass Was Just the Beginning

A   CALIFORNIA, Pennsylvania, Texas and Virginia may be quite different in many ways when it comes to the presidential primaries, but they do have one thing in common: all are grappling with how to collect tolls from the drivers who use their highways. Electronic toll collection is increasingly the obvious answer. Pennsylvania, which is trying to turn Interstate 80 into a toll road, is considering going completely electronic and not including cash lanes.

B   By charging tolls on an Interstate that had always been free, Pennsylvania hopes to generate the money needed to maintain this vital east-west artery, a major thoroughfare for trucks. Other states are also looking for ways to raise the money needed for highway repair, upkeep and expansion. Because resistance to raising taxes on gasoline and diesel remains strong, lawmakers are instead turning to tolls or, in governmental parlance, 'user fees'.

C   While Interstate 80 might appear to be a good place to go entirely electronic, the state may be forced to install some cash lanes because many drivers – including some in rental cars and those from states without toll roads – still pay with cash. Cash transactions are costly, though, because highway agencies must pay toll-takers, maintain plazas and safely transfer the cash to banks.

And for drivers already faced by a multitude of distractions, fumbling through pockets for nickels, dimes and quarters to pitch at toll collectors is not only frustrating, it can be dangerous.

D   Like fast-food restaurants, department stores and other businesses that handle cash, tolling agencies are introducing a variety of technologies to streamline the process and increase profits. The most common substitute for human toll collecting uses a combination of radio-frequency identification transponders, high-speed cameras and networked computers that read tags in windshields and instantaneously charge the driver's account, usually billed to their credit cards. Toll plazas are being redesigned so vehicles do not need to slow down.

E   E-ZPass, one of a growing array of technologies that are changing the way agencies collect tolls, is the ubiquitous version, available to drivers in a dozen states from Maine to Virginia. In just New York State, nearly 10 million tags are in use, three times the number in 1999.

F   The spread of electronic tolling is having a subtle and unexpected impact on motoring. Drivers need not weave through toll plazas in search of a lane that accepts cash, a particularly difficult task for those on motorcycles. Travel across many states no longer requires a hoard of change for tolls. And because they can check their toll payments online, businessmen do not need to save fistfuls of receipts for their expense reports.

G   Increasingly, electronic tags will be embedded into windshields, license plates and other places so drivers will no longer have to send off for a portable tag from a tolling agency. And because they are part of the car, they will be harder to steal.

H   Electronic tolling is changing the way drivers view tolls too. A study by an economist at M.I.T, Amy Finkelstein, found that drivers who pay their tolls electronically are less aware of the rates they pay.

She also found that rates at the tollbooths included in the study were up to 40 per cent higher on roads that accepted electronic tolls compared with those that did not. Drivers rarely like tolls, but they are willing to pay them – even if they are unaware of how much they are paying – if they are getting something in return, like less crowded lanes or a shorter wait at a tollbooth.

I   The more costly alternative would be to build at least one lane for a manned booth with offices nearby to store the cash. While fewer than half of Pennsylvania's drivers have an E-ZPass, the lanes would be designed with an eye toward removing them as the percentage rises. 'We're treating these cash lanes as temporary,' said Barry J. Schoch, vice president at McCormick Taylor, the engineering firm hired by the Pennsylvania Turnpike Commission to prepare a list of possible sites. 'In 50 years, there will be transponders built into the car, so if we build tollbooths, we will be able to convert them to some other use like rest or maintenance areas'.

J   Some of the oldest and largest tolling agencies, like the Port Authority of New York and New Jersey, are studying how to phase out their cash lanes too. Because more than 71 per cent of transactions at the Port Authority's tunnels and bridges include an E-ZPass – up from 52 per cent in 2000 – Anthony E. Shorris, the agency's executive director, expects cash booths to disappear from those crossings over the next five years. The future, in fact, may be on display in places like Stockholm, where drivers do not need tags at all. There, cameras take pictures of every license plate, video recognition software reads the numbers and the owner is charged. While E-ZPass and other radio-tag systems are likely to remain because of their widespread use, agencies introducing tolls for the first time are looking more at these video-only systems, according to Naveen Lamba, a specialist in traffic management systems at I.B.M, which provides much of the technology for Stockholm's system. While there are concerns about the reliability of these systems and the privacy of the data they collect, Mr. Lamba said that drivers are increasingly comfortable with electronic tolling.

Questions 1–5

The reading passage has ten paragraphs, **A–J.**

Which paragraph contains the following information?

1 an unforeseen effect of electronic tolls on the way people drive
2 tolls as a means of increasing revenue to fix the roads
3 a technological method of paying tolls without using tags in cars
4 an explanation of why cash tolls are still needed
5 why using cash lanes will only be very short-term

Questions 6–9

Do the following statements agree with the claims of the writer in the reading passage?

Write:

YES   if the statement agrees with the claims of the writer

NO   if the statement contradicts the claims of the writer

NOT GIVEN   if it is impossible to say what the writer thinks of this

6 It is clear that taking tolls from road users is best done electronically.
7 Cash tolls are expensive to administer because of the expense of employing security guards at toll plazas.
8 The removal of cash tolls is only for financial gain.
9 Business people will benefit the most from the use of electronic tolling.

Questions 10–13

Choose the correct letter **A**, **B**, **C** or **D**.

10 One reason for having electronic tags implanted in the vehicles themselves is

    A   to reduce the administration costs of using electronic tolls.

    B   to increase the reliability of making toll payments.

    C   so that vehicles will be easier to monitor by toll agencies.

    D   so that they will not be removed easily by thieves.

11 Research by Amy Finkelstein showed that drivers

    A   do not know how much they pay.

    B   are more price-conscious when they pay.

    C   do not care how much the tolls are.

    D   are less tolerant than they were previously.

12 The proportion of E-ZPasses used in the Port Authority of New York and New Jersey has

    A   experienced a sizeable increase.

    B   remained fairly stable.

    C   seen a noticeable fall.

    D   fluctuated slightly.

13 According to Mr Lamba, electronic tolling is

    A   taking time to implement properly.

    B   meeting with some resistance among drivers.

    C   gaining greater acceptance among drivers.

    D   proving to be an expensive option.

⭕ Reacting to the text

Are electronic collections devices just another way of raising money from the public?

Do you think toll systems control and restrict our lives or do they help us?

Word building: Modal verbs to adjectives

Look at the extract below from the reading passage on page 184.

While E-ZPass and other radio-tag systems are likely to remain because of their widespread use …

The meaning of the adjective *likely* can be expressed in the following ways:

… will probably remain …
it is probable that … will remain …
… should remain …

1   Work in pairs. For **1–9** below, <u>underline</u> the most suitable word in *italics*.

    1 Can the communications systems be improved? Yes, it's *possible/probable/certain*.

    2 They wouldn't build an extension of the railway line. They were very *unwilling/willing/likely* to do so.

    3 They didn't need to build more refineries. It was *unnecessary/necessary/possible*.

    4 The satellite should improve communications dramatically. At least that's the *expected/certain/unlikely* result, but nobody is sure.

    5 The government should hit its target. But that's only a *possible/probable/obligatory* outcome, not a certainty.

6 The oil company could do what it wanted without any interference from the government. They were *able/willing/possible* to do anything they wanted.

7 Do safety measures have to be imposed on every construction project? Yes, I think it's *compulsory/optional/certain*.

8 Oil will run out some time. It can't last for ever; that's *certain/essential/obligatory*.

9 They don't have to build a motorway through the nature reserve; it's not *essential/possible/probable*.

2 Work in groups. In the following extract from IELTS Speaking Part 3, <u>underline</u> the modal verbs that show possibility, probability and obligation. Choose a suitable adjective from exercise 1 to replace each one. Make any other necessary changes.

> **Examiner:** Can faster communication systems like broadband have an impact on people's lives?
>
> **Candidate:** I think the development of faster communication systems than we have now can have an impact on local as well as national economies, as they should enable people to do business faster. Obviously, they can't solve every problem, but they can at least help. For a while, governments wouldn't invest in fibre optics, but now the cables are being installed everywhere. For example, in my home country they provide jobs for local people …

3 What developments of infrastructure do you think there will be in your country in the near future?

Which developments do you think are necessary?

Listening

IELTS Section 3

1 For **1–7** below, tick (✓) the items that are related to the research process. For each, decide what they mean and how they relate to the process.

1 aims and objectives **5** data analysis
2 lectures **6** teaching
3 research question **7** literature review
4 research findings

2 Work in pairs. Decide which you think is the most difficult. Give reasons.

> 2.9 **SECTION 3** **Questions 21–30**
>
> **Questions 21–23**
>
> Choose the correct letter, **A**, **B** or **C**.
>
> **21** Ahmed's research is connected with the
>
>   **A** impact of roads in urban areas.
>   **B** link between people and urban infrastructure.
>   **C** reasons behind system breakdowns.
>
> **22** Janice is finding the examining of her data
>
>   **A** a lot of effort.
>   **B** an easy task.
>   **C** a slow process.
>
> **23** What did Janice think as she commenced her research project?
>
>   **A** She assumed that it was going to be very hard.
>   **B** She imagined she would never be able to begin.
>   **C** She felt relaxed about the whole process.

Don't forget!

• <u>Underline</u> the words in the questions that warn you that the answer is coming soon.

Questions 24–28

What comments does Janice make about the various aspects of her research?

Choose five answers from the box and write the correct letter, **A–G**, next to questions 24–28.

> **A** fairly easy
> **B** very easy
> **C** fairly difficult
> **D** very difficult
> **E** most difficult
> **F** tiring
> **G** time-consuming

24 research question   ....

25 literature review   ....

26 research proposal   ....

27 designing the methods   ....

28 aims and objectives   ....

Questions 29 and 30

Choose **TWO** letters, **A–F**.

Which **two** of the following does Janice recommend Ahmed should contact for help with writing?

> **A** language centre
> **B** private teacher
> **C** student union
> **D** research supervisor
> **E** main library
> **F** course tutor

Language focus: Concession

1 In IELTS Speaking and Writing you can make your argument more persuasive by conceding or agreeing with a point of view and then adding your own.

Look at the reading passage on page 184 and find an example of *may* used as a concession in the first paragraph. Which of the structures below can also be used?

> **1** *Although ... may, ...*   **2** *While ... , might ...*

🔊 Read more about concession in the Grammar reference on page 225.

2 Work in pairs. Rewrite **1–8** below so that they contain the words in brackets. Make any necessary changes and be careful with punctuation.

Example:

I can't deny this is an admirable idea. We will have to wait and see what the future holds.   (though)

Though I can't deny this is an admirable idea, we will have to wait and see what the future holds.

1 Increasing the capacity of the phone network is a good solution to the problem. It is not the only one. (although ... may)

2 This is a sound argument. I think I'd want to see more funds made available for new carriages as well.   (may ... but)

3 The facilities available are endless. Inner city conditions are cramped.   (while ... may)

4 I don't like the idea of computers controlling systems like transport. They perform a vital function.   (nevertheless)

5 I agree with the creation of high-speed communication systems. I can't help thinking that they will lead to more demands on workers and hence more stress.   (much as)

6 They are expensive to maintain and upgrade. Extensive metro systems exist in many major cities.   (may ... but)

7 I partly agree with the opinion expressed here. I think it is naive to suggest that increasing the fares will in the end lead to a better transport service.   (but)

8 It's clear the quality of public services is improving. More needs to be done.   (nonetheless)

3 Sentences **a–e** below develop the idea of five of the sentences in exercise 2. Match **a–e** below with a suitable idea in exercise 2.

  a It'll just put more cars on the road, and then revenue will decrease and there will be another problem.

  b The trains themselves could also be refurbished.

  c We need to ensure they are working for us and not us for them.

  d The line rental, for example, could be reduced.

  e This, in turn, will increase costs for companies.

4 Use your own ideas to develop the other three sentences.

5 Work in pairs. Think of at least three issues in the news at the moment that you partly or largely agree with. Prepare reasons and examples to support your opinion and then add an outcome. Use the words and phrases for conceding and adding your opinion in exercises 1 and 2.

6 Explain your opinions on the issues you have chosen to another pair of students.

Speaking
IELTS Part 2

1 Work in pairs. In each sentence of the following extract from a Part 2 topic, a phrase is in the wrong place. Decide which phrases are in the wrong place and where they should go in the sentence.

What I would like to describe is a journey that I made to see in France last winter a friend. The trip was a short five-day break to a small village, which is full of the most wonderful castles, in the Loire valley. To Paris I took the train and then to Tours, which is the largest city near the village I was visiting. The journey was exciting because it was to France my first visit. Which goes through the Channel Tunnel to Paris I was able to catch the train and take another train to Tours. The journey was very smooth, because the train network in France exceptionally well runs and the Eurostar train is well integrated with the French system. What made the special for me journey was the fact the trip marked my first journey to France, and my first time in the tunnel under the English Channel. But what it magical made, not just special or thrilling, was the snow. As we passed the snow fell through the countryside on the fairytale castles along the Loire. It was a time truly enchanting …

2 Decide which of the following topics is being discussed in exercise 1.

1 Describe a journey you made which was special to you.

You should say:

  when it took place

  where you went

  what happened during the journey

and explain why it was special to you.

2 Describe a trip you made where something went wrong.

You should say:

  when it took place

  where you went

  what happened during this journey

and explain why this trip went wrong.

3 Spend one minute making notes for the topic that wasn't discussed in exercise 1.

4 ⬤ With a partner, take turns talking about the topic. When you have finished, look at each other's notes and decide whether you think your partner followed their notes or adapted them as they spoke.

Don't forget!

- Keep your notes to a maximum of ten words so you do not read them.
- Write words or phrases vertically on the page so they are easy to see at a glance.
- Keep talking until the examiner indicates that you should stop.

1 Look at the Task 1 question below and then answer questions 1–6.

Writing:
IELTS Task 1

WRITING TASK 1

You should spend about 20 minutes on this task.

> *The table shows spending in the UK by visitors from North America and purpose of visit between 2002 and 2006.*
>
> *Summarise the information by selecting and reporting the main features, and make comparisons where relevant.*

Write at least 150 words.

Spending in UK: visitors from North America and purpose of visit 2002 to 2006

	Spending (£ million)					Growth 2005-06
	2002	2003	2004	2005	2006	%
North America						
Holiday	1,053	982	1,063	1,012	1,130	11.6
Business	859	815	866	896	1,108	23.6
Visiting friends or relatives	539	533	547	522	585	12.1
Miscellaneous	318	318	388	382	557	45.9
All visits	2,780	2,658	2,877	2,822	3,390	20.1

1 How many different visitor purposes are mentioned in the table?
2 What is the trend for each purpose?
3 How does the growth column relate to the other data?
4 Which line of information will help you write the overview?
5 What is the clear trend of the overview?
6 Is there an exception to the general trend that is evident in this line?

2 Decide which two of the following introductions are suitable for the question in exercise 1?

1 The table provides a breakdown according to the purpose of their visit of how much American visitors to the UK spend between 2002 to 2006.

2 The table illustrates spending in the UK by American tourists and purpose of visit between 2002 and 2006.

3 The table gives data on the expenditure of American visitors to the UK according to the purpose of visit from 2002 to 2006.

3 You can add data to your answer in the following ways:

- *from ... to*: *Spending on holidays rose over the period* **from** *£1,053 million* **to** *£1,230 million.*

- *with + noun + verb + ing*: *Spending on holidays rose over the period* **with expenditure increasing** *from £1,053 million to £1,230 million.*

- *verb + ing*: *Spending on holidays rose over the period,* **increasing** *from £1,053 million to £1,230 million.*

- *with + noun*: *Spending on holidays rose over the period* **with an increase** *from £1,053 million to £1,230 million.*

For **1–5** below, combine the two sentences using the structure in brackets.

Example:

It is clear that the growth in expenditure increased steadily. The biggest rise occurred between 2005 and 2006.   (*with + noun + verb + ing*)

It is clear that the growth in expenditure increased steadily with the biggest rise occurring between 2005 and 2006.

1 There was a rise in expenditure on holidays over the period. Spending increased from £1,053 million to £1,230 million.   (*with + verb + ing*)

2 The general trend for miscellaneous expenditure was clearly upward. It rose from £318 million to £557 million, a near 60% increase.   (*verb + ing*)

3 Spending on business trips also went up. It climbed from £859 million to £1,108 million.   (*with + noun*)

4 Climbing from £539 million in 2002, expenditure on visiting friends or relatives rose only slightly to £585 million. Most of the growth took place one between 2005 and 2006.   (*with + noun*)

5 The overall money spent went up. It was £2,780 million in 2002 and £3,390 million in 2006, a 20.1% increase. It is clear miscellaneous expenditure accounted for the bulk of the rise.   (*from ... to ...*)

4 ⬤ Work in groups. Use the checklist for Task 1 on page 209 to discuss the task below.

WRITING TASK 1

You should spend about 20 minutes on this task.

The table shows spending in the UK by visitors from Europe and purpose of visit between 2002 and 2006.

Summarise the information by selecting and reporting the main features, and make comparisons where relevant.

Write at least 150 words.

Spending in UK: visitors from Europe and purpose of visit 2002 to 2006

| | Spending (£ million) | | | | | Growth 2005-06 |
	2002	2003	2004	2005	2006	%
Europe						
Holiday	1,640	1,784	2,141	2,373	2,655	11.9
Business	1,833	1,848	1,994	2,237	2,614	16.9
Visiting friends or relatives	1,061	1,273	1,471	1,655	1,830	10.5
Miscellaneous	1,001	962	1,002	1,365	1,454	6.5
All visits	5,549	5,882	6,623	7,656	8,573	12.0

5 Write your own answer for the question. When you have finished, check your answer using the checklist on page 209.

Vocabulary

1 Answer **1–10** below, as quickly as you can. Write no more than two words for each answer.

    1 What are built over rivers?

    2 What can be laid underground to carry optical fibres?

    3 What can be accessed from a computer to get information?

    4 What beams information to earth from space?

    5 What fuels can be found in fields?

    6 What is carried on tall towers or on cables under the ground?

    7 What is sometimes burned as fuel to cook food in an oven?

    8 What is filtered, treated and purified before being supplied to houses?

    9 What is each house connected to that supplies electricity?

    10 What is one possible term for a series of interconnecting roads?

2 Write a sentence for each of the questions above, use the verb in the question.

    Example:

    1 What are built over rivers?

    Bridges are built over rivers.

3 Find and replace the jumbled words in the following extract from IELTS Speaking Part 3. Then decide which of the questions below the candidate was answering.

    1 Do people have access to a wide range of services in your country?

    2 Is the infrastructure of cities more important today than it used to be? Why do you think this is the case?

'Mmm … I think it is. It's rccuali because without certain aspects of the stureinfraruct in modern cities people nowadays would be totally lost. The tenkwor is very complex and made up of fefrendit cesvseri, but I think people take many of them like relectictyi and water for tngrade and do not really prapetecia them until they are cut off for one reason or another. At one time, and not that long ago, people were able to mend many things that broke down themselves. Now a whole series of cevseri itrindesus exist to connect us to the water slypup or the nonaialt ridg or to nnrctecoe the telephone when it is cut off.'

Reading

In the following text based on part of an IELTS Speaking Part 3 answer, replace the words in *italics* with a word from the reading passage on page 184.

I am not sure that people can cope with *struggling* with yet another electronic service like toll roads. I personally can't see why *lanes where people pay with money* cannot be kept. Why does everything have to be done in the interest of a few companies. They say they want to *make* the service *much more efficient*, as the roads are like *large veins in the bodies that carry blood to and from the heart*. I can understand they want more money to repair and *maintain* and even expand the road network. Yet I can't see how phasing out *situations where money changes hands* will help. And booths *that have people in them* bring a personal touch. So do we really want something up in space looking down at chips on the *glass at the front of the car* and reading *the metal plates with the car's numbers on them*?

Word building

1 Match **1–7** below with a suitable response **a–g**.

1 He wouldn't do it for any amount of money.	**a** I'm not sure if it's allowed.
2 May I park here?	**b** Do you think that's likely?
3 The company didn't need to increase access fees.	**c** Yes. You're right it wasn't necessary.
4 The train should arrive on time.	**d** Oh yes, it's possible.
5 Do you think it can happen?	**e** Mmm, they were a bit critical.
6 The government shouldn't have said that.	**f** Well yes, they are compulsory.
7 Do safety measures have to be adhered to?	**g** He doesn't sound very willing.

2 Complete the gaps with an adjective that reflects the modal verb in the first sentence.

1 Maintaining communication systems is vital for modern economies. This is not optional; it's _____ .

2 Old buildings don't have to be knocked down in today's cities. It's not _____ as they can be incorporated into a modern landscape.

3 I wouldn't agree to his suggestion. In fact, I was very _____ to do so.

4 They might build more roads. It's _____ , but I'm not sure.

5 The problem of satellite debris in space has to be dealt with. It's _____ for the safety of everyone.

6 Cities will soon be dealing with highways in the air for flying cars. It's almost _____ to happen.

Concession

In sentences **1–6** below, find the error that confuses the meaning. Decide what the correct sentence should be.

1 Clean water may be taken for granted in the West, but fortunately there are places in the world where it is rare.

2 Although the chances of bringing electricity to every home looks possible, it's a worthy aim.

3 While delays may not be as frequent as they were, the rail network is not as chaotic as it used to be.

4 Much as I love surfing the web, I feel safe while doing so.

5 He says he's an expert in water purification, but he has made serious mistakes.

6 While the neighbourhood may be as safe as people say, I will go near it.

(14) Money and happiness

Vocabulary: Money matters

1 ○ Work in groups. Describe each of the photographs. Then discuss the questions below.

- Where were coins first used?
- Do you know of any places or situations where people exchange or barter goods? Have you ever bartered or exchanged goods?
- What is your reaction to the following quote from Benjamin Franklin?

'Money makes the world go round.'

2 Make a list of words and phrases associated with the word *money*. Then compare your list with a partner.

3 Work in pairs. The word *money* collocates with the words *government* and *problems* to form the compound nouns *government money* and *money problems*. Is it possible to say *money government* or *problems money*? Decide whether the following words go before or after the word *money*.

1 management	**3** taxpayers	**5** paper	**7** counterfeit
2 market	**4** laundering	**6** sponsorship	**8** public

4 Work in pairs. For **1–12** below, (circle) the noun that is in the correct position.

Example:

	finance	government/state/capital	(finance)
1	finance	director/minister/department	finance
2	finances	company/government/state/family/household	finances
3	cash	reserves/flow/payment/settlement/limit/crisis/crop	cash
4	currency	conversion/markets/speculation/fluctuation/reserves/crisis	currency
5	credit	agreement/arrangement/facilities/terms/limit/transfer	credit
6	debt	collection/collector/burden/mountain	debt
7	savings	account/plan/bank	savings
8	spending	consumer/government/public/welfare/education	spending
9	spending	programme/target/cut/limit/money/power/spree	spending
10	expenditure	consumer/government/public/welfare/education	expenditure
11	price	war/range/increase/cut/tag	price
12	income	capital/investment/household/family	income

5 For **1–8** below, cross out the incorrect words in *italics*.

Example:

More g*overnment money* ~~government~~ was allocated to improve local bus services.

1 A *cash crop cash* is a valuable source of income for many families in agricultural communities, but *cash flow cash* can be a problem because produce is usually seasonal. This can lead to a *cash crisis cash* for local farmers.

2 *Money paper money* was invented by the Chinese.

3 *Education expenditure education* has declined at a time when few working in the field think it should. The current *expenditure level expenditure* should at least be maintained.

4 *Family finances family* are often the concern of the *finance minister finance*, especially when making funding decisions.

5 *Management money management* needs to be taught as much to adults at work and students in university as to school children.

6 A fall in a country's foreign *currency reserves currency* can trigger a *currency crisis currency*.

7 Many prominent individuals have called for the *burden debt burden* of poor nations to be reduced by cheap loans or complete cancellation.

8 Normally I don't have so much *spending money spending* available. But one of the happiest days I have had recently was when I won a large sum of money and I went on a *spree spending spree*.

6 ⬭ Work in groups. Think of at least three ways that money has directly or indirectly affected your life in the past week. For example, paying for transport with cash or an electronic card, giving you a place to sleep, etc. Take turns describing your experiences. Ask questions about each other's experiences.

Listening
IELTS Section 4

1   Work in pairs. Skim questions **31–40**. Decide what the topic of the talk is.

2   ⬤   What do you think companies can do to make their workers happy? For example, what types of in-house training programmes can companies provide for staff?

◉ 2.10   **SECTION 4   Questions 31–40**

Questions 31–34

Choose the correct letter, **A**, **B** or **C**.

31 What point does the speaker make about people's attitude to business?

    A Their understanding of business practices is fairly limited.

    B They wrongly believe that it is only about financial gain.

    C Some people are changing their attitude to wealth creation.

32 According to the speaker, one positive aspect of business is that

    A people profit from the jobs it creates.

    B its attitude to employees is changing.

    C it gives young people discipline.

33 What does the speaker say about how her company helps local communities?

    A Care is taken to focus support where needed most.

    B It tries to put some money back into the local areas.

    C Help is given to improve numeracy standards.

34 How does the speaker say the company's training programme changed?

    A It was managed very carefully.

    B It grew in its own way.

    C It developed very fast.

Questions 35–40

Complete the sentences below.

Write **NO MORE THAN THREE WORDS AND/OR A NUMBER** for each answer.

Further developments in the training scheme

35 Workers were encouraged to put their own .... first.

36 Full-time staff members were each allocated .... weekly for training.

37 Some more experienced workers decided to .... for nothing to various organizations who need professional help.

The effects of the scheme

38 .... from work through illness have been reduced enormously.

   • Productivity was not affected.

39 The company has seen its profit go up by ....

40 A reduction in staff turnover has led to a cut in ....

   • And the cost of training new staff members has lessened.

3   ⬤   Some people think the best way to improve productivity is to help employees enjoy their work. Others think that productivity can be raised by increasing salaries. Which view do you agree with? Give reasons.

Word building: Values and beliefs

1 Look at the following quote from the speaker in the listening practice on page 196.

... our accountancy firm adheres to a strict ethical code ...

Can you say *moral code* instead? What is the difference between 'ethics' and 'morals'?

2 Match the words below to their meaning **a–g**.

1	standards	a	ideas that people believe are true
2	ethics	b	ideas or theories on which a system of beliefs is based
3	values	c	traditional practices that people in a society follow
4	customs	d	principles of right and wrong accepted by a society
5	beliefs	e	a set of principles that people use to decide what is right or wrong
6	principles	f	traditional principles of good behaviour
7	morals	g	principles and beliefs that influence how a community lives morally

3 Work in pairs. Make a list of as many words as you can from the word *values*. When you have written down all the words you know, check your answers in a dictionary.

4 Complete the gaps in the text below with words relating to the word *valuable*. Use the prompts given to help you.

_____ (plural noun) are standards that individual people attach great importance to. If you _____ (verb) something in your life then you treasure it enormously. _____ (plural noun) like precious objects made of gold and diamonds may be _____ (adjective) to some people as status symbols, but they are _____ (adjective) when compared to attributes like honesty, integrity, loyalty and trust.

5 Complete the gaps in the text below with words relating to the word *principle*. Use the prompts given to help you.

Philosophy can teach people the _____ (plural noun) of right and wrong, but it is becoming increasingly difficult for people to be _____ (adjective) in life and maintain a high moral standard. Unfortunately, _____ (adjective) people are found in all walks of life, whether it be business or politics, so one must be on one's guard to make sure one doesn't do anything that compromises one's _____ (plural noun).

6 Complete the gaps in the text below with words relating to the words *ideal, moral* and *ethics*. Use the prompts given to help you.

People are often accused of being _____ (adjective) rather than realistic when pursuing their _____ (plural noun). It is easy to attack someone whose personal _____ (plural noun) or _____ (adjective) stance you don't agree with.

7 ⬤ Work in groups. Discuss the question below. Half of the group should talk about the advantages and the other half should talk about the disadvantages.

'People today get their values from national figures like politicians and celebrities such as sports stars and pop stars. What are the advantages and disadvantages of this? Give reasons and examples.'

Language focus: Substitution and ellipsis

1 Look at the following quote from the speaker in the listening practice on page 196. Then answer the questions below.

It is also about bringing people together and making links and contributing to the economy of the country. But in doing so our accountancy firm adheres to a strict ethical code.

1 In the second sentence, what does the word *so* replace from the first sentence?

2 What happens if the words are repeated?

3 What happens if people use substitution like this a lot in writing or speaking?

4 Which common expression in speech do you know where the word *so* is used like this?

🔍 Read more about substitution and ellipsis in the Grammar reference on page 226.

2 Work in pairs. Match texts **1–8** below with a suitable continuation **a–h**.

1 Companies can help local communities to develop by putting back some of the profits they have made from the local people.

2 My grandmother told us how to behave when we were young

3 People follow the traditions and ways of the society they belong to.

4 The government should introduce philosophy into the school curriculum.

5 I left home when I was 18 to go to university.

6 Detailed analysis has been done on what makes people happy,

7 My family have always adhered to the traditions of the community we came from and

8 According to some people, moral standards on television are declining and should therefore be raised.

a and continued to do so when we were adults.

b but ways need to be found to apply such research for the benefit of the public.

c I suppose I will continue to do so in spite of the pressures to the contrary.

d In doing so they believe that the general behaviour in society will be improved.

e I did so with some trepidation, but it turned out to be exciting in the end.

f Doing so would have a beneficial effect on student behaviour.

g Handing down such customs from generation to generation is important if a community is to survive.

h Such philanthropic behaviour would set a good example for other organizations.

3 For **1–8** in exercise 2, <u>underline</u> the words and phrases of substitution and the words they replace.

4 For sentences **1–7** below, cross out any unnecessary words.

1 Although the government wanted to stop funding the railway venture, they weren't able to stop funding it.

2 The banks didn't want the policy on extending loans to small businesses to change, but the government did want the policy to change.

3 Some people don't believe that there is a clear link betwee happiness and money, while others do think there is.

4 The fact that health, wealth and happiness are often linked together when people talk about happiness must mean they are linked.

5 The college was praised for student behaviour and success as it hoped it would be praised.

6 The university didn't invest as much in delivering subjects like philosophy as it could have invested.

7 My father laid down the law with us when we were children, but my mother didn't lay down the law.

Speaking
IELTS Part 3

1   Work in pairs. Read the following Part 3 questions. Then match the ideas in the list below to a suitable question.

Money and happiness

Do you think people associate money with happiness? Why?

Do you think it's possible to lead a happy life without money? How?

What advantages does money bring to people's lives?

What other factors do you think are necessary to lead a happy life?

The influence of money

Do people attach too much importance to money nowadays? Why?

How can money sometimes control people's lives?

In what ways can money be used for the good of humanity?

technological gadgets

overemphasize/overrate money

it controls/restricts/governs every aspect of people's lives

redistribution of wealth

allows people to do things they want

brings freedom

money not everything other factors

indulge in buying consumer goods

life can be difficult without

health/work/friends

having more time

reduces/increases anxiety

richer nations helping poor nations/people

2   Work in pairs. Use the ideas in the list to discuss the questions. Then take turns asking each other the questions. When you have finished, give each other feedback using the checklist on page 210.

Reading
IELTS Reading Passage

1   Scan the reading passage on page 200 for words that are synonyms of **1–8** below.

1 deal with	**3** complete	**5** poverty	**7** move
2 happiness	**4** unceasing	**6** step	**8** community

2   Work in pairs. Each choose one paragraph to skim. Then briefly explain what it is about to your partner. Find another pair of students that have chosen the same paragraph and check that you agree.

Don't forget!

• As there is no title, look at the last question and skim the questions to get the gist of the passage. Then skim the text.

READING PASSAGE

You should spend about 20 minutes on **Questions 1–13**, which are based on the reading passage below.

A All in all, it was probably a mistake to look for the answer to the eternal question – 'Does money buy happiness' – from people who practice what's called the dismal science. For when economists tackled the question, they started from the observation that when people put something up for sale they try to get as much for it as they can, and when people buy something they try to pay as little for it as they can. Both sides in the transaction, the economists noticed, are therefore behaving as if they would be more satisfied (happier, dare we say) if they wound up receiving more money (the seller) or holding on to more money (the buyer). Hence, more money must be better than less, and the only way more of something can be better than less of it is if it brings you greater contentment. The economists' conclusion: the more money you have, the happier you must be.

B 'Psychologists have spent decades studying the relation between wealth and happiness,' writes Harvard University psychologist Daniel Gilbert in his best-selling 'Stumbling on Happiness,' and they have generally concluded that wealth increases human happiness when it lifts people out of abject poverty and into the middle class, but that it does little to increase happiness thereafter.

C That flies in the face of intuition, not to mention economic theory. According to standard economics, the most important commodity you can buy with additional wealth is choice. If you have $20 in your pocket, you can decide between steak and peanut butter for dinner, but if you have only $1 you'd better hope you already have a jar of jelly at home. Additional wealth also lets you satisfy additional needs and wants, and the more of those you satisfy the happier you are supposed to be.

D The trouble is choice is not all it's claimed to be. Studies show that people like selecting from among maybe half a dozen kinds of pasta at the grocery store but find 27 choices overwhelming, leaving them chronically on edge that they could have chosen a better one than they did. And wants, which are nice to be able to afford, have a bad habit of becoming needs (iPod, anyone?), of which an advertising and media-saturated culture create endless numbers. Satisfying needs brings less emotional well-being than satisfying wants.

E The nonlinear nature of how much happiness money can buy – lots more happiness when it moves you out of penury and into middle-class comfort, hardly any more when it lifts you from millionaire to decamillionaire – comes through clearly in global surveys that ask people how content they feel with their lives. In a typical survey people are asked to rank their sense of well-being or happiness on a scale of 1 to 7, where 1 means 'not at all satisfied with my life' and 7 means 'completely satisfied.' Of the American multimillionaires who responded, the average happiness score was 5.8. Homeless people in Calcutta came in at 2.9. But before you assume that money does buy happiness after all, consider who else rated themselves around 5.8: the Inuit of northern Greenland, who do not exactly lead a life of luxury, and the cattle-herding Masai of Kenya, whose dung huts have no electricity or running water. And proving Gilbert's point about money buying happiness only when it lifts you out of abject poverty, slum dwellers in Calcutta – one economic rung above the homeless – rate themselves at 4.6.

F Studies tracking changes in a population's reported level of happiness over time have also dealt a death blow to the 'money buys happiness' claim. Since World War II the gross domestic product per capita has tripled in the United States. But people's sense of well-being, as measured by surveys asking some variation of 'Overall, how satisfied are you with your life?', has barely budged. Japan has had an even more meteoric rise in GDP per capita since its postwar misery, but measures of national happiness have been flat, as they have also been in Western Europe during its long postwar boom, according to social psychologist Ruut Veenhoven of Erasmus University in Rotterdam. A 2004 analysis of more than 150 studies on wealth and happiness concluded that 'economic indicators have glaring shortcomings' as approximations of well-being across nations, wrote Ed Diener of the University of Illinois, Urbana-Champaign, and Martin E. P. Seligman of the University of Pennsylvania. 'Although economic output has risen steeply over the past decades, there has been no rise in life satisfaction … and there has been a substantial increase in depression and distrust.'

G If money doesn't buy happiness, what does? Grandma was right when she told you to value health and friends, not money and stuff. Or as Diener and Seligman put it, once your basic needs are met 'differences in well-being are less frequently due to income, and are more frequently due to factors such as social relationships and enjoyment at work.' Other researchers add fulfillment, a sense that life has meaning, belonging to civic and other groups and living in a democracy that respects individual rights and the rule of law. If a nation wants to increase its population's sense of well-being, says Veenhoven, it should make 'less investment in economic growth and more in policies that promote good governance, liberties, democracy, trust and public safety.'

Questions 1–5

The reading passage has seven paragraphs, **A–G**.

Which paragraph contains the following information?

NB You may use any letter more than once.

1 a suggestion that less emphasis ought to be placed on economic development

2 evidence that the lack of money does not necessarily lead to unhappiness

3 some suggested non-monetary grounds for being happy

4 an explanation of the monetarist's assumption that wealth breeds happiness

5 proof that an increase in a country's wealth does not make people more content

Questions 6–9

Do the following statements agree with the information given in the reading passage?

Write:

TRUE	if the statement agrees with the information
FALSE	if the statement contradicts the information
NOT GIVEN	if there is no information on this

6 According to the general conclusion of psychologists, people are not made much happier by an increase in wealth after a certain threshold.

7 Research indicates that a narrow range of options increases shopper anxiety.

8 More multimillionaires took part in one survey than was expected.

9 Up until the Second World War money influenced people's happiness more profoundly.

Questions 10–12

Complete the sentences below.

Choose **NO MORE THAN TWO WORDS** from the passage for each answer.

10 Diener and Seligman claimed that there were clear .... when using the economy to gauge the relationship between money and happiness.

11 Despite improvements in the economy in recent years, ... has not increased.

12 People's take-home pay has less impact on happiness than .... and pleasure derived from employment.

Question 13

Choose the correct letter **A**, **B**, **C** or **D**.

Which of the following is the most suitable title for the reading passage?

A How self achievement affects happiness

B Why money doesn't buy happiness

C How happiness has declined since World War II

D What economists think about happiness and money

⬤ Reacting to the text

What is your reaction to the reading passage. Does money make people happy? Give examples from your own knowledge and experience.

Writing:
IELTS Task 1

1 Work in pairs. Check that you understand all the words in the table and the pie chart.

WRITING TASK 1

You should spend about 20 minutes on this task.

The table provides information about satisfaction with living standards in England by age in the year 2007. The pie chart shows how confident people are about the future.

Summarise the information by selecting and reporting the main features, and make comparisons where relevant.

Write at least 150 words.

Satisfaction with standard of living

England   **Percentages**

	16–21	50–59	60 and over
Very satisfied	34	32	34
Fairly satisfied	49	52	55
Neither satisfied nor dissatisfied	13	9	6
Fairly dissatisfied	4	5	4
Very dissatisfied	0	2	1

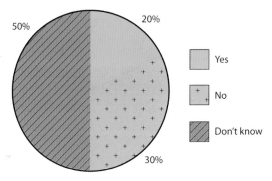

Do you think your living standards will improve in the near future?

50%   20%

□ Yes

⊞ No

▨ Don't know

30%

2 Work in pairs. Underline mistakes **1–5** below in the following sample answer and correct them.

1 an extra word that is not necessary

2 an example where an adjective and adverb are not in the correct position in the sentence

3 a noun that is spelt incorrectly

4 a definite article that is missing

5 a verb that is not in the correct form

The chart shows how happy various age groups were about living standards in England in 2007 with pie chart indicating people's optimism about the future.

Overall, people indicated that they were very content with their living standards, with only a few expressing dissatisfaction. For example, the positive rating for those 60 and over stood at 89 per cent against only 5 per cent for the latter. The youngest age group were similarly happy with 83 per cent be satisfied with their standard of living (34 per cent for very and 49 fairly satisfied). As regarding the disatisfaction rating, only 4 per cent were fairly dissatisfied with none very dissatisfied. By contrast, the 50-59 age group were content less slightly (7 per cent), but the greater part (84%) were fairly or very satisfied (52 against 32 per cent). A refusal to take sides about their standard of living was most obvious in the youngest category (13%), followed by the 50-59 age group (9%) and the 60 and over (6%).

Turning to the pie chart, optimism about the future is shared by fewer people, 30% compared to 50% who are pessimistic and 20% non-committal.

3   Work in pairs. For **1–5** below, decide which part of the sample answer in exercise 2 the suggested rewrites **a** and **b** relate to. Decide whether one or both of the suggestions improve the text.

1 a gives you an idea about the satisfaction level of people about living standards
   b provides a breakdown of the degree of satisfaction about

2 a expressed more satisfaction than dissatisfaction with
   b were kind of more satisfied with

3 a Take those who are 60 and over. Their positive rating
   b An example is the 60 and over, they

4 a the biggest number
   b the overwhelming majority

5 a a smaller proportion of the public
   b by a tinier part of people

4   Write your own answer for the Task 1 question below. When you have finished, check your answer using the checklist on page 209.

WRITING TASK 1

You should spend about 20 minutes on this task.

The chart below gives information about the Daily Happiness-Stress Index in the USA during one week in 2008.

Summarise the information by selecting and reporting the main features, and make comparisons where relevant.

Write at least 150 words.

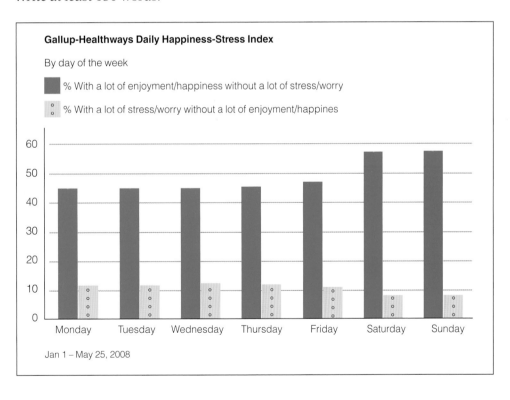

Gallup-Healthways Daily Happiness-Stress Index

By day of the week

■ % With a lot of enjoyment/happiness without a lot of stress/worry

▫ % With a lot of stress/worry without a lot of enjoyment/happines

Jan 1 – May 25, 2008

14 Review

Vocabulary

1 Match each noun **1–10** below with a noun **a–j** to make a compound noun. There may be more than one possible answer.

1	paper	**a**	limit
2	currency	**b**	mountain
3	price	**c**	war
4	state	**d**	bank
5	debt	**e**	spending
6	family	**f**	income
7	cash	**g**	reserves
8	savings	**h**	crop
9	consumer	**i**	money
10	credit	**j**	finance

2 For sentences **1–10** below, complete each gap with a compound noun from exercise 1.

1 When the older children and both parents were working, the _____ increased and they were able to save some money.

2 Rich as well as poor countries can be weighed down with a vast _____ .

3 Over-reliance on a _____ like maize or bananas for income is precarious because of price fluctuations.

4 I deposited all my money in a _____ .

5 The _____ soared after the rise in the value of the dollar.

6 Just like coins, _____ is in danger of disappearing as people pay even for small items electronically.

7 _____ is often used a means of gauging people's confidence in the health of the economy.

8 A _____ erupted on the high street among clothes retailers to attract customers to their shops.

9 I try not to exceed my _____ , though sometimes it is difficult to resist.

10 _____ for major projects is often cut off at the whim of politicians.

Word building

1 In the following extract from an IELTS Writing Task 2 answer, underline the correct word in **bold**.

… It is crucial for children to be taught the traditions, including the **beliefs/ ethics** and customs of their community so that they can learn the basic **principles/standards** of what is right or wrong. The aim of teaching people about morality is not to make them **moralistic/amoral**, but so that they can behave in a way that shows respect to others. If children, for example, are taught a code of behaviour without going deeply into **ethics/morality** which is more theoretical, then **standards/principles** of behaviour will be improved …

2 Use the words in brackets to help you complete the gaps in the following response to an IELTS Speaking Part 3 question. Then decide what the examiner's question was.

> *I don't think so. I think young people are more _____ (an adjective connected with 'real'), because they are more in tune with what's going on in the world. So no I wouldn't say they are _____ (an adjective that indicates the person is naive and is used as a criticism). I don't see anything wrong with young people pursuing their _____ (a noun that is related to the previous adjective) and trying to change the world as long as they don't harm others. I think it's a question of having the right _____ (an adjective connected with principles of right and wrong) upbringing and applying that to better oneself and others.*

Substitution and ellipsis

1 For **1–5** below, complete the sentences with a word or phrase from each box **A** and **B**.

A	B
while others	do
but clearly	do
I think everyone else	didn't
but the audience	they are
but fortunately there are many who	should

1 The television presenter claimed that work was a very important factor in making people happy,
2 Some people don't believe in the need to save money for the future,
3 Many people don't want to do volunteer work to help others,
4 Politicians often think the opinions of ordinary people are not important when they are in power,
5 Just as I have had the chance to have a free education,

2 Complete the gaps in the following extract from an IELTS Writing Task 2 answer using substitution or ellipsis.

> Good health is a major factor in making people happy. For example, when people are ill, they are not able to function properly even if 1 _____ . 2 _____ obstacles can induce mental as well as physical illness, which can be difficult to stop no matter how hard people try to 3 _____ . Although someone has apparently recovered from a car accident, it may not be obvious for a long time that he or she in fact 4 _____ for a long time .

Additional material

Unit 8 Writing Task 1 (page 112)

1

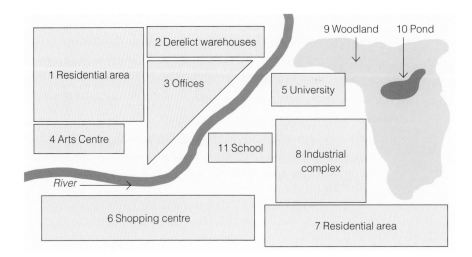

1 Residential area
2 Derelict warehouses
3 Offices
4 Arts Centre
5 University
11 School
8 Industrial complex
6 Shopping centre
7 Residential area
9 Woodland
10 Pond
River

Unit 8 Writing Task 1 (page 112)

3 Student A: Sandring 2009

N

1 _____
2 _____
3 _____
4 _____
5 _____
6 _____
7 _____
8 _____
9 _____
10 _____

Unit 8 Writing Task 1 (page 113)

4 Sandring 2000

N

Residential area
School
Hospital
Quarry
Coach station
Park
Industrial wasteland
Fields
Public gardens

Ready for Writing   Describing a graph (page 129)

1 Is the overview good? Why/ Why not?

2 Does the student use a range of complex sentences? Give examples.

3 Does the student list pieces of data or does he summarize the information? Give examples.

4 Is there a range of linking devices? Give examples.

5 How many examples of comparison and contrast can you find? Give examples (including verbs).

6 Are there more verbs or nouns of rise and fall? Give examples. What is the effect of this?

7 In the third paragraph, find examples of verbs of rise and fall.

8 Find examples of a variety of noun phrases used to avoid repetition when referring to the age groups.

Unit 12   Writing Task 2 (page 173)

Checklist for articles

1 **Is the noun countable?** → Is it singular? → Is the context in which it is used inside and outside the text general? → **Use the indefinite article, a (or an).**

2 **Is the noun countable?** → Is it plural? → Is the context in which it is used inside and outside the text general? → **Don't use the zero article and put the noun in the plural.**

3 **Is the noun countable?** → Is it plural? → Is the context in which it is used inside and outside the text specific? → Use the definite article and put the noun in the plural.

4 **Is the noun uncountable?** → It is therefore singular → Is the context in which it is used inside and outside the text general? → **Use the zero article.**

5 **Is the noun uncountable?** → It is therefore singular? → Is the context in which it is used inside and outside the text specific? → **Use the definite article.**

Remember: You need to recognize whether the context in which you write, read or hear the noun is general or specific.

Unit 13 Vocabulary: Nouns related to systems (page 182)

Questionnaire

Have you used each of the following systems today?

	You	Student 1	Student 2	Student 3
1 transport system	☐	☐	☐	☐
2 road network	☐	☐	☐	☐
3 water service	☐	☐	☐	☐
4 electricity grid	☐	☐	☐	☐
5 electronic network	☐	☐	☐	☐
6 telephone network	☐	☐	☐	☐
7 radio network	☐	☐	☐	☐
8 satellite system	☐	☐	☐	☐
9 Internet	☐	☐	☐	☐
10 GPS system	☐	☐	☐	☐
11 Other _____	☐	☐	☐	☐

Unit 8 Writing Task 1 (page 112)

3 Student B: Sandring 2009

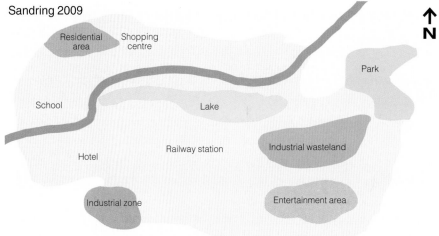

Unit 9 Writing Task 2 (page 125)

built/natural environment   educate in general about the past

understand history   respect buildings/property   appreciate beauty

pride in one's heritage   protect environment   helps relaxation

promote mental/physical health

IELTS Writing checklists

IELTS Writing Task 1

1 Have you written at least 150 words?
2 Have you completed the task according to the rubric?
3 Have you paraphrased the rubric in your introduction or just copied it?
4 Have you summarized the information and not listed every piece of data?
5 Have you written an overview?
6 Have you included any information that is not there?
7 Have you left any important data out?
8 Have you just listed information or have you compared it?
9 Have you divided your answer into paragraphs?
10 Have you written too many words? You don't need to write more than 180 words. You won't be penalized for writing too much, but you may be penalized for not summarizing.
11 Have you mentioned any striking features?
12 Have you avoided repetition of words and structures?
13 Have you used a range of grammar, vocabulary and complex structures ?
14 Have you used the correct tenses?
15 Have you checked your writing for mistakes?

Additional questions for maps

1 Have you included an overview?
2 Have you used appropriate adverbs/adverbial phrases of location ?
3 Have you used a range of synonyms?

Additional questions for processes

1 Have you used the passive correctly?
2 Have you used the correct tenses?
3 Have you used the appropriate linking devices?

IELTS Writing Task 2

1 Have you written at least 250 words?
2 Have you completed the task according to the rubric?
3 Have you paraphrased the question in your introduction?
4 Have you given reasons and examples as requested in the rubric?
5 Is your answer abstract as required or does it contain personal examples?
6 Have you developed your ideas by expressing contrasts, causes, effects, purposes and conclusions?
7 Are your ideas just listed or organized with a range of linking devices to reflect the development in 6?
8 Have you divided your answer into paragraphs?
9 Have you written 4/5 paragraphs?
10 Do your ideas fit well together?
11 Have you included any irrelevant ideas?
12 Have you avoided the repetition of words and structures?
13 Have you used a range of grammar, vocabulary and complex structures ?
14 Have you checked your writing for mistakes?

IELTS Speaking checklists

IELTS Speaking Part 1

See the checklist for Part 3. Remember this section is personal not abstract.

IELTS Speaking Part 2

See checklist for Part 3 and 1–5 below.

1   Did you make notes?
2   Were your notes short – no more than about ten words?
3   Did you answer all the parts of the question?
4   Were your notes easy to read as you spoke?
5   Did you refer to your notes as you spoke?

IELTS Speaking Part 3

1   Is your answer organized?
2   Did you develop your answer by giving reasons and examples?
3   Was your answer abstract as required or was it too personal?
4   Were your ideas relevant to the question?
5   Did you paraphrase the question?
6   Did you avoid repetition of words and structures?
7   Did you use a range of grammar, vocabulary and complex structures ?
8   Did you concentrate too much on accuracy at the expense of fluency?
9   Did you speak clearly?
10   Did you speak too quickly or too slowly?
11   Were you relaxed enough to breathe properly?
12   Did you speak using the correct rhythm or sentence stress?
13   Did you use the correct word/phrase stress?

Wordlist

Unit 1

A Describing people

Adjectives

artistic
adventurous
chatty
conscientious
considerate
creative
dynamic
hard-working
helpful
sporty
supportive
talkative
wise

Nouns and adjectives

respect/respectful/respectable

ambition	ambitious
care	careful/caring
calmness	calm
cheerfulness	cheerful
generosity	generous
loyalty	loyal
sense of humour	humorous
sociability	social
punctuality	punctual
reliability	reliable
talent	talented

B IELTS Reading

Choosing headings for paragraphs or sections

Nouns and their synonyms

aims
effect
emphasis
lack
need
reason for
result
use
what . ... is based on

C Verbs of movement

Verbs

dip/fall slightly and quickly recover
fall slightly and then level off
fall gradually/decrease steadily
fluctuate/be erratic
hit a low/reach their lowest point
hit a peak/reach a high
plummet/plunge
remain stable/stabilize
rise gradually/increase slowly but surely
soar/rocket

Nouns

a climb
a decline
a dip
a drop
a fall
an increase
a peak
a plunge
a rise
fluctuations

D Useful words and phrases from the reading passage

settle into university life
integrate into university life
draw on internationally recognized expertise
settle down more easily into university life
ascertain (students') views about ...
pioneering research
key factors influencing ...

Unit 2

A Verbs of cause and effect

Verbs	Nouns
achieve	achievement
advance	advancement
affect	effect
attract	attraction
damage	damage
destroy	destruction
deteriorate	deterioration
enhance	enhancement
foster	fostering
harm	harm
improve	improvement
impact	impact
increase	increase
influence	influence
produce	production
promote	promotion
reduce	reduction
result	result
ruin	ruin
shape	shape

Phrases to describe cause and effect

bring about an increase in …
bring about the destruction of …
cause (enormous) damage to …
change the shape of …
do harm to …

have a/an	(dramatic) effect (on …)
	(huge) impact (on …)
	(positive/negative) influence (on …)
lead to a	(significant) improvement (in …)
	reduction in …

lead to the ruin of …
make better links between …
result in a (sharp) deterioration in …

B Qualifying adjectives

Positive and negative adjectives

appealing	unappealing
convenient	inconvenient
effective	ineffective
harmful	harmless
important	unimportant
inspiring	uninspiring
necessary	unnecessary
practical	impractical
significant	insignificant
useful	useless
valuable	invaluable
worthwhile	worthless

Synonyms

important $\longrightarrow$ critical/crucial/essential/key/vital
unimportant$\longrightarrow$insignificant/trivial

C Linking devices

although/but/however
as/because/since
also/furthermore/moreover/similarly/what is more
accordingly/as a result/and so/so/for instance/
consequently/therefore
in order to
for example/for instance

D Useful words and phrases from the reading passage

the process of urbanization
go hand in hand with …
emerge as the center of …
become the seat of …
exercised a certain degree of …
there is reason to believe that …
can be regarded as the culmination of …

Unit 3

A Sports

Sport	Place	Equipment
bodybuilding	gym	weights
boxing	ring	gloves/shorts
diving	sea/reefs	oxygen tank
fishing	lake	rod
football	pitch	ball/goal
golf	ourse	clubs/irons
horse riding	course	saddle
running	track	shoes/spikes
swimming	pool	costume/trunks
tennis	court	racquet/ball

Types of sports
combat
equestrian
field
indoor
motor
outdoor
racquet sports
water
winter

B Adjectives ending in -ed/ing

Verbs and adjectives

annoy	annoying/annoyed
bore	boring/bored
challenge	challenging/challenged
electrify	electrifying/electrified
excite	exciting/excited
exhilarate	exhilarating/exhilarated
fascinate	fascinating/fascinated
interest	interesting/interested
invigorate	invigorating/invigorated
irritate	irritating/irritated
motivate	motivating/motivated
thrill	thrilling/thrilled

C Adjectives with prepositions
addicted to …
bored with …
capable of …
enthusiastic about …
fanatical about …
fond of …
indifferent to …
interested in …
keen on …
mad about …
passionate about …

D Useful expressions to describe data
a smaller proportion of …
a third of (the number of) …
a quarter of …
half of …
three-quarters of …
twice as many …
three times as many …
five times the number of …
half as many …
forty/40% of …
over fifty/50% of …
the bulk of …
three/four out of every ten …

E Useful words and phrases from the reading passage
build the foundation of …
become a guinea pig
create the illusion of …
ensure the experience is memorable
experience a few seconds of thrills
figure out how to …
push the boundaries of …
relive their (terrifying) experiences
suppress
trigger the release of a …
understand the broad effects of …

Unit 4

A General category nouns

Nouns and collocations

adverse/unfavourable/trying	circumstances
(face a) terrible	dilemma
significant/political/momentous	event
profound	impression
amusing	incident
burning/controversial/thorny	issue
memorable/festive/state	occasion
golden/excellent/perfect	opportunity
unexpected	outcome
faint	possibility
acute/serious/insurmountable	problem
ideal/happy/dangerous/sticky	situation
imaginative/effective/perfect	solution

B Useful expressions

It was too good an opportunity to miss.
It is a rather awkward situation.
It is a divisive issue that arouses passion.
It was an annoying incident.
It was the happiest event of her life.

C Uncountable nouns with countable nouns as examples

accommodation like flats
cash like coins
clothing like shirts
crime like burglaries
equipment like computers
fruit like oranges
furniture like chairs
information like bank details
litter like bottles/cans
luggage like suitcases
media like magazines
(bad) weather like storms

D Linking devices

although
but
despite the fact that
even if
even so
however
in spite of the fact
much as
nevertheless
nonetheless
still
though
while
yet

E Developing ideas by expanding the meaning of adjectives

Adjectives and verbs

alarming	frighten
appealing	attract
interesting	fascinate
motivating	encourage
satisfying	please
shocking	stun
worrying	trouble

F Useful words and phrases from the reading passage

grow at an alarming rate
cover an area twice the size of …
stretch from …
debris/junk/trash/garbage/rubbish
come across …
unless consumers cut back on …
so durable it is not detectable
constitute (90 per cent) of …

Unit 5

A Adjective/noun collocations

agricultural society
dominant culture
general public
governing elite
indigenous people
modern civilization
thriving community
urban population

B Forming adjectives from nouns

Adjectives ending -al

agriculture	agricultural
industry	industrial
nation	national
technology	technological
tradition	traditional

Adjectives ending -ous

danger	dangerous
luxury	luxurious
population	populous
space	spacious

Adjectives ending -ful

beauty	beautiful
success	successful
use	useful

Verbs of prediction

Verb		Noun
anticipate	it is anticipated that …	anticipation
estimate	it is estimated that …	estimation
expect	it is expected that …	expectation
forecast	it is forecast(ed) that …	forecast
predict	it is predicted that …	prediction
project	it is projected that …	projection

C Useful words and phrases from the reading passage

become the undisputed leader in …
become saturated with images of …
concentrate/focus on …
have a clear lead
the issue for … is whether …
narrowly targeted to …
represent radically different approaches
recently rated the most …
… sole purpose is to …
win the race

Unit 6

A Conservation

Collocations
admire the scenery
breathtaking view
derelict factory
dominate the landscape
planting season
tree conservation
panoramic view
spoilt/unspoilt countryside
spectacular scenery
tranquil countryside
visit open spaces

B Transitive and intransitive verbs

Transitive	Intransitive	Both
bear	appear	break
collect	become	break up
create	bloom	decrease
crush	blossom	disperse
cultivate	come out (of)	grow
eat	disappear	increase
gather	emerge	prune
harvest	exist	ripen
lay	fall	roast
make	flow	smell
plant	go down	
pollinate	happen	
produce	look	
reap	occur	
transplant	open up	
utilize	rise	
weave	sprout	
sow		
pick		

C Describing sequences

Linking words and phrases
initially/first
then/next/following that/after that
as soon as/once/after/before
finally
when/where

Nouns to summarize stages in sequences
assembly
collection
delivery
harvesting
packaging
pasteurization
recycling
separation
storage
transportation

D Useful words and phrases from the reading passage
belongs to the family …
peculiar to …
it has a strong tendency to …
characterized by the …
native from … to …
cultivated since ancient times throughout …
was featured in …
production declined from lack of …
naturally adapted to …

Unit 7

A Work
(a teacher) by profession
career ladder
earn a livelihood
have a good job/occupation
hold down a job
improve their job prospects
job opportunities
(academic) qualifications
work ethic

B Collocations

Adjective/noun collocations
impressive/outstanding/proudest   achievement
good/fair   chance
considerable/huge   advantage
considerable/financial   benefit
total/complete   failure
distinct/obvious   disadvantage
huge/massive   improvement
ample/career/once-in-a-lifetime   opportunity
career/employment/excellent/long-term   prospects
enormous/large amount of   success

Verb/noun collocations
a lack of/represent   achievement
enjoy/gain/outweigh/take   advantage
accrue/derive/enjoy/gain   benefit
arise/come up/deserve/give somebody/grab/take/throw away   a chance
end in/expect/result in   failure
have/offset/suffer   disadvantage
constitute/make/room for/scope for/show improvement
provide/seize/squander   opportunity
boost/damage/have/offer   prospects
achieve/depends on/enjoy/guarantee   success

C Useful words and phrases from the reading passage
apply (their) knowledge
(employers') opinions have to be treated with caution
part with money
play an increasingly important role in …
reflect (that) change
reflect on their own learning
remain a key part of …
rigorous/accurate assessment
take a Masters in …
take account of …
through sheer love of learning
there is a move away from …
well rounded people
work as part of a team

Unit 8

A Nouns relating to places

Adjectives and nouns
(residential) area
(business) district
(magnificent) location
(safe) neighbourhood
(beautiful) place
(northern) region
(spectacular) setting
(derelict) site
(open) space
(tourist hot) spot
(pedestrian) zone

B Useful expressions for describing places
covered with …
fed by …
overlooking …
surrounded by …
stretching into the distance
teeming with …

C Verbs relating to changes in maps
chop trees down/down trees
convert … into …
create a …
demolish
give way to …
knock … down/down …
make way for …
pull … down/down …
replace … with …
… take (their) place
tear … down/down …
(completely) transform
turn … into …

Verbs and nouns

build	building
change	change
construct	construction
develop (into)	development
expand	expansion
extend	extension
transform	transformation

D Location

Location phrases

North	in the north of … , north of …, to the north of …
South	in the south of … , north of …, to the south of …
East	in the east of … , east of … , to the east of …
West	in the west of … , west of … , to the west of …

Verbs of location
there is …
lies …
is situated …
is sited …
is located …
stands …
runs/flows …

E Useful words and phrases from the reading passage
it necessarily involves not only, … but also …
possess a complex spatial knowledge of …
can broadly be identified
with their strong (Western) overtones
share characteristics
record for posterity
show a profound knowledge of …

Unit 9

A Beauty

Adjectives relating to reactions
beautiful
dazzling
ecstatic
emotional
evocative
humbling
impressive
magnificent
majestic
melancholic
nostalgic
overjoyed
overwhelmed
thoughtful

Useful expressions for describing reactions
be taken aback by …
evoke memories of …
fill (someone) with …
humble (someone)

impress (someone)
make an enormous impression on (someone)
make (someone) feel …
make (someone) thoughtful about …

B Prefixes *over-* and *under-*
overawed
overcome
over/underestimated
over/underpriced
over/understated
overtaken
over/underrated
overrun
over/undervalued
underfunded

C Useful words and phrases from the reading passage
inspired by …
transformed the … from what was then seen as … into …
become a popular (London) landmark
attempts to popularise industrial buildings by …

Unit 10

A Art

People in the arts

ballet	dancer/choreographer/composer/musician
newspaper	journalist/columnist/editor/printer/contributor/reader
novel	novelist/writer/author/editor/reader
orchestra	conductor/musician/pianist/violinist/percussionist etc
play	actor/actress/lead (role)/playwright/director/producer/costume designer/set designer
sculpture	sculptor/artist
song	singer/songwriter
symphony	composer/musician/conductor

B Useful words and phrases from the reading passage

graffitti
street art
the (riverside) facade of …
covered in giant murals
display of (street art) at a major museum
… recently featured in a retrospective exhibition
compete with each other
after a (police) crackdown on …
… is a highly polarising phenomenon

Unit 11

A The family

Words relating to family members

ancestor
family
family tree
young/old generation
godfather/mother
grandparents
household
niece/nephew
offspring
orphan
parents
relatives
siblings
widow
widower

B Suffixes -hood and –ship

Nouns and and relevant verbs

(reach) adulthood
brotherhood
(spend) childhood
draughtsmanship
fatherhood/motherhood
(face) hardship
(show) leadership

membership
(reach) nationhood
parenthood
professorship
(cultivate/maintain) relationship
(withdraw) sponsorship

Collocations with the word *relationship*

broken	
build	
close	
family	
long-lasting	relationship(s)
network of	
parent-child	
professional	
special	

C Useful words and phrases from the reading passage

it takes a village to bring up …
kinship
a wide network of relatives
responsible for his or her upbringing
the interests of the entire community
take precedence over …
that role transcends age and gender
socialization contributes to cohesion

Unit 12

A Adjectives with multiple meaning

alien	strange/extraterrestrial
curious	inquisitive/unusual
different	dissimilar/several/diverse/unusual
foreign	from or in another country/unfamiliar
fresh	new/cold and windy/recently made or prepared
novel	book/original
new	recently arrived/inexperienced
odd	unusual/irregular
pristine	new and untouched/morally good
strange	unexpected/unfamiliar/odd
unique	treasured/happening only in one place/not the same as anyone else

B Words related to memory

memento (n.)
memo (n.)

memorabilia (n.)
memoirs (n.)
memorable (adj.)
memorial (n.)
memory (n.)
memorize (v.)
remember (v.)

C Useful words and phrases from the reading passage

… diversity reflects the maturity of the ecosystem
… also supports a variety of …
… which are all listed as vulnerable
… is also of cultural importance
… are of cultural and historical significance
… have a cooperative and integrated approach to managing …

Wordlist

Unit 13

A Words related to systems

electricity grid	cables/generator/national/pylons
gas supply	appliance/fields/industry/pipelines/works
oil industry	exploration/field/refineries/slick/wells
railway/train infrastructure viaducts	bridges/lines/tunnesl/
satellite system	channel/communications/dish/receiver/weather
water supply	filter/pressure/purification/tap/treatment

B Modal verbs to adjectives

can/may	possible
could/can	able

didn't need	unnecessary
don't/didn't have to	not essential
have to be	compulsory
may	permissible
should	expected/probable/likely
will	certain
wouldn't/won't	unwilling

C Useful words and phrases from the reading passage
highways/roads/lanes/artery/thoroughfare/toll road
go entirely electronic
to streamline the process
the ubiquitous version
have a subtle and unexpected impact on …
because of their widespread use
while there are concerns about the reliability of …
be increasingly comfortable with …

Unit 14

A Money matters

Collocations with *money*

counterfeit government paper public sponsorship taxpayers'		credit
money	laundering management market	currency

Collocations with words relating to money

consumer education government public welfare		debt
capital state government	expenditure/spending	expenditure
company family government household state	finance	finance
capital family household investment	finances	income
	income	price
cash	crisis crop flow limit payment reserves settlement	savings

agreement
arrangement
facilities
limit
terms
transfer

conversion
crisis
fluctuation
markets
reserves
speculation

burden
collection
collector
mountain

cut
level
pattern

department
director
minister

bracket
group
statement
tax

cut
increase
range
tag
war

account
bank
plan

B Values and beliefs

Nouns
(a high) moral standard
individual morals
invaluable objects
moral stand
personal morals
set of principles
standards of behaviour
system of ethics
traditional values
valueless objects

Adjectives
principled
unprincipled

Collocations
accuse someone of being moralsitic
adhere to a strict ethical code
attach importance to one's beliefs/values
compromise one's principles
follow customs
take a moral stand
treasure valuables
value something

C Useful words and phrases from the reading passage
look for the answer to the eternal question
tackle the question
lift people out of abject poverty
do little to increase happiness
there is a direct correlation between … and …

Grammar reference

Unit 1

Present simple, present continuous and past simple

A Present simple

You use the present simple:
- for an habitual action
  *I **get up** before 8 am every day.*
  *Lectures **start** at 9 am every day.*
- to show how frequently people do things
- *I sometimes **arrive** late, because the buses are not reliable.*
- for facts
  *The sun **rises** in the east.*
  *Water **boils** at 100°C at sea level.*
- to describe states
  *I **have** a pen.*
  *I **agree** with you wholeheartedly.*

B Present continuous

You use the present continuous:
- to describe actions and events which are happening 'around now' (the actions and events may not be apparent at the time of writing or speaking)
  *The earth **is becoming** warmer year by year.*
  *More and more students **are applying** for the course.*
  *I'm **doing** a course on pottery at the moment.*
- to describe an action that is in the process of happening as you speak or write
  *You **are preparing** for IELTS if you are using this book.*
  *The baby's **sleeping**. Try not to wake her.*
- to talk about the future (see Unit 5)

C Present simple or present continuous?

1 You use 'state' verbs like *know*, *promise* and *understand* only in the present simple.
  *I **promise** I'll come to the party.*
  *I **understand** what you are saying.*
2 For verbs that have a 'state' and 'action' meaning, you use the present simple to describe 'states' and the present continuous to describe 'actions'.
  State: *I **think** studying languages is important.*
  Action: *I'm **thinking** about this problem. Give me a few minutes.*
  State: *I **have** a pen.*
  Action: *The government **is having** difficulties.*
  State: *This perfume **smells** nice.*
  Action: *The cat **is smelling** the food. Maybe he'll eat it.*
3 **With *always***
  Present simple: He **always gets up** at 7 am. (He does it as a matter of routine.)
  Present continuous: He's **always talking** about his health. (He does it more than I think he should.)
4 **With the verb *to be***
  Present simple: She **is** very persistent. (This is part of her personality.)
  Present continuous: She **is being** very persistent at the moment. (This is unusual for her. This is not her normal behaviour.)

D Past simple

You use the past simple:
- to describe a completed action, event or state in the past which is not connected with now. The time in the past may be clear from the information around the sentence
  *At one time, people **believed** that the world was flat.* (But they don't now.)
  *He **lived** in China for a long time.*
  *Dickens **wrote** many brilliant novels.* (He wrote them a long time ago.)
- to describe an action or event at a particular time, or during a particular period of time
  *I **stayed** in London for two months in 2008.*
  *Sales **rose** between 2005 and 2009.*
- to describe habitual actions in the past
  *I **attended** classes in pottery for three months.*

Likes and dislikes

1 The verbs *like, love, enjoy, can't stand/bear, detest, dislike, hate* and *loathe* can be followed by a noun.
  *I **like football**.*
  *I **hate spiders**.*
2 The verbs *enjoy, fancy, dislike, detest, loathe* can be followed by a verb + *-ing* only.
  I enjoy swimming. (NOT ~~I enjoy to swim.~~)
3 The verbs *can't stand/bear, like, hate, love* and *prefer* can be followed by a verb + *-ing* or *to*.
  *I like **playing/to play** baseball.*
  *I can't bear **watching/to watch** sport on TV.*
4 You can use *like* with a verb + *-ing* or *to* to express a particular meaning.
  *I **like to go** for a swim every morning.* (I think that this is a good idea but don't necessarily enjoy it.)
  *I **like going** for a swim every morning.* (I enjoy it.)
5 *prefer*
  You can use the following to express a preference for one thing compared to another:
- *prefer* + noun + *to* + noun. Use the *-ing* form if the things are activities.
  *I **prefer books to** computer games.*
  *I **prefer surfing to** sailing.*
- *prefer* + *to* + infinitive + *than* + infinitive without *to*
  *I **prefer to read** novels **than play** computer games.*
6 *I'd rather*
  You can use the following to express that you *would rather* do one thing compared to another:
- *would/'d rather(not)* + verb
  *I'd **rather go** to the concert.*
  *I'd **rather not watch** the horror film.*
- *would/'d rather* + verb + *than* + verb
  *I'd **rather** play the piano than go out.*
7 *would like/love/prefer/hate*
  Would like/love/prefer/hate must be followed by *to* + infinitive.
  *I'd **love to go** to a live concert.*
  *I'd **prefer to eat** in than go to the restaurant.*

Unit 2

Past simple and present perfect

1 **Past simple**
For use, see Unit 1.

2 **Present perfect**
You use the present perfect:
* to describe actions or events that have a connection with the present
  I **have just passed** my exam. Look at my certificate.
  I'**ve just** fixed the TV! Look, it's working!
* to talk about an action or event that has happened at any time up to now, but you don't know or mention when. The emphasis is on the fact the action or event has happened, not the time that it happened
  I **have lived** in West Africa.
  He **has visited** France.
* to talk about periods that continue to the present
  My parents **have lived** in their house **since 2001**.
  I **have studied** hard **for the past month**.
  Note the contrast between the past simple and the present perfect.
  I **did** a lot of work yesterday (no connection with the present), but I **haven't done** much today (connection with the present).
  I **visited** Spain ten years ago, but I **haven't been** to Italy.
  When **did** you **finish** the book?
  Or
  Haven't you **finished** it yet?

3 **Present perfect continuous**
You use the present perfect continuous to describe periods up to and including the present.
She'**s been watching** that film all afternoon.
I **have been learning** English since I was ten.

Habit in the past - *used to* and *would*

You use *used to* and *would* to describe habitual actions and events in the past.
1 You use *used to* to describe habits or states in the past which no longer happen or exist.
  I **used to** live in the countryside.
  I **used to** play chess quite a lot when I was a child.
  Note that *used to* becomes *use to* with questions and negatives.
  I **didn't use to** play outdoor games much.
  Did your parents **use to** travel much when they were younger?
2 You use *would* to describe past habits but not states.
  I **would** work for my uncle every Tuesday evening when I was 16.
  I **used to** own a collection of antique clocks.
  (NOT ~~I would own a collection of antique clocks.~~)
  Would is often used to reminisce about the past and in descriptive writing.
  On spring afternoons, I **would** go for long walks with my friends and look at the wildlife.
  Note that you usually don't use *would* in negative or *yes/no* questions.

Adverbs of frequency

1 You use adverbs of frequency to indicate how often something happens. Common adverbs of frequency are *always, usually, normally, regularly, often, frequently, sometimes, occasionally, rarely, hardly ever, seldom, never*.

2 You use adverbs of frequency after *be* and auxiliaries, but before all other verbs.
  I **am always** on time for lectures.
  He **has never eaten** noodles before.
  Politicians **rarely pay attention** to the opinions of the people.
3 You can invert the subject and the verb when you use *never, rarely* and *seldom* at the beginning of a sentence.
  Never have I seen such an impressive PowerPoint presentation from a student.

Unit 3

Comparison

A **Comparative adjectives**
1 **One syllable adjectives**
  You form the comparative from adjectives with one syllable by adding *–er*.
  high → high**er**

  For one syllable adjectives ending in *–e*, you add *–r*.
  larg**e** → larg**er**

  For one syllable adjectives ending in a consonant, you double the final consonant.
  big → big**ger**

2 **Two or more syllable adjectives**
  You normally form the comparative from adjectives with two or more syllables with *more/less*.
  exciting → **more/less** exciting

3 **Adjectives ending in consonant + -y**
  You form the comparative from adjectives ending in consonant + *y*, by changing *-y* to *–i*.
  dr**y** → dr**ier**
  eas**y** → eas**ier**
  Note some adjectives can be formed with *–er* or *more/less*.
  The river **is shallower/more shallow** here than over there.
  Theme parks with thrilling rides are becoming **commoner/more common** than in the past.

B **Superlative adjectives**
1 **One syllable adjectives**
  You form the superlative from adjectives with one syllable by using *the* before the adjective and adding *–(e)st* to the adjective.
  long → **the** long**est**

2 **Two or more syllable adjectives**
  You form the superlative from adjectives with two or more syllables by adding *the most/least* before the adjective.
  interesting → **the most/least** interesting

3 **Adjectives ending in consonant + -y**
  You form the superlative from adjectives ending in consonant + *y*, by changing *-y* to *–i*.
  dr**y** → the dr**iest**
  eas**y** → the eas**iest**

C **Irregular comparatives and superlatives**
  Some common adjectives have an irregular comparative and superlative form.
  good → better → the best
  bad → worse → the worst
  far → farther/further → the farthest/the furthest

*She is a **better** player than he is.*
*The performance of the team was **worse** than last time.*

D Comparative adverbs

Like comparative adjectives, you form comparative adverbs by adding – *(e)r* to one syllable adverbs and using *more* with two or more syllable adverbs.
*Computer sales rose **faster** over the last decade compared to the previous one.*
*Attendances at the cinema fell **more dramatically** in the first quarter than the second.*

E Comparative structures

1 *than*

You can make comparisons by using *than*.
*Sales were **greater** in 1980 **than** in 1990.*

2 *as + adjective + as* to compare two equal things

You can compare two equal things by using *as* + adjective + *as* .
*I'm **as tall as** my sister.*

3 *not as + adjective + as* to compare two things that are not equal

You can compare two things that are not equal by using *not as* + adjective + *as*.
*Computer sales were **as high** in June **as** they were in January.*

F Words to strengthen or weaken comparisons

You can add words and expressions to strengthen or weaken comparisons.

1 Comparatives

Words and expressions that can be added to comparatives include: *a bit, a little, slightly, much, (quite) a lot, far, significantly, considerably, a great deal, twice, three times*.
*Book sales rose **much/a lot/far more slowly** in the last quarter.*
*The number of shoppers was **a little lower** last month compared to this month.*

2 Superlatives

Words and expressions that can be added to superlatives include: *by far, easily, a long way*.
*The Indian architect's building was **by far the most popular** in the competition.*
*Sweden is the company's **smallest** market, **by a long way**.*

3 With *as ... as ...*

Words and expressions that can be added to modify the structure *as ... as ...* include: *(not) nearly, not quite, almost, just, half, twice, three times*.
*The population of the town **is three times as** big **as** it was in 1960.*
*The rest of the team were **not nearly as** good **as** the captain.*

Adjectives with prepositions

Some adjectives are followed by a particular preposition when used with the verb *be*. Sometimes a different preposition is used depending on whether you are referring to 'people' or 'things'. You can check this in a dictionary but they include:
*angry/annoyed/happy/upset **about** (things)*
*good/bad **at***
*late/famous/ready **for***
*different **from***
*interested **in***
*afraid/fond/frightened **of***
*keen **on***
*kind/married/used **to***
*angry/annoyed/bored **with** (people)*
When you use a verb after the proposition, you use the verb + -ing form.
*He's **keen on playing** football.*
*I'm **interested in learning** about other cultures.*
When you learn new adjectives which are followed by prepositions, try to learn the adjective and the preposition together.

Unit 4
Countable and uncountable nouns

1 Countable nouns

Countable nouns have a singular and a plural form. They are used with the singular or plural form of a verb.
*I have **a car**. The **car works** well.*
*I have **two cars**. The **cars work** well.*
Note some common countable nouns only have a plural form. These include *goods, means, trousers, stairs*.
*The **goods are** already with the customer.*

2 Uncountable nouns

Uncountable nouns only have one form and are used with the singular form of the verb.
*The **information is** in the leaflet.*
(NOT ~~The informations are in the leaflet.~~)
In order to quantify uncountable nouns you use phrases like *a piece of/a bit of/a slice of/a sheet of,* etc.
*The leaflet contains **several pieces of information**.*
*Can I borrow **two sheets of paper**?*

Note that *news* is followed by a singular verb.
*The news **is** on in a few minutes.*

3 Some nouns can be countable or uncountable depending on the meaning. The countable meaning is specific and the uncountable meaning is general. Examples include:

a business (a company)	*business* ('business' in general)
a painting (a work of art)	*painting* (the activity)
a noise (a specific noise)	*noise* ('noise' in general)
a fruit (a specific type of fruit)	*fruit* ('fruit' in general)

***Fruit is** good for you.*
***Two fruits**, apples and pears, **are** grown in this region.*

4 Many common nouns are uncountable in English, but countable in other languages.
***Accommodation is** expensive in London.*
***Information is** available on the website.*
***The furniture is** very modern.*
***The weather is** very good today.*

5 Some nouns can be used with the singular or plural form of a verb. These include *army, class, company, crowd, data, family, government, group, public, team*.
*The government **is/are** preparing for the next election.*
*The family **is/are** very happy with the new house.*
Note that in Australian and American English the singular verb is used with *government* etc.

Making suggestions

You can use the following to make suggestions:
* modal verbs like *should/ought to* to make strong suggestions
  *Shopkeepers **should/ought to** be made responsible for cleaning the area around their shops.*

Note that you can use *must* to express a very strong suggestion.
*Shopkeepers **must** be made responsible for cleaning the area around their shops.*

- modal verbs like *could/might* to make weak suggestions
  *A new body with strong powers **could/might** be set up to tackle the problem of international pollution.*
- fixed phrases that introduce suggestions. These are followed by *would be ... /is to ...*
  ***The best way to/A good way to/One way to** improve the environment **would be/is to** ...*
  ***A good idea would be/is to** ...*

Unit 5

Ways of looking at the future

1   Simple future
You use the simple future to make predictions.
*The train **will** arrive late.*
*I'**ll** be better this evening, don't worry.*
*Attendances at the cinema **will** continue to rise.*
You can use the simple future with the following verbs to describe graphs:
predict
forecast
project
estimate
anticipate
*It **is predicted** that sales **will** rise.*

2   *going to*
You use *going to* for plans and intentions in the near and distant future.
*I'm **going to** train to be an accountant after I finish my university course.*
Going to is also used to make predictions when there is evidence in the current situation.
*There's **going to** be a storm – look at those clouds.*

Note *going to* should not be used to make predictions in graphs in IELTS Writing Task 1 answers.

3   Present continuous
You use the present continuous for arrangements or plans that have already been made. There is usually a time expression.
*We'**re all flying** to Bangkok next Sunday.*
(We have planned the trip and bought the tickets.)

4   Future perfect
You use the future perfect to make predictions about actions that will be completed before a certain point in the future.
*Everyone **will have left** by 9pm.*
*Sales **will have reached** 2000 a month by the middle of next year.*

5   Future continuous
You use the future continuous to talk about actions or events that will be happening at a particular point of time in the future.
*Sales **will be rising** at the rate of ten million units per year at the end of the decade.*
*I'll **be writing** my dissertation by then.*

6   Future perfect continuous
You use the future continuous to emphasize the duration of actions or events that will be happening at a particular point of time in the future.
*People **will have been living** on other plants for a long time by then.*

7   Present simple
You use the present simple to talk about future events that are based on a fixed schedule or timetable.
*The train **leaves** at 8.00.*
*The film **starts** in 15 minutes.*
You also use the present simple to talk about the future after the following words: *when, after, before, unless, in case, as soon as, until, by the time, the next time*.
***When** I **visit** Dubai again, I'll take more photographs.*

8   Common phrases to talk about the future
You can use the following common phrases to talk about the future:

- ***... be about to ...*** for the immediate future
  *The world of technology **is about to** undergo another major change.*
- ***... be bound to ...*** for certainty
  *She **is bound to** succeed as she is very intelligent.*
- ***... be to be + verb ...*** for fixed arrangements
  *He **is to be made** into chairman of the company.*
- ***... be set to ... / ... be (un)likely to ...*** for probability. These are useful for IELTS Writing Task 1.
  *Shopper numbers **are set to** rise dramatically.*
  *Sales **are likely to** fall in the coming months.*

Unit 6

Transitive and intransitive verbs

1 A transitive verb has an object.
*The tree **produces fruit** every year.*
An intransitive does not have an object.
*I usually **walk** to class.*

2 You can use transitive verbs in the active and the passive.
*Farmers **produce** much of the food we eat.* (Active)
*Much of the food we eat **is produced** by farmers.* (Passive)

3 You cannot use intransitive verbs in the passive.
Car sales fell over the period.
(NOT ~~Car sales are fallen over the period.~~)
The sun rises in the east.
(NOT ~~The sun is risen in the east.~~)

4 Some verbs can be either transitive or intransitive.
*The farmers **grow fruit** on the hillside.* (transitive active)
***Fruit is grown** on the hillside.* (transitive passive)
*Fruit **grows** on the hillside.* (intransitive)

5 Certain verbs like *become* can be followed by a noun or an adjective.
The flowers become seeds. ('become' + noun)
The fruit becomes ripe. ('become' + adjective)

Note the old-fashioned use of the verb *become* as a transitive verb.
The hat becomes you. ('The hat suits you.')

Unit 7

Conditionals 1

1 First conditional: *if* + present simple + *will* + infinitive
You use the first conditional to talk about situations in the present or future and their possible results.
*If young people **focus** on skills for the modern age, they **will never be** out of work.*
You can also use *may/might/going to/can* instead of *will* in the main clause.
*If it is difficult, I **can** help you.*
*If the train is late, we **may** miss the beginning of the concert.*

2 Second conditional: *if* + past simple + *would* + infinitive
You use the second conditional to talk about imaginary or unlikely situations in the present or future.
*If he **learnt** to drive, it **would open up** new job opportunities.*
*If I were you, I'**d learn** to drive.*
Note that in speech *If I was you* is becoming more common.
You can also use *could/might* instead of *would* in the main clause.
*If he **learnt** to drive it **could/might open up** new job opportunities.*

3 Third conditional: *if* + past perfect + *would have* + past participle
You use the third conditional to hypothesize or speculate about the past.
*If I **had spent** more time studying, I'**d have been** less nervous about the exam now.*
You can also use *could/might* instead of *would* in the main clause.
*If I **had spent** less time studying, I **could/might have been** less nervous about the exam now.*

4 You can begin with *were* in the second conditional and *had* in the third conditional and change the word order as follows:
***Were** he to learn to drive, it would open up new job opportunities.*
***Had** I spent less time studying, I'd have been less tired before the exam.*
This form is more formal.

5 You can use *unless* instead of *if not* in conditional clauses.
***Unless** I get some money, I won't be able to travel abroad to study.*
*If I **don't** get some money, I won't be able to travel abroad to study.*
***Unless** he had saved a lot of money, he could have never managed to travel abroad.*
*If he **hadn't** saved a lot of money, he could have never managed to travel abroad.*

Unit 8

Referring in a text

1 You use the following pronouns to refer back to a noun:
- ***it*** for singular nouns
  *The **neighbourhood** where I was brought up used to be very busy, but now **it** is very quiet and peaceful.*

*The **place** I like to visit when I go home is near my parents' house. **It** is a very secluded spot on a hill by the river.*
In the example above, it is clear that *it* refers back to the noun *place*. The word *spot* helps you to understand this.
- ***they*** for plural nouns
  *A **number of sites** are still lying idle, yet **they** could be used for houses.*

2 You can use the following to refer to a noun, event or idea, or the latter part of the previous sentence.
- ***this***
  *The government brought about **a massive transformation of the area**, but **this** (change) needs to be further supported.*
  In the example above, *this* refers to the *massive transformation of the area*. The word *change* can be added. *It* cannot be used because it might not be clear whether it refers to the government, the transformation or the area.
  The district has become more prosperous in recent years. This has led to an increase in house prices in the area.
  In the example above, *this* refers to the idea that *the district has become more prosperous in recent years*. *It* cannot be used.
- ***these***
  *Many new buildings were constructed in the district in the last few years. **These** have brought many new people into the area.*
  In the example above, *these* refers to the *many new buildings*. *They* is not correct as it might refer to 'the last few years'.
- ***that***
  You can use *that* to refer back to a noun, event or idea, but it is not as common as *this*.
  *The region has many wild animals roaming around the plains. **That** is what makes **it** very exciting to visit.*
  In the example above, *that* refers to the *many wild animals roaming around the plains*. The pronoun *it* refers to *the region*.
- ***those***
  *The speakers' **recommendations** were endless, but only **those** that were cost-effective were adopted.*
  In the example above, *those* refers to some of the speakers' recommendations not all of them.

3 You can use the pronoun *it* to refer back to *this* or *that* in a text.
*The setting for the film was decided upon at the last minute, but **this** did not cause any serious problems. **It** did, however, mean it cost a lot more.*
In the example above, *this* refers to *decided upon at the last minute* and *it* refers to back to *this*.

4 You can often use *this, that, these, those* followed by a noun to refer back to nouns, events or ideas.
*The committee suggested that **the financial district should be expanded. This recommendation** was accepted.*
*Wildlife like tigers and lions are often held in captivity, but **these creatures** need to be allowed to roam freely.*
*In the past, people used to believe **strange things** about the natural world. However, **those ideas** went out of fashion years ago.*

Unit 9

Modal verbs for evaluating

1 Expectations and suggestions

You can use *should/ought to* to express suggestions.
*The government **should** increase taxes to fund education.*
You can also use *should/ought to* to express expectations.
*The increased investment in education **should** help improve standards.*

2 Drawing conclusions

You can use *must* to draw conclusions about the present.
*The house **must** be very expensive. Look at the size of the garden!*
You can use *must/musn't have* + past participle to draw conclusions about the past.
*The paintings **must have cost** a lot of money.* (They are by a famous artist and look very expensive.)
*They **mustn't have spent** a lot of time preparing for this production.* (It wasn't very good.)

3 Making criticisms

You can use *should/shouldn't have* + past participle to make criticisms about the past.
*The council **should have protected** the building as it was very important historically.* (They were wrong not to protect it.)
*They **shouldn't have knocked** the building down as it was very important historically.* (They knocked it down which was not the right thing to do.)
You can also use *could have/might have* + past participle to make criticisms or show annoyance.
*They **could have protected** the building!* (It was worth protecting, but they didn't.)
*Private companies **might** at least **have contributed** to the cost of the new building!* (They didn't contribute and I think they should have!)

4 Weak possibilities and weak suggestions

You can use *could/might* to express weak possibilities and suggestions.
*The coins we found **could** be worth a lot of money.* (It is possible, but I'm not sure.)
*They **might** put works of art like sculptures to make the city more attractive.* (I'm not saying they should do it, but it is a possibility.)
*They **could/might** like to build a new art gallery to help improve the area.* (I'm suggesting this would be a good idea.)

Unit 10

Defining and non-defining clauses

Relative clauses contain a relative pronoun: *which, that, where, who, whose, whom.* You can use them in sentences to provide additional information about nouns.
There are two types of relative clauses: defining and non-defining.

A Defining clauses

Defining clauses provide essential information which identifies 'who' or 'what' is being referred to. You do not use commas at the beginning or end of the clause.
*The artist **who** painted the pictures in this gallery has used very vibrant colours.*
*The film **that/which** we saw last week was very exciting.*
You can leave out the relative pronoun only if it is the object of the clause and only in defining clauses.

*The water-colour **(that/which)** she painted in her teens has just sold for a record sum.*
*The artist **(who/whom)** I saw this morning was very famous.*
In speech you can use *that* instead of *who/whom*.
*The artist **(that)** I saw this morning was very famous.*

B Non-defining clauses

Non-defining clauses provide additional information, which can be left out. You need to use commas at the beginning and the end of the clause. In speech, you indicate a non-defining clause by pausing briefly at the commas.
*The square, **which** is very small with many old buildings, is my favourite place in Paris.*
You cannot leave out the relative pronoun in non-defining clauses when it is the object of the clause.
*The square, **which** I visit very frequently, is my favourite place in Paris.* (NOT ~~The square, I visit very frequently, is my favourite place in Paris.~~)
You cannot use *that* to introduce a non-defining clause.
~~The square, that is very small with many old buildings, is my favourite place in Paris.~~

1 that/which

You use *that* or *which* when referring to things. You use *which* rather than *that* with prepositions.
*My mobile phone, **for which** I paid a lot of money, has been stolen.* (NOT ~~My mobile phone, for that I paid a lot of money~~)

2 who/whom

You use *who* or *whom* when referring to people. You can use *whom* as the object of the word *who*. *Whom* is more formal and it is not often used in speech.
*The artist **who/whom** I saw this morning was very famous.*
You use *whom* with prepositions. This is quite formal and is only used in formal writing.
*The manager **to whom** I sent the cheque has disappeared.*
*The manager **who** I sent the cheque to has disappeared.*

3 whose

You use *whose* to show that something belongs to someone.
*That's the film director **whose** film just won the award.*

4 when/why/where

You use *when* when referring to a time and *why* when referring to a reason. You can leave out *when* and *why* in defining clauses
*The reason **(why)** the bridge looks so elegant is the materials used.*

5 where

You use *where* when referring to a place.
You cannot leave out *where* in defining clauses.
*The town **where** I was brought up has expanded.* (NOT ~~The town I was brought up has expanded.~~)

Unit 11

Conditionals 2

1 Even if ...

You can use *even if* for emphasis.
***Even if** it doesn't solve the problem, it's surely worth a try.*
***Even if** they spent a lot of the money on the programme, it would be worth it.*

2 Supposing/what if/imagine/let's say ...

You can use *supposing/what if/imagine/let's say ...* for speculation.

Supposing *you inherited a lot of money, what would you do?*
Imagine *you could do any job for a day, what would you choose?*

3 *Otherwise*
You can use *otherwise* as an alternative to *unless/if not*.
More money needs to be put into upgrading the broadband system; ***otherwise****, it will slow down.* ('Unless more money is put into upgrading the broadband system, it will slow down.')

4 *If only*
You can use *if only* to express regret.
If only *I had spent more time learning to play the violin when I was younger, I'd be much better now.*

5 *If … should …*
You can use *if … should …* as a variation of the second conditional.
If the government ***should*** *introduce a law to promote electric cars, there will be a lot of support for it.*

6 *On condition that/provided/provided that/as long as*
You can use *on condition that/provided/provided that/as long as* as a variation of *if*.
Provided that *the roads are clear, traffic will move freely.*

Unit 12

Articles

There are two types of articles that are used with nouns: definite and indefinite. The indefinite article – *a/an/zero* article with *s* – is used with countable nouns and the zero article without *s* with uncountable nouns. The definite article – *the* – is used with countable nouns in the singular and plural and with uncountable nouns.

1 Indefinite article: *a/an*
You use *a/an*:
- when you introduce a countable noun for the first time
  He bought ***a book*** *this morning.*
  A new car *was launched today.*
- with a countable noun which is one of a group
  I played ***a song*** *from the CD.*
- for someone's occupation
  He's ***an artist****.*
- with certain numbers/quantities
  I bought half ***a kilo of*** *tomatoes.*
  I invited about ***a dozen*** *people.*
- with hours, days, weeks, years and decades
  I visit him once ***a week****.*
  She earns nearly $50 ***an hour****.*

2 Definite article: *the*
You use the definite article:
- with uncountable and countable nouns that have been mentioned before
  He bought ***a book*** *this morning.* ***The book*** *was very expensive.*
- when it is clear what the context is for the noun
  I had lunch in a restaurant near home today. ***The food*** *was fabulous.* ('The food' in the restaurant)
- when there is only one in a system
  The sun *was hidden by clouds this morning.*
- with plural countries and abbreviations of countries names
  the Netherlands   the UAE

- with mountain ranges, rivers and oceans/seas
  the Alps   the Amazon   the Pacific
- with nationalities
  The Irish *have migrated to many different countries.*
- with groups of people
  the *young*
- with instruments
  I have played ***the piano*** *since I was ten.*
- with superlatives
  the best/worst
- with time
  in ***the past/future***

Note *at present*

3 Zero article (no article)
You use the zero article:
- with countable and uncountable nouns when you are talking generally
  I buy ***apples*** *every week.*
  Happiness *is easy to find.*
- with names of cities, countries, states and roads
  Sao Paulo   Germany   Oxford Street
- with geographical areas, lakes, mountains and islands
  Northern Europe   Lake Victoria
  Mt. Kilimanjaro   Corfu
- with days, months and years
  Tuesday   February   1979
- with meals when you talk about them generally
  Let's go out for ***dinner****.*
  Compare:
  The dinner *we just had was very cheap.*
- with company names
  Yahoo

3 Using articles in a text
When you write, use the Articles checklist on page 207 to check you are using articles correctly.

Unit 13

Concession

1 Conjunctions
You can use linking words like *although/though/while* to highlight your ideas. You concede or agree with someone else's idea and then add your own.
Although/though *I agree with the proposal, I think it is better to increase pensions for those over 75 years of age.*

You can use *while* and *whereas* to compare two things and emphasize the difference between them.

While *the home team was slow and clumsy, the away team was fast and precise.*

2 *may/might* with *although/though*
You can use the modal verbs *may* and *might* with *although/though* to make concessions.
Although/Though *this idea* ***may*** *be sound, there are better ways to tackle the problem.*

3 *may/might* with *but*
You can use *may/might* with *but*.
This ***may*** *be a very good way to improve the cohesion of society,* ***but*** *it must be done in conjunction with other measures.*

4 *much as*
You can use *much as* with verbs of feeling, approval and agreement to express concessions.

__Much as__ I approve of the solution to the problem, I don't __believe__ it is the best way to deal with the situation.

5 Adverbs

You can use adverbs like *nevertheless/nonetheless*.
The policy is not popular with the general public.
__Nevertheless/Nonetheless__, it needs to be continued.

Unit 14

Substitution and ellipsis

A Substitution

You can use the following for substitution in speech and writing to avoid repetition:

- **so**
  Are you coming to the party this evening? I think __so__.
  Here *so* is replacing *that I am coming to the party*.
  Note that you do not use *it* instead of *so*.
  You can also use *so* at the beginning of a clause.
  Many people think the situation is getting better and __so__ do I.

- **do/don't/did/didn't**
  The public didn't support the idea of privatizing health care in any way, but the government at the time __did__.
  Here *did* is replacing *did support the idea of privatizing health care*.
  The government's advisors wanted to reduce investment in health provision, but ministers __didn't__.
  Here *didn't* is replacing *didn't want to reduce investment in health provision*.

- **to do so/doing so**
  The social care provided needs a complete overhaul. __Doing so/to do so__ would require considerable sums of money.
  Here *doing so/to do so* is replacing *to overhaul the social care provided*.

- **neither/not**
  I have not visited any cities outside London, __nor/neither__ has my family.
  Here *neither/nor* replaces *not visited any cities outside London*.

- **not**
  Do you think that people need money to be happy? I hope __not__!
  Here *not* replaces *people do not need money to be happy*.

B Ellipsis

1 You can use the following to avoid repetition:

- Leave out words to avoid repetition after *and/but*
  I live in the countryside and commute to work in the city.
  (INSTEAD OF *I live in the countryside and **I** commute to work in the city*.)
  I go to museums in Lisbon a lot and to the street markets.
  (INSTEAD OF *I go to museums in Lisbon a lot and I go to the street markets.*)

- *used to* to avoid repetition of verbs
  I think people don't read books a lot now, but they __used to__.
  Here *used to* is replacing *read a lot of books in the past*.

- modal verbs to replace the main verb
  The government don't put much effort into finding ways to increase the happiness index of the population but I think they __should__.
  Here *should* replaces the *government should put much effort into finding ways to increase the happiness index of the population*.

2 You cannot leave out:

- main verbs after the verb *be*
  Many people are involved in volunteer work, but more could be done.
  (NOT *Many people are involved in volunteer work, but more could be*.)

- *been* after a modal verb in the perfect passive
  People of my generation were not given enough information about focusing on quality of life as opposed to money, when they should have been.
  (NOT *People of my generation were not given enough information about focusing on quality of life as opposed to money, when they should have*.)

Listening scripts

1 We are all friends now

 1.1

(C = clerk; V = volunteer)

C: Hi. Charles Lewis speaking.
V: Hi. Am I through to Mr Lewis?
C: Yes, you are. How can I help you?
V: I'm, er, phoning about the notice I saw saying that you are looking for helpers for the <u>charity event</u> being held next month.
C: Yes, we are. We need a number of people. Em … we need about 20 volunteers to help out as guides, ticket collectors and to work on stalls, and some people to take charge of a range of children's events. The venue of the show will be <u>Andrews</u> Hall. I take it you're interested?
V: Yes, definitely. It says here the event will take place between Friday and Sunday on the 15th to the 17th of <u>July</u>. Is that correct?
C: Yes, it is. The event is open each day – Friday to Sunday at 10 am … and runs until <u>8</u> pm every evening that it's open.
V: OK. The times sound OK. Am I right in thinking you're only looking for part-time helpers?
C: Yes, that's right. We have lots of full-time volunteers, but we need <u>part-time</u> helpers to fill empty slots in the schedule.
V: I'd be interested in helping out part-time rather than doing the whole event anyway.
C: Yes, that's fine.
V: What do I have to do now?
C: I just need to take down a few details. Right … First of all, I need your name?
V: It's Andrea Davenport.
C: Is that D-E- … ?
V: No, it's em … , <u>D-A-V-E-N-P-O-R-T</u>.
C: Davenport. OK. And can I take some contact details?
V: Yes.
C: Let's start with your address?
V: It's 90 Fordenham Mansions, 62 Park Avenue.
C: Could you spell that for me?
V: It's <u>F–O–R–D–E–N–H–A–M</u> and then Mansions.
C: OK.
V: 62 Park Avenue. And that's London SW1 4PQ.
C: And a contact telephone number?
V: My home number is <u>887 6451</u>. I work in the afternoons, so the best time to ring is in the <u>morning</u>.

....

C: Right. That's all that done.
V: Do I need to come along for an interview or anything?

C: Yes. We're seeing people at the moment. Can you come next Saturday from 9 am onwards?
V: Yes, that's fine.
C: Well Andrea, do you have any more questions about the work?
V: Em … oh, can I just ask if experience is necessary?
C: No, but it certainly helps. We're just looking for people <u>who get on with others</u> and who are independent. For example, we need people we can leave in charge on their own if nobody else is available.
V: I think I can do that. I like working with other people, but I am able to work on my own without anyone around.
C: That all sounds really very useful and the sort of thing we're looking for. And we also need people who <u>are always on time</u>.
V: I think I'm OK with that.
C: Fine. I'll send you an event pack with all the event details, address, application form, etc. to go through. You can bring the completed application form along with you on Saturday.
V: OK.
C: I've got a slot at 9 am for an interview.
V: That's fine.

2 Technology–now and then

 1.2

Welcome to Radio South here in South London. My name is Darren Timpson, and I'm here with you for the next hour to bring you some local cultural news. Our first item is about a group of seven young people packing in the visitors of all ages at Penwood Museum. <u>They have won first prize in the sixth summer show art competition, and their installation is on display along with the other four prize winners</u>. In case you don't know, the museum runs a competition as part of the yearly summer show. Each year the competition has a specific theme. The theme of this year's competition has been '<u>improving links between the local community and the museum</u>'. The competition was open to groups of young people from organizations like schools and youth clubs, who were aged <u>between 15 and 19 years of age</u> on the final entry date for the competition, which was the 13th of May. While preparing their competition entry, the competitors

<u>were allowed to use the educational facilities at the museum</u> and to look for help from local sponsors but were not allowed to buy any equipment. The first prize was won by a group of youngsters from Tigers Community Centre, who called their entry *Technology – now and then. What use is it?* They took various exhibits from the museum's collection of equipment from the 1950s to the 1970s and arranged them with modern versions. The teenagers then recorded their own reactions and comments to the exhibits and did the same with the comments made by older people in their seventies and eighties. The prize-winning exhibits are having a big impact on Penwood Museum attendances, which <u>have been up 45 per cent</u> since the summer show opened. Some of the video commentaries are very moving and some very funny.

....

I particularly liked seeing the recording of the reaction of several elderly people in their seventies when they talked about an early wooden-framed TV. They remembered the excitement of their first TV, which they thought <u>still fitted in with today's trends</u>. They remembered how they would sometimes all go round to someone's house to watch TV as a special treat. But they thought the modern TV plasma screen with the remote was much easier to watch. As for the collection of old radios, it has to be seen. They are really huge old wooden frame radios in perfect working order and in perfect condition. The youngsters' reactions to the radios were very funny; they couldn't believe how big they were. And the older people, all of whom used to have one, said they liked them. But they also thought they <u>were too big to fit into living rooms</u> these days. A few more items worth looking at from the display are old kitchen items. The young people thought the cooker from the 1950s looked funny. The older interviewees nearly all used microwave ovens, which they thought were <u>much handier</u>. Seeing old typewriters on display next to slim laptops made them look weird and cumbersome. Even the older people preferred the laptops, which they thought were <u>thrilling</u>. The other electronic items on display were a collection of old and fairly recent cameras. The older people thought the older cameras were '<u>well made, and better than the newer ones</u>'.

227

3 Thrill seekers

 1.3

(T = tutor; M = Marcello; V = Vicky)

T: Right, Vicky and Marcello. We arranged this tutorial so you could give me an update of your joint project, the, er … case report on the work you've been doing at a local sports club. Is that right?

M: Yes. That's it. Mmm … it's Stars Club – the one that's been in the news a lot lately. It's not that far from the Kennedy Campus.

T: Right … Yes, I have it here. Fire away.

M: Well, at first we were going to look only at the management structure of the club, but, em … we decided to include what's made it more successful than other local clubs. The club's success has not just come from its many sporting achievements: it's also attracting so many young people. Mm … we talked to staff and members and …

T: How many people did you talk to?

V: There're just over 600 members overall and 23 staff, including freelance workers. So far we've talked to mm … ooh, about 173 people.

T: Didn't you think of giving a questionnaire to everyone?

V: We decided against it.

T: Why was that?

V: Well, we thought that face-to-face interviews, however brief, would be better as we'd be able to probe people gently to give us more details if need be.

T: And your findings so far?

M: The club's actually very well run. The managers're very focused and work well together. And the management team also includes representatives from the various teams at the club.

V: This means that when decisions're made, they're not taken in isolation of the members, as so often happens in other organizations. The management team's in touch with the members and vice versa.

T: You seem to have learnt a lot so far.

M: I agree. It's a really exhilarating experience being there. I can't wait to go in every day.

....

T: OK. Would you like to tell me a bit about the reasons behind the success of the club? Vicky, would you like to go first?

V: OK. Mmm … well … when we asked the people we questioned to say what they thought were the most important reasons for the club's success, many people gave loads of reasons without being prompted, but it was clear that there were three factors that stood out from all the others.

T: Can you say something more about each of these specific points? Marcello, would you like to go on?

M: Well, as Vicky said, we isolated three main factors; though some are more important than others. We found that for most people having financial help from the government, private individuals and companies was absolutely crucial. They felt that it was important to … have money to pay for facilities, em … for travelling expenses and, em, for any absences from their job.

T: Yes. That doesn't sound surprising considering the costs the athletes incur. We can't expect them all to be rich amateurs. And the next factor?

M: Mmm … I personally thought the quality of facilities would come next but a close second was the quality of the coaching, which is more professional.

V: Like Marcello, I expected facilities to come next, and …

M: And most people said the club managed to attract some really top quality people working as coaches. And the coaches saw their job as pushing athletes to realize their full potential. The most influential coaches were those preparing athletes for the track events, swimming, weightlifting and climbing. They also had coaches for more esoteric areas like rock climbing and rowing.

T: And the other items? … Vicky?

V: Er … the next factor is the motivation and dedication of the athletes themselves, which has been necessary for them to become the best in their field. It was really thrilling to see this in action.

T: And success breeds success.

M: Yes, definitely.

T: It sounds as if you've got a lot out of this experience.

M: It's the sort of place I'd like to work after I've graduated.

V: Me too. I'd like to train as a coach there.

T: Brilliant. And have you started writing up the case study yet?

M: Yes, we've done quite a bit and …

Ready for Listening

Section 1

 1.4

(S = sales person; C = customer)

S: Good morning, Jackson's Bookstore. You're through to the book search department. How can I help you?

C: Hi. Mm … I'm looking for a book. I've found the title on the Internet, but I can't find a copy of it anywhere. I understand you undertake a book search to locate copies of books.

S: Yes we do. Can I just take down a few details of the book title, etc?

C: Yeah sure.

S: First of all, what's the title and the author?

C: It's called *The Judgement* by Dayne Wight.

S: *The … Judgement*. OK. That's typed in. Hmm, I'm afraid the computer's being a bit slow this morning.

C: They're always causing problems.

S: And the author is Dayne Wight?

C: Yes, that's it. It's Dayne Wight. That's W–I–G–H–T not W–H–I–T–E.

S: OK. Wight. Em … this computer is being really slow. And, er … the ISBN number?

C: 978-0-691-08879-9. And it's a paperback not hardback.

S: … 08879-9 and a paperback. OK. Em … I can see from the computer that it has never been in print in this country. It's only been published in North America, but it's out of print now.

C: Yes. I read part of it at a friend's house a while back, but couldn't find a copy of it. I'm not sure what you'd put it under, but I suppose you could call it … er … biographical fiction, if such a category exists.

S: Hmm … the computer's showing that we don't have any copies in our own collection of second-hand books or our overseas books either.

C: Ah, OK.

S: But I can do a book search for you through other collections and try distributors in the United States, but it might take some time.

C: I see. How much will that cost?

S: Well, it depends on the search. We offer two types: gold or silver.

C: OK.

S: For the gold we search around the world, and for the silver we only look in America, Europe and in this country. The gold search is £25.

C: £25. That's more than the book costs!

S: Yes probably, but it depends on how much you want the book. And the silver is £17.

C: OK. I'll go for the silver. How long will it take?

S: I can't say. With this service we go on until we come up with something, but I can't guarantee that we'll find anything.

C: No. I realize that.

....

S: Right. I'm afraid the computer's not working. I'll write everything down by hand and copy it in later. OK, I need your contact details.

C: The best way is probably by mobile or email.

S: OK … your mobile number?

C: 08967 54 65 36

S: 54 65 36. And … your email address?

C: And my email address is

mandythompson9z all one word
...@yahoo.fr all lower case.

S: OK. Is that mandy with a 'y' and
thompson9z?

C: Yes, that's it.

S: And, er … I need to take a home
address for our records.

C: It's 90 Chaucer House, Ludlow Park
Drive, Richmond, SW20 9RL.

S: OK. And do you want to receive
notification by email about special
offers?

C: I'd rather not.

S: OK. I'll just tick this box …

Ready for Listening

Section 2

 1.5

Hi everyone, and welcome to the local
evening news. I'd like to start with an
exciting new development on this side
of the city – the redevelopment of the
old Regal Cinema on Duncton Street.
Last night was the official opening of
the new Regal Cinema Complex, as it is
now known.
And what a transformation! The
venue has changed from being a
rundown, depressing building to a
state-of-the art cinematic experience,
and it's wonderful to see so many of
the original features still intact. The
building which housed the old cinema
has been completely renovated, while
managing to incorporate some of the
old features of the cinema like the
façade, which is still there, but all the
dirt has been completely removed
with a few modern touches added.
Multicoloured glass panelling has been
added to the facade so the entrance
now looks really snazzy.
The old auditorium, which was like
a huge cavern and not particularly
welcoming, has been partitioned to
create three screens. This means that
there is now one large cinema screen
– 'Screen 1' – which has a capacity of
500 people. The two smaller screens
– Screens 2 and 3 – have a capacity
of 175 and 150. There are fewer seats
overall compared to the old cinema –
about 150 actually – but there is a now
a greater variety of shows to choose
from.
The foyer to the cinema has been
totally brought up-to-date and made
bigger with a much larger ticket office
and machines for collecting tickets that
have been booked in advance. People
will no longer have to stand outside in
the rain as they had to in the past while
they were waiting to buy tickets. And
where there was a bar serving coffee
and cold drinks with a few stools and
high tables there is now a restaurant.
The roof terrace, which used to have
just a few benches and seats, will be
opening shortly with a landscaped

garden with a bar which is open all
year round. This will be a welcome
addition to the centre.
The basement, which leads out into
a garden at the back, has been totally
renovated and turned into a members'
room with a bar-restaurant and a
small display area for artwork or stalls.
The cinema shop is no longer beside
the ticket office; it is now next to the
entrance to the restaurant. It doesn't
just sell sweets, as it did before, but
cinema-related memorabilia including
programmes and books, DVDs, CDs,
posters …

....

And I've got a leaflet here about the
programme for the opening week of
the newly refurbished cinema, em …
which is the week beginning the 14th of
July. As it's during the school holidays,
there will be a special promotion.
For the matinee performance each
day the cinema is offering free tickets
to the first 100 children up to and
including 16 years of age, and to all
pensioners. And there will be special
rates for cinema goers who book a
meal in the restaurant as well. Plus
there will be special nights where there
are child-free performances, and also
each Wednesday tickets will be half-
price for members of the cinema. I
see here the membership is only £30 a
year and gives you access to member-
only previews and to the members'
restaurant in the basement.
But perhaps the biggest innovation at
the cinema is the monthly programme
of lectures where not just actors
and actresses, but producers and
writers, will be involved in delivering
talks about a particular film. This is
certainly a major development which
will definitely pull in many cinema
enthusiasts, and hopefully revitalize
the area.

Ready for Listening

Section 3

 1.6

(Z = Zahra; T = Tim)

Z: Hi Tim.

T: Zahra, hi. So, have you decided
yet what you're going to do your
tutorial paper on?

Z: Yes, actually I have. I agonized over
it for ages, as you well know. You
had to listen to me.

T: Well, that's true, but you've had to
listen to me too! … So, what's it on?

Z: Electronic gadgets, but from a
particular angle: 'must-carry'
gadgets. You know, gadgets that
people cannot leave the house
without, er … like mobiles phones,
etc. It's not particularly original.

T: That's really very neat.

Z: Oh. Do you think so?

T: Yes, actually I do.

Z: I thought it was really quite
ordinary.

T: And how are you going to do the
research for the paper?

Z: I thought of interviewing people in
the age groups 20–25 and 50 plus,
so I can ask students for the first
group and I'll have to ask lecturers
and people in the street or people
working on campus for the other
group. But I haven't made up my
mind yet which groups to choose.

T: Em … and what are you setting out
to show?

Z: I'm not sure at this stage, but
something along the lines of …
er … the idea that we are making
ourselves more stressed, and it has
reached such a stage that we are
so dependent on the gadgets that
leaving the house without them
makes us ill. I'm just thinking
on my feet here. I haven't really
thought it right through to the end.

T: What about your questionnaire?

Z: Mmm … , yes that's another thing.
What I'm not really decided about
is the length the questionnaire
should be.

T: The best thing is to keep it short.

Z: Maybe. But I'll finalize the length
when I sit down to type it up.

....

Z: I need to find someone to try out
my questions on. I've got some
already written.

T: I can be your guinea pig if you
want.

Z: Great!

T: Fire away!

Z: First … question number one. What
electronic gadgets are you carrying
with you now?

T: Let's see. I've got my mobile phone,
… my iPod, my laptop.

Z: Which do you carry with you every
day?

T: All of them!

Z: What do you use your mobile
phone for generally?

T: Em … apart from phoning, mostly
for texting and downloading music.
But I also use it for video-phoning,
sending emails … and I talk to my
family now using the video on the
phone.

Z: On a scale of 1–10, where 1 is not
at all difficult and 10 very difficult,
how difficult would you find it to
leave your mobile at home for a
whole day?

T: Very difficult, so 10. I'd be
completely lost without it.

Z: And what about the laptop? What
do you use it for?

T: I use it for em … writing up
assignments, but mainly for
browsing the Internet.

Z: Using the same scale, what about
your laptop?

T: Well, let's see … It's not as essential

as my mobile phone, but it's still important. A score of … <u>8</u>. This one's not heavy, but I can do without it, if necessary. I seem to use my mobile for most of the things I used to use the laptop for. Soon I probably won't need it.

Z: What about the iPod?

T: I can use my mobile for music as well, so it's not essential, but I carry it everywhere with me because it's light and it's got my whole music collection on it that I can listen to on the move. And, mmm … well, for that, I'd give a score of <u>5</u>.

Z: Is there any gadget you intend to get in the near future?

T: Yes. I'd like to get a newspaper reader when they become lighter and cheaper and more readily available. <u>I think I'll end up using it for everything</u>, even to replace the mobile.

Z: Do you think so?

T: Oh yeah. They'll be perfect for video messaging.

Z: And the score?

T: Definitely <u>10</u>. And I'd like a pair of …

Ready for Listening

Section 4

 1.7

Good morning everyone. The topic of my seminar paper this week is a rather unusual method of bringing water to drought-ridden regions of the world. The methods people most think of, or read about in newspapers and or see on TV, mmm … are preventing deforestation and encouraging reforestation to prevent water run-off from barren land and hence to stop flooding. Another method is … er … drilling bore holes to bring water from aquifers deep in the ground <u>to irrigate the land</u>.

But the method I would like to talk about today is the production of rain through *seeding clouds*. For those of you who are not familiar with this practice, it is basically a process where nature is *coaxed*, as it were, to produce rain. In many places in the world attempts have been made throughout history to produce rain in times of drought <u>through magic</u>, but from the latter part of the last century scientists've been endeavouring to come to the rescue by chemical means. And in some places they've been trying not just to produce rain but also to divert it so that it does not rain on special days, such as national or international ceremonies.

Cloud seeding has been carried out since the middle of the last century, but no scientist can confirm that the practice is actually responsible for cloud seeding and not nature itself.

Because who can confirm that the clouds would not let loose a deluge anyway? Having said that, there is some evidence that seeding clouds to produce rain can lead to <u>a 15% increase in rainfall</u>.

But what would happen, for example, if the actions of cloud seeding in one place led to a disastrous deluge in another? It would also be tricky to prove that any damage was the responsibility of cloud seeders. Some people are understandably against the practice of cloud seeding as <u>we do not really know the consequences of interfering with nature</u>.

Cloud seeding has apparently been used by Californian officials to replenish reservoirs. In other parts of the US, electricity utility companies are especially fond of seeding to bring more water to hydroelectric plants. And the practice is also popular with authorities in Russia and China too. For years the Russian air force has tried to coax moisture out of clouds to ensure sunshine on national holidays. <u>But no country is more committed to researching weather modification than China</u>, with a national budget in the tens of millions of dollars and thousands of miles flown by rain seeding aircraft every year.

....

Last year the university agricultural and meteorology departments were given a 20 million dollar grant, funded in part by the government and various companies in the food and agricultural industry, to conduct research into cloud seeding to increase precipitation. While the research is aimed primarily at the US, it is hoped that the benefits accrued will have far-reaching consequences for other drought-ridden regions of the planet.

Now … let's see, mmm … if we look at this slide here, we can see how cloud seeding works. There are two basic methods: from the air and from the ground. Looking first at seeding from the air, we can see that <u>an aeroplane flies above the clouds from where it fires silver iodide into clouds by dropping chemical flares</u> in order to increase precipitation. <u>Silver iodide crystals then attach themselves to water droplets which makes the water freeze and fall as rain or snow</u> over high ground. If we now look at the diagram showing cloud seeding from the ground, we can see that there is a <u>ground seeding generator</u> here on the right of the slide, which has a tall chimney, and em … next to this is on the left is a … em … this structure here which is <u>a fuel tank containing propane</u>. <u>Heat generated from the burning of the propane lifts the silver iodide crystals up to cloud level</u> again leading to precipitation.

4 Global problems and opportunities

 1.8

Good morning. Last week we had a broad overview of the development of early forms of transport up to the late 18th century in Europe, and also looked at how the problems faced by various communities provided new opportunities for innovation and progress. Now, this week we are going to continue with this theme as we examine a number of significant events in the evolution of modern railways – events which took place in England in the first four decades of the 19th century.

If you look at the timeline here on the left of the screen, mmm … you can see the first significant date is the year 1803. <u>This was the year an engineer called William Jessop opened the first public railway</u> in south London, England – to carry industrial goods. Although the railway was horse-drawn and not really what we would consider a railway today, nonetheless it's still regarded as the world's first public railway. The railway was constructed as a cheaper alternative to building a canal, then a common means of carrying freight.

The first railway steam locomotive was built in 1804 by an English engineer, Richard Trevithick, to whose work later pioneers like George Stephenson are seriously indebted. Richard Trevithick died a poor man, and <u>what he had achieved went largely unnoticed</u>. His engines were not commercially successful, partly because the locomotives he built were too heavy for the railway tracks of the time.

Wars in Europe led to an increase in the cost of feeding the horses which pulled the coal on horse-drawn railways like the Surrey Iron Railway. With this and the cost of using the canals, which were run by private companies, the time was now right to introduce a locomotive that was economically viable.

In the year 1812, <u>the first commercially successful steam locomotive, the Salamanca,</u> appeared on the scene at Middleton in Yorkshire in the north-east of England. Apparently, the Salamanca was even visited by Tsar Nicholas 1.

But probably the most important year was 1825 when the engine *Locomotion*, created by George Stephenson, ran on the Darlington to Stockton Railway. <u>The line was initially built to connect inland coal mines to Stockton, where coal was loaded onto boats</u>. Initially the Railway was to be horse-drawn, but permission was granted to use a locomotive or 'moveable' engines. <u>Provision for transporting passengers was made, although at the time</u>

they were regarded as being of little importance.

....

The year 1831 saw the opening of the successful Liverpool to Manchester line with Stephenson's locomotive *The Rocket*. The Liverpool to Manchester Railway is thought of as the first modern railway. The reason for this is that both goods and passenger traffic were carried on trains according to a scheduled timetable. After the success of the Stockton to Darlington Railway, money poured into the north-west of England as the region went through a period of rapid industrialization, with the railway linking the rich cotton manufacturing town of Manchester and the thriving port of Liverpool. Up to now the canals, which were constructed in the previous century, were felt to be making too much profit from their fees on trade using the canals and thereby to be hindering the development of the conurbations in the region.

And the effect of the opening of the Liverpool and Manchester Railway? It was quite dramatic. By 1834 nearly half a million passengers were being carried each year, a significant increase. Also more merchandise, including cotton, coal and other goods, was transported between the two cities using the railway. The age of the railway as a means of ferrying people from one place to another had arrived. The increase in passenger numbers and in the movement of goods led to a drop in toll prices on the roads, as well as a decrease in charges for the use of canals.

It's hard for us to appreciate the opportunities these early pioneers seized in the face of difficulties in construction and in changing people's attitudes. Perhaps we can end for today with a brief quote from Dr Larder, author of the *Steam Engine Familiarly Explained and Illustrated* in 1823, 'Rail travel at high speed,' he said, 'is not possible, ... because passengers, unable to breathe would die of asphyxia.' Next time you take a train ...

5 The future

 1.9

(M = Marcus; C = customer)
M: Good morning, exhibition booking office. Marcus speaking. Can I help you?
C: Is that the booking centre for 'Robots: the end of modern civilization?'
M: Yes madam, that's correct. How can I help you?
C: Well, mmm ... I'm attending the exhibition and I'd just like to check a few details if that's OK.
M: Yes, sure.

C: OK. I understand the exhibition opens the week after next on the Tuesday, and ... the preview is on Monday.
M: Yes, that's right. There is a preview on Monday, but the exhibition is not open to the general public on that day. But for the rest of the week it is.
C: OK, I see. That's fine. I've got two complimentary day passes for the exhibition; can you tell me if I can use the tickets on any day?
M: Well, I'm not sure if there are any restrictions, ... let's see ... Yes, here we are.
C: Yes?
M: You can use them on any day including the preview day, except Saturday. But you need to sign up for the days you want to attend in advance.
C: Oh, I see. I haven't decided what days to attend yet.
M: Mmm ... well ... Saturday you can't attend with the tickets you have, and Thursday is already completely booked. I think the other days'll book up fairly quickly now as there's a lot of interest in the exhibition.
C: You mean I won't be able to attend on Saturday even with a free ticket.
M: I'm afraid not. So it's better to book your days now.
C: OK. I suppose, mmm ... I'll attend on the Tuesday and Friday. Do you need my name?
M: No, I just need to take a reference number with the day passes. Your name will come up with the number; it'll be the same number on each one. I'll register them for both days, and then when you use one it'll automatically cancel.
C: OK, the number is S–F–6–7–3–3.
M: ... 3–3. Thank you, I've got that.
C: What about services like cafés and so on?
M: Oh, there are 15 restaurants in all, that's three cafés and the rest are different types of dining areas round the Exhibition Centre. Some restaurants around the centre will be doing special promotions at the Exhibition Centre itself, so you won't go hungry.

....

C: Is there somewhere nice to stay nearby?
M: Oh yes. There're rooms at the nearby halls of residence, which are part of the university. They're just across the road from the Exhibition Centre.
C: How much are they?
M: A single room is £30 per night, which includes breakfast in the cafeteria. And there are some very pleasant hotels in the area. They range from around £30 to about £60. It depends how much you

want to spend really.
C: What about getting there? Has the Exhibition Centre got good transport links?
M: Yes. We're very well located – about 20 minutes' walk at most from the station, and about 45 minutes from the airport. There are lots of buses; the best one, which stops just by the Exhibition Centre's main entrance, is bus 17. No, sorry, it's bus 70. I keep getting them mixed up. It only costs £3 from the station.
C: And taxis? Just in case.
M: Er ... you'll pay a maximum of £17.
C: Mmm ... well that all sounds OK.

6 Fruits and seeds

 1.10

Good morning and welcome to the Fairbridge Countryside and Woodland Centre. I'd like to give you some information about the centre and the short programmes we run for young people on woodland therapy. We're actually a centre run by volunteers, and we were set up 15 years ago to educate people of all ages and backgrounds about nature. And for the past two years we have been taking groups of youngsters in their teens on educational programmes on Fridays, Saturdays and Sundays, em ... from schools mainly from around the area, ... but some have come from much further afield. Initially the youngsters are not very impressed by the setting because there is no way for them to get in touch with friends, etc., as there is no mobile phone signal, so it throws them quite a bit. But almost without exception, by the end of the three days they're here the young people don't want to leave and want to come back again. In fact, two of the workers here came with student groups five years ago, and when they left school they came straight to work for us. The centre is self-sufficient due in part to the sales from the nursery and we also get donations, but the bulk of our income is now from running the educational courses.

This is a basic map of the centre. We are here at the entrance to the centre, and you can see the cabins run along the east side of the path as you go north. The first cabin, Oak Lodge, is for students. It's quite large and can accommodate 16 students in bunk beds. Then the next four cabins are for families, and the cabin after that, Ash Lodge, is for teachers, which can hold up to six adults. On the west side of the path, directly opposite the student cabins, are the educational facilities. They are quite up-to-date with all the latest wizardry. And next to that is the cafeteria, which is shared with visitors to the centre. Just beside the cafeteria is a picnic area with climbing frames for children. We don't allow open-air cooking here, because of the trees. <u>The plant nursery is that complex you can see that runs all the way along the north part on the map.</u>

....

If you go over here, between the picnic area and the nursery, the path leads to the woodland itself. As we are on a hill here, we are quite high up and so you have quite breathtaking <u>views</u> of the countryside. You can see the river stretching for miles through rolling countryside. Fortunately the whole woodland is safeguarded, so nobody can chop down any trees. The <u>landscape</u> here has not changed for hundreds of years. Some of the trees have been growing here a rather long time, and the aim of the centre and the volunteers is to keep it that way. We advise people to stick to the paths, as it's very easy to get lost. As you walk through the woodland you will see workers removing dead wood and chopping down trees. I would ask everyone not to remove anything like <u>seeds or flowers</u> from the woodland so we can conserve it for future generations.

7 The world of work and training

 1.11

(T = tutor; J = Jack; V = Olivia)

T: We've got some time left for a feedback tutorial on your joint presentation today, if you have time.

J: Yeah, we can do it now while it's fresh in our minds.

T: So, Olivia how do you think it went?

O: Well, em … I was really happy with it actually, but I'm glad it's over. I think the main advantage of doing the presentation was that we both learnt quite a lot about training and skills development for the workplace and how they improve people's opportunities in life.

J: And we learnt a lot from delivering it as well.

O: Yeah that was important too. Mmm … as I said, I was pleased with it, but if I had to do it again, I'd change a few things.

T: Like what?

O: Well, mm <u>the first thing I'd do is improve the speed of the talk by making the delivery slower.</u> And I'd keep a clock in front of me so that I was aware of the speed and … and the next thing is mmm … the length of the talk … <u>I'd make the presentation time 20 minutes for each of us, because I think ten minutes was much too short.</u> If we had given ourselves more time, it

would have flowed better.

J: Yes, I agree. I thought the timing was a bit tight. I'd say maybe even 30 minutes each.

T: Mmm … 30 minutes might have been a bit long for both you and the audience.

J: Maybe you're right; 20 minutes is probably better.

O: And the next thing is <u>connected with the order of the data.</u> I thought the sequence was bad – it could have been a lot better.

T: Yes. If I had to give some particular advice, I'd say you need to give yourselves a run through once or twice using the equipment, just to see what it's like. Doing it without preparation like that is not that easy.

O: No it isn't. We were a bit stupid there. And another thing for me is that <u>we forgot to give out the handouts</u> with the copies of our slides on them for people to take notes. <u>I should have given them out before we started.</u> And one final thing is … is I'd check that everyone can see the screen properly as a few people were sitting in awkward places, so <u>I'd check the arrangement of the chairs in the room.</u>

T: And Jack. What about you? How did you feel about it all?

J: Well, mmm … I agree with Olivia. Yeah … in everything she said. It's very difficult to make the delivery smooth. If I do it again, I'll spend more time practising to make it run more smoothly.

....

T: But would you add anything to what Olivia said?

J: Er … perhaps <u>I'd try not to pack too much information into the time given.</u> Em … I thought at first it would be the opposite. Em … <u>I was afraid that we would end up looking foolish.</u> And also I think I'd spend less time on the information gathering phase because unless people devote time to practising, they won't give a good performance.

T: Yeah, I think I'd agree. Anything else?

J: Yeah. I get very <u>nervous</u> when I speak in front of people. Were I to do it again, I'd make sure I practised speaking. I think the key for me is learning to reduce my nerves.

O: But you were very calm!

J: Not inside I wasn't!

T: Well, it didn't show.

O: I think you need the nerves to keep you going, but maybe try to take your mind off it beforehand by exercising or something.

T: Is that everything?

J: Yeah.

T: OK. Well, you'll be pleased to

know the feedback from the class questionnaires was <u>good</u> from everyone, so well done. I have to say that I agree with them.

O: Oh, thanks.

T: And after the tutorial I'll make a copy for both of you of the <u>questionnaires</u> from the class, if you want. And if you do give a talk again, you can keep them to refer to.

8 The history of geography

 2.1

Well, today we are going to look at early human migration out of Africa to colonize the world.

Throughout history there've been waves of humans migrating as people have moved from one locality to another, sometimes quickly over very short distances … and sometimes slowly over very great stretches of land, mmm … in search of a new or different or better life. There now appears to be general agreement that the first movement of people of any real significance in any part of our planet originated in East Africa about <u>100 000 years ago</u>. If we look at the first slide here, we can see the route this first group of modern humans took as they made their way across the Red Sea here, which was then a dry bed. Then through Arabia and into what is now the Middle East. But these early pioneers soon died out. <u>But at that time, just like today, the earth was subject to shifts in temperature. About 70 000 years ago the planet became warmer</u> and another group of modern humans migrated out of their homeland of Africa, following basically the same route, and then moving on to South Asia. If you look at this second slide, you will see here that by about 50 000 years ago modern humans had colonized China, and about <u>45 000 years</u> ago they had reached Europe. These early humans settled in the wide open spaces of Siberia about 40 000 years ago. And this line here on the map shows that about 20 000 years ago modern humans reached Japan, which as you can see from the map on the slide, was connected to the main <u>land mass</u> at that time.

Now, on this map on the next slide you can see that there was no land connection between Australia here and South East Asia here, so the first Australians who arrived around 50 000 years ago must have made the journey across the sea in <u>simple boats</u> to settle on the Australian continent, as evidence shows here, here and … here on the map.

This next map shows the route which modern humans took from Asia to North America, which as you can see was reached across what is now the Bering Strait through Alaska. This migration happened between 15 and 13 000 years ago. There is also some evidence to suggest that modern humans came across pack ice via the North Atlantic, but this theory has been discounted by some. Since that time, the American continent has been the destination of waves of human settlement.

....

Before we look at more modern examples of human movement, like the Anglo-Saxon migrations to Britain in the 5th century AD, the migration of Turks during the Middle Ages and the migration of the Irish to America in the mid-19th century, I'd like to look at a migration within the continent of Africa itself, that I'm personally very interested in.

If we look at the map of Africa here on this next slide, we can see some patterns that are common to other waves of human movement throughout history. The routes here show what is probably the most significant migration in Africa itself: that of the Bantu, who spread out from a small region in West Africa near the present day border of Nigeria and Cameroon, just around here on the map … to occupy roughly 30 per cent of the continent by the year 1 000 AD.

A trigger for this movement may have been the result of cultivation of the yam, a starchy root vegetable, which Bantu farmers started to grow as part of their staple diet. This cultivation began around 2 750 BC, resulting in the expansion of the population. The Bantu people then spread out into the neighbouring territories, which were then sparsely populated. As the land of the rainforest could not sustain the farmers and their families for longer than a few years, they moved on, felling trees and creating new clearances in the forest to cultivate yams. With the numbers of the Bantu on the increase between 2 500 and 400 BC the people were constantly on the move, migrating south down through modern day Congo … here in central Africa, and reaching Zimbabwe here and modern-day South Africa by about 100 AD.

It was contact with Sudan in north Africa that introduced the Bantu to iron production, in which they excelled. Once they had exchanged knowledge of working in iron from Sudan, the quality of their work rivalled that produced by the Mediterranean people of the time. The Bantu now had better tools to fell trees, clear forests and work fields. And there is one other benefit iron gave the Bantu, and that was a military advantage over their neighbours. I'd say that migration has transformed

the world from early times, and we all reap the benefits of different peoples coming into contact with each other.

9 What is beauty

 2.2

(T = tutor; M = Malcom)

T: Hi Malcolm. How are you?

M: Fine, thanks. And you?

T: Yes, I'm OK. You left a message when you booked this tutorial to say that you wanted to talk about your film project. Am I right?

M: Yeah.

T: So, how can I help you?

M: Well, I'm having difficulty getting started. I should have been about halfway through about now, but I haven't done anything at all really. I think I'm feeling a bit overwhelmed.

T: Overwhelmed? In what way?

M: Mmm … I don't know. I may have chosen something too abstract.

T: Which is? Remind me … ?

M: It's 'Perceptions of beauty in India'.

T: Yeah. That's a good subject; it's probably quite challenging, but very appealing.

M: I wanted to put together a moving digital photo collage of my travels around India last summer showing the beauty of the place. I was completely overawed.

T: How many did you take in all?

M: At least 600.

T: That is a lot. I'm sure it's a wonderful photographic record, but I think your problem lies there. Can you tell me? What did you take photographs of?

M: Buildings like palaces and official places like the government buildings in New Dehli by Lutyens – I think they're really underrated. People just think of the Taj Mahal and poverty, but India's not all like that. It's huge: it's got tradition, colour and beauty at every corner. I've also got some dazzling images of places like the Ganges at Varanasi; the grandeur and splendour of the images simply take your breath away.

T: OK, I have a suggestion.

M: Yeah?

T: What about going through your digital stills on the computer and selecting the ten images which appeal to you the most? And …

M: I don't know if I could narrow it down to that.

T: Well, you'll be surprised. Select the top hundred, and then narrow that down to 25. And then you could …

M: I've just thought of an idea.

T: Yes?

M: I could mmm … Yes that's it! I could select the top ten as you

suggest, and then find various people's views on these … and then do a video collage with the pictures swirling around like a pop video. Why didn't I think of that before! That's it!

T: Problem solved?

M: Yes, but now I have to do all the work!

....

M: Can the film be longer than 15 minutes?

T: I wouldn't advise it. There might have been a few people on the course last year who made 20-minute, or even 25-minute films, but I have to say they were the least successful. I think you'll find that it's good discipline to try to work within a time limit.

M: Mmm …

T: And I'd say that ten minutes might be good …

M: Ten minutes! That's almost nothing.

T: You'll be very surprised. One minute per place fading out and in. It could be very effective. Remember the work we did on adverts and the short attention span of people generally, especially these days.

M: Yeah, I suppose you're right. I'm just thinking of all the materials – 600 plus stills down to ten, and then reduced to a ten-minute film. What about the format? How do I need to submit it?

T: Mmm … all the information is on the department website. You access it as per usual.

M: What's it under?

T: Go to 'Digital Photography'. Then 'Year One', and then click on 'Film Project', and everything is there. And don't forget you have to fill in a submission form detailing the project's background.

M: Yeah, I … I know all that. But can't I just email it to you when it's done?

T: You can. But we also want copies burned on DVD, … four copies are needed with the submission form.

M: OK, I can do that.

10 Is it art?

 2.3

Welcome on this lazy Saturday morning to Radio Hope here in Australia. This is Davy Chester, your host on your favourite show *Your Chance*, and boy do we have a lot for you on the show this week. There's the new Street Art exhibition; a new exhibition, which opened last weekend at the Horn Gallery in George Street, and which has caused a sensation judging by our email survey. And then we have the decision by the government to make all museums and art galleries free of charge from next

January. And for families and kids there's the new theme park, which has opened just outside the town.

But first to the Street Art exhibition. We've had many people saying how brilliant the exhibition is, and others saying what a load of rubbish it is, and that public money was being misspent. Apart from the criticism regarding the waste of money, some people complained that the exhibition would encourage graffiti and vandalism all over town. I put this point to Mrs Cook, the director of the art gallery, which, incidentally, I visited myself on Thursday evening, and she said that graffiti was already appearing without the Street Art exhibition. Some people who emailed in said that instead of promoting graffiti, the gallery could have used the opportunity to support local artists, who get no help from the council. And Mrs Cook did point out that when there were attempts to remove the huge mural based on Aboriginal art at the end of Coin Street there was a huge public outcry – thousands of people turned out to stop the authorities removing the mural, and there was a vigil with volunteers for three weeks until the local council reversed their decision.

While I was at the exhibition, I asked Mrs Cook what she thought about the decision to make all museums and art galleries free of charge. She said that there had been a fierce debate about this over the past year or so, because people were deterred from visiting places of a cultural nature like the Horn Gallery because of the cost. And while children were able to get in free, they rarely came with their parents, and this was a bad thing. So, basically, she was for the change. From the email survey we've had on the show website, I think about 70 per cent said that they would agree with Mrs Cook, only ten per cent were very definitely against and 20 per cent said they didn't know, which I think reflects the national consensus, give or take a few points. Now, er … when I spoke to Mrs Cook she said that there was one thing she and other people working in the gallery world were worried about and that is the level of government funding. They have always had subsidies from the government to run the galleries, but this was always topped up by entrance fees. They're waiting to see if this will be reflected in the government's arts funding for next year.

....

Now, as you all know, we have been wanting to do a walk-about on the show for a long time, and this week for the first time we will have two reporters on the street. We have one reporter, Angie Hunter, standing by outside the Horn Gallery with Mrs Cook to test opinions on the Street Art

exhibition itself. And we'll see what people really think about their art galleries being free or not. To make sure we get as wide a spectrum of people as possible we have another reporter, Alex Grey, who's standing outside the department store in White's shopping precinct in the pedestrian area. So, if you are listening and want to make your views known, pop down to the precinct or the gallery. We'll be starting the walk-about in 15 minutes at 12.45, after we have got through the other items today, so …

11 Psychology and sociology

 2.4

(S = school administrator; P = parent)

S: Headmaster's office, Damian speaking. How may I help you?
P: Yes, hi. It's Margaret Williams here.
S: Oh. Hi there.
P: My daughter Helen is in the fifth year and …
S: Ah yes, I know her…
P: Mmm … well, I understand that the International Friendship Club is planning a trip this year and just wanted to know more about it.
S: Yes, well, we normally print a factsheet for pupils to take to their parents, but that won't be done for another … month I don't think, but I can still help you with some details from the information I have.
P: OK.
S: Well, let's see … Now, mm … school trips 2000 and … ah, here it is. It hasn't been entered into the computer yet. But what exactly would you like to know?
P: Em … well, first of all, where's the trip to, how much is it and when is it?
S: The trip in the current school year will be to … South America, … to Peru specifically.
P: To Peru, wow! That sounds thrilling. That never happened in my childhood.
S: Nor mine either! Mmm … it says here the group will be staying with families connected with a school just outside the capital, Lima, and then will be making trips to the surrounding areas.
P: OK. Will each of them be on their own with the family?
S: No, there'll be no students on their own; students will all be in pairs.
P: I see. What about the cost?
S: It's surprisingly cheap actually. At the moment it's … £495 for the 15 days all inclusive, but obviously not including gifts for the host families and spending money.
P: Mmm … , it's still a lot as I'm a single parent.
S: Well, there are some bursaries, and it may be that the price comes

down; this is only the initial price. Last year, if it were not for the school fund, it would have been a lot more. Last year it came down by about £120 per student, so it depends on how much is available in the school hardship fund.
P: Oh, I see. And when is the trip?
S: Em … it takes place during the spring holidays.

....

P: OK. Can I ask you … how Helen goes about applying?
S: Applying? Well, the application is quite simple. There will be a deadline to get the application in ten days after the date of the advert, which will come out on the 29th of September.
P: OK.
S: And then when the applications are received, each student will have to have an interview to assess whether they are suitable or not.
P: How many places are there?
S: 20 with a minimum age of 16, so it's restricted to the upper years.
P: And are any teachers going?
S: Oh yes. There'll be places for six adults, four of whom will be teachers, and two parents, who will go free.
P: Right. Do they apply as well?
S: Yes. You interested?
P: Yes! And when it comes to paying, provided Helen's application is successful, can we pay by instalments? Say, £50 a month?
S: Oh yes, that's not a problem provided you make a deposit of £100, and then pay the rest by instalments with the final balance due three weeks before the departure date. Students will only be allowed to go on the trip if all the money is paid in advance – I'm afraid we've had problems in the past with money not being paid, so we are very strict about it now.
P: I see. That's totally understandable.

12 Travelling around the world

 2.5

Now that the main summer holiday season is almost upon us, we are devoting this week's Health Spot in our programme to all of you young people who are setting off on backpacking holidays to sunny shores. We hope you have the time of your life, but to help that dream come true we've got a few tips for you before you head off.

The first thing to do is to make yourself a checklist of all the things you need to do and take with you, especially if you, like me, are very forgetful. Apart from the usual things like checking you have your tickets and passport and the necessary visas, there are practical things that you need to do. I'm going to pick a few things at random from the checklist we've made here, but you can get extra information from our website, where you can download the details. Or, if you would rather have someone to listen to, you can download the podcast for free with all the information from the website. So, the first item that I think is important is sun protection, especially if you are fair-skinned. To protect yourself you can buy sun creams and special clothing and a hat – a wide-brimmed hat – and sunglasses. Provided you are well protected, you'll be OK. But the best form of protection against ultraviolet rays is to stay out of the sun. Stick to the shade; especially between 11 and 4 pm, as this is the most dangerous time. You can also buy special clothing that has built-in protection like sun cream.

Mmm, now … ah, OK, another tip here about clothing, em … is … besides a hat and so on, one item on the checklist that is indispensible is a good pair of walking shoes. Good walking shoes do not come cheap, but it is money well-spent, because if you're walking around a lot your feet will need some support. Some sandals are OK for walking, but you may be better off with shoes.

Customs? Ah yes … make yourself familiar with the customs of the country you are going to, so that you don't cause problems. It's easy to assume that people everywhere behave like ourselves. You cannot know everything, but you can find out about the main types of behaviour like what to wear and where to wear it.

....

Now, a very important point. When you are away, it's easy, if you're enjoying yourself, to lose contact with your family at home. But try and prevent this from happening so your family don't experience any anxiety unnecessarily and mmm, er … possibly waste resources. One good tip here is to remember to have a particular time to make contact. You can use a mobile phone to text your family. In these days of the Internet there is no excuse for at least not sending a quick message or a quick text on the mobile.

Let's see … Some kind of waterproof cover: something that is light but effective … And yes another good tip here – an essential for your backpack is a simple first aid kit with plasters in case you cut yourself, or tread on something sharp – and if you do, some antiseptic wipes would be very handy too, so you can clean the skin to prevent infection and so on …

And yes, this is a good piece of advice. Remember to keep valuables like cameras safe at all times. As tourists you can't be careful enough, and don't let your guard down for a second.

Remember to enjoy yourselves. Look out for novel experiences, and open your minds to the strange and the new!

Ready for Speaking
Part 2 and 3

🔘 2.6

(E = examiner; C = candidate)

E: Now, I'm going to give you a card with a topic to look at. You have one minute to make notes and then I'm going to ask you to talk about the topic.

E: Can you talk about the topic?

C: The skill that I'd like to talk about is playing a musical instrument, mmm … like the piano, and I'd like to learn it in the near future. I know it's possible to go to a class to learn to play the piano, but mmm … I know I'd find that very annoying. I think learning to play the piano's one of those skills that'd be better to learn … to acquire by paying for individual tuition. I realize that it might be expensive, but it'd be mmm … very rewarding in other ways.

Why I'd like to be able to take up the piano is because … it's mmm … very soothing to play and to listen to. It's a wonderful feeling to lose yourself in the music as you're playing. I've got several friends who are mad about music, and I've listened to them many times. They've played both classical and pop music to me, and they've found it thrilling to play for someone. And to me it is a very peaceful experience just sitting there and listening. As well as helping to calm people down, playing an instrument like the piano's er … very good for the brain as it keeps it active. One of my friends, who plays the guitar and the piano, says that he plays for about … half an hour before he does any homework, and it helps him to focus on his work and concentrate more. And it's healthy, because it helps take away part of the stress of modern lifestyle. Friends've also told me that it improves their ability to focus, and so they play before they study or do any work, which I think would mm … benefit me too.

E: OK. Thank you. Which type of music would like to learn to play?

C: Er … I'd like to start with classical, but I'd like to learn jazz music later on and maybe some pop music.

E: Do you think it's important to keep acquiring new skills throughout one's life?

C: Yes, I think it is.

E: Why do you think so?

C: Well, mmm, at the moment life is changing so fast with the

advances that have been made in technology, and also through em … globalization in the past few decades, so it's important for people of all ages to keep up-to-date with skills of all kinds.

E: How essential do think it'll be for workforces in the future to be proficient technologically?

C: Mmm, I'd say it is vital, because more and more of the work that is done nowadays requires a lot of input using one form of technology or another, so that in the near future it will be almost impossible to find work, even basic work, without practical computing skills. Take car design, for example. It seems that technical drawing done by hand is less important now than knowing how to create new products on the screen. Soon designers'll be creating holograms of cars not just three-dimensional computer images. And the same applies to architecture and teaching too.

E: In what way do you think learning only computing skills can be a disadvantage in life?

C: Em … first of all, people are already becoming over-reliant on computers for virtually everything. In the current knowledge-based society, where information is available literally at people's fingertips, there's a danger that people's knowledge'll decrease and accessing information'll become just like switching on the light without necessarily understanding what's happening. And people're in danger of losing their ability to do basic things.

E: Mmm, er, should preparation of children and young people for work focus on computing skills at the expense of practical skills?

C: Mmm … I think it's a matter of balance, because we need the people to build computers and so on, and the people to learn to be able to use them for their work. Also, if any machines break down, we need people to be able to fix them. And so if education concentrates on training people to use machines to access knowledge at the expense of training technicians etc., then there'll be a major problem.

E: Do you think people will have to work longer in the future?

C: At one time it was thought that people would have more leisure time in the future, but it seems that the opposite is true. As people are living longer worldwide, they're also being asked to work longer with the result that the age at which people will be drawing a pension, if they have one, will be later than it is now. And in fact it's already starting

235

to happen in many countries like the UK and France.

E: How can people ensure that work does not control their lives?

C: It's not easy, but not impossible either. One way is to ensure that one has interests outside work, and that these interests are not connected with work in any way. For example, if people are involved in working in computers all day, they could find something that requires manual skills like pottery.

Part 2

 2.7

(E = examiner; C = candidate)

E: Now, I'm going to give you a card with a topic to look at. You have one minute to make notes and then I'm going to ask you to talk about the topic.

E: Can you talk about the topic?

C: The skill that I'd like to talk about is playing a musical instrument, mmm ... like the piano, and I'd like to learn it in the near future. I know it's possible to go to a class to learn to play the piano, but mmm ... I know I'd find that very annoying. I think learning to play the piano's one of those skills that'd be better to learn ... to acquire by paying for individual tuition. I realize that it might be expensive, but it'd be mmm ... very rewarding in other ways.
Why I'd like to be able to take up the piano is because ... it's mmm ... very soothing to play and to listen to. It's a wonderful feeling to lose yourself in the music as you're playing. I've got several friends who are mad about music, and I've listened to them many times. They've played both classical and pop music to me, and they've found it thrilling to play for someone. And to me it is a very peaceful experience just sitting there and listening. As well as helping to calm people down, playing an instrument like the piano's er ... very good for the brain as it keeps it active. One of my friends, who plays the guitar and the piano, says that he plays for about ... half an hour before he does any homework, and it helps him to focus on his work and concentrate more. And it's healthy, because it helps take away part of the stress of modern lifestyle. Friends've also told me that it improves their ability to focus, and so they play before they study or do any work, which I think would mm ... benefit me too.

E: OK. Thank you. Which type of music would like to learn to play?

C: Er ... I'd like to start with classical, but I'd like to learn jazz music later on and maybe some pop music.

Part 3

 2.8

(E = examiner; C = candidate)

E: Do you think it's important to keep acquiring new skills throughout one's life?

C: Yes, I think it is.

E: Why do you think so?

C: Well, mmm, at the moment life is changing so fast with the advances that have been made in technology, and also through em ... globalization in the past few decades, so it's important for people of all ages to keep up-to-date with skills of all kinds.

E: How essential do think it'll be for workforces in the future to be proficient technologically?

C: Mmm, I'd say it is vital, because more and more of the work that is done nowadays requires a lot of input using one form of technology or another, so that in the near future it will be almost impossible to find work, even basic work, without practical computing skills. Take car design, for example. It seems that technical drawing done by hand is less important now than knowing how to create new products on the screen. Soon designers'll be creating holograms of cars not just three-dimensional computer images. And the same applies to architecture and teaching too.

E: In what way do you think learning only computing skills can be a disadvantage in life?

C: Em ... first of all, people are already becoming over-reliant on computers for virtually everything. In the current knowledge-based society, where information is available literally at people's fingertips, there's a danger that people's knowledge'll decrease and accessing information'll become just like switching on the light without necessarily understanding what's happening. And people're in danger of losing their ability to do basic things.

E: Mmm, er, should preparation of children and young people for work focus on computing skills at the expense of practical skills?

C: Mmm ... I think it's a matter of balance, because we need the people to build computers and so on, and the people to learn to be able to use them for their work. Also, if any machines break down, we need people to be able to fix them. And so if education

concentrates on training people to use machines to access knowledge at the expense of training technicians etc, then there'll be a major problem.

E: Do you think people will have to work longer in the future?

C: At one time it was thought that people would have more leisure time in the future, but it seems that the opposite is true. As people are living longer worldwide, they're also being asked to work longer with the result that the age at which people will be drawing a pension, if they have one, will be later than it is now. And in fact it's already starting to happen in many countries like the UK and France.

E: How can people ensure that work does not control their lives?

C: It's not easy, but not impossible either. One way is to ensure that one has interests outside work, and that these interests are not connected with work in any way. For example, if people are involved in working in computers all day, they could find something that requires manual skills like pottery.

13 The importance of infrastructure

 2.9

(J = Janice; A = Ahmed)

J: Hi Ahmed. How is the research project going?

A: I've just started, and it's giving me a headache already. I didn't really think it would be like this at all really, but then ...

J: The beginning is always the worst part. I always hate getting started.

A: Yeah, it's always a real problem.

J: So ... you're doing something ... on the relationship between the public and systems like roads and transport in cities?

A: Yes, that's it. And you are doing ... ?

J: Cityscapes and their impact on people's moods.

A: Ah, yes.

J: It has given me lots of headaches too. What's your problem?

A: Oh, everything basically. I am just trying to get my head around everything and don't know where to start.

J: Mmm ... I'm in the middle of looking at data analysis, and I am having a bit of a struggle myself at the moment.

A: You're at the data stage. Oh right. You're quite far on then.

J: Yeah. I am ...

A: Could you tell me what your experiences have been as you are further along than me? It might make me feel a bit better.

J: Yeah sure. <u>Looking back I don't know how I got to this stage, but mm ... I found it really difficult to get going. I thought I was never going to get started</u>, but then it all came together.

A: That's good to hear. I thought I was the only one. But can you tell me about your experience say of em ... doing the research question?

J: <u>I thought I would have difficulty turning my ideas into a research question, but it wasn't as bad as I thought. In fact, I found it extremely easy.</u>

A: OK ... I might ask for your help on that then. What about the literature review?

J: <u>The literature review? That I found really took up a lot of time.</u> Although it can eat into the time, I actually like digging into things and getting to the bottom of problems.

A: Yes, I agree it can be fun. I'm reading a lot to try and get myself to frame my research question, and I'm really getting into the literature.

J: <u>Well, the thing I was very glad to get out of the way was writing the research proposal. I was exhausted after that,</u> because it's important to make sure the research proposal is really clear on the focus of your research. It's not easy summarizing everything and bringing it together.

A: <u>And designing the methods?</u>

J: <u>That was quite easy to do</u> – I enjoy analyzing systems and putting them together, so I think I sorted the methods design out really quickly. <u>But what I found really agonizing was writing the aims and objectives. That was probably the most difficult thing of all.</u>

A: Yeah ... they aren't easy.

....

J: Is all of this any help Ahmed?

A: Oh yes. One of the problems is that it's OK to see things written on paper but it's the thinking behind it.

J: Yes, of course. It is.

A: Yeah. I appreciate it. My spoken English is not a problem, I think, but I've not done much writing and I'm going to find that bit difficult.

J: Well, you can get help you know.

A: Yeah? Mm, do you think I need a private tutor?

J: Oh no, that's not necessary, I'm sure. <u>I know there's language support in the university if you are not a full-time student; you just need to contact the Language Centre.</u>

A: OK, thanks for that.

J: <u>And you can get help through the main library.</u> It's not just for lending books you know.

A: Really? I never thought of that.

J: It's so easy to get isolated and not know everything that's available.

14 Money and happiness

 2.10

Good afternoon to you all. My name's Diana Simpson, and I'm from the City Business Forum. I'm managing director of a firm of accountants which employs over 2 000 people here and abroad. I'd like to thank you for coming today, and I'd like to thank Professor Beacon for inviting me here to talk to you today about an example of a training scheme to create a happy workforce, which we are trying to promote as a model of good practice. Before I say something about our training scheme I'd like to tell you a little bit about business values and the values of our company. <u>When people think of business they often mistakenly think of money and profits</u>, and at times businessmen and women have a negative press. However, business is not all bad; not just about making profits, though there is no denying that this is important. It is about creating something, often out of nothing, building it up from scratch. <u>And an obvious plus is that business is about providing new employment opportunities</u> that in turn enrich people's lives. It is also about bringing people together and making links and contributing to the economy of the country. But in doing so our accountancy firm adheres to a strict ethical code. We have set ourselves high standards, and <u>we seek to improve the communities we work within by returning some of the profits back into those communities</u>.

The training scheme I'd like to talk about is one we have been developing within our company for the past seven years. At the beginning of the training scheme, before I actually became managing director of the company we had, like many companies, staff meetings and training sessions, which were conducted by staff in-house on financial matters.

<u>But the training scheme has evolved almost naturally</u> to its present state using minimal resources. Initially we allocated a certain number of hours per year for staff to follow their own training by company trainers paid for by the company. This was delivered in-house once a fortnight during office hours at different times of the day including early morning and late evening. This development worked very well with courses being offered on languages, stress-busting, arts and crafts and physical exercise. Vouchers or discounts were also offered to staff to go to local gyms, and some staff members formed their own running and swimming clubs.

As the scheme has further evolved, we have actively encouraged staff in our company to aim for personal <u>fulfilment</u> and not just to focus on their professional development. About 18 months ago we decided to devote more time to training by giving each full-time worker <u>two hours</u> a week for training, and a proportionate amount for part-time workers. A further development has been that some of the more experienced staff decided to use the time they were allocated to <u>give training</u> free of charge to various organizations who need professional help.

....

And the results of the company's move from professional development on work-related matters to a focus on staff happiness? Well, quite frankly, they are startling. Staff absences? Well the number of <u>staff absences</u> from sickness have been reduced substantially – a 25 per cent decline as you can see from the bar chart here. The fact that working hours have been reduced has not affected productivity; actually, it is the reverse. Company profits have increased with a rise of <u>15 per cent</u>. So the company profits are in a healthy state now. But the most important impact on the company as a whole has been the drop in staff turnover. All companies, large or small, have some staff turnover, but we have managed to reduce ours by a whopping 90 per cent. The knock-on effect has been reduced <u>recruitment costs</u> and the expense on training new staff with a further impact on profitability. We are looking at other ways of developing this further and promoting the model as a means of good practice.

Sample answer sheets

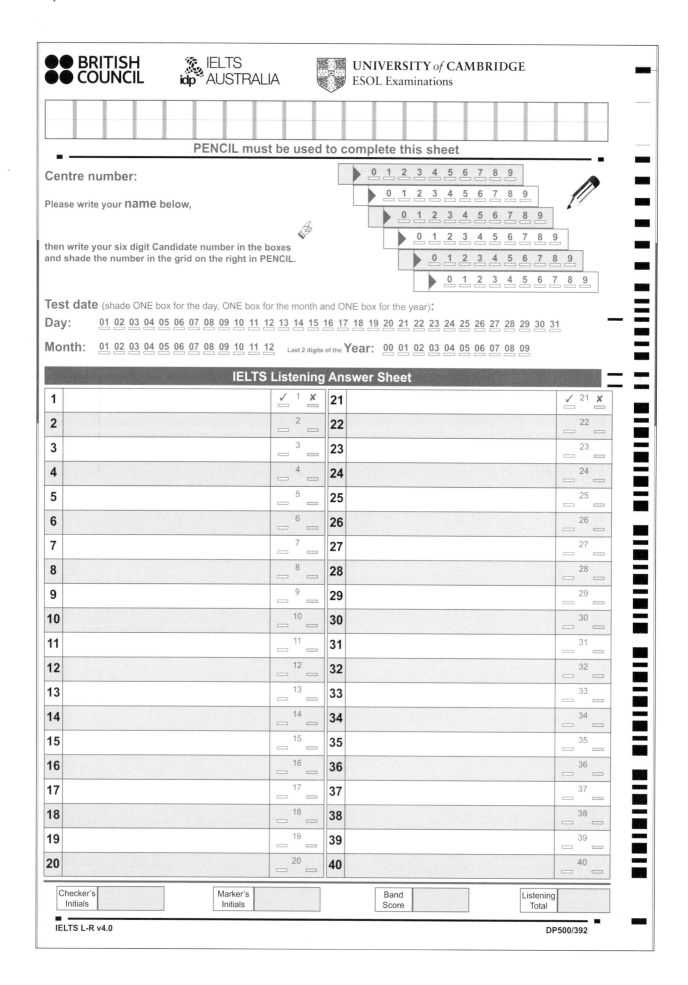

Are you: Female? ⊐ Male? ⊐

Your first language code: ▶ 0 1 2 3 4 5 6 7 8 9
▶ 0 1 2 3 4 5 6 7 8 9
▶ 0 1 2 3 4 5 6 7 8 9

IELTS Reading Answer Sheet

Module taken (shade one box): Academic ⊐ General Training ⊐

		✓ 1 ✗			✓ 21 ✗
1			21		
2		2	22		22
3		3	23		23
4		4	24		24
5		5	25		25
6		6	26		26
7		7	27		27
8		8	28		28
9		9	29		29
10		10	30		30
11		11	31		31
12		12	32		32
13		13	33		33
14		14	34		34
15		15	35		35
16		16	36		36
17		17	37		37
18		18	38		38
19		19	39		39
20		20	40		40

Checker's Initials		Marker's Initials		Band Score		Reading Total	

Macmillan Education
Between Towns Road, Oxford OX4 3PP
A division of Macmillan Publishers Limited
Companies and representatives throughout the world

ISBN 978-0-2307-3214-8 (+ key edition)
ISBN 978-0-2307-3215-5 (- key edition)

Original design by Andrew Jones
Page make-up by xen. http://www.xen.co.uk
Illustrated by Fred Blunt, Julian Mosdale, Oxford Designers and Illustrators,
and Alan Rowe
Cover design by Barbara Mercer
Cover photograph © Getty/Sean Dary

Author's acknowledgement

I would like to say a very special thank you to Alison Ross and Amanda
Anderson for their great patience, guidance and insight and to say to thank you
to Liz Hunt, Jo Kent, Debra Emmett, Mary Jane Hogan and Phil Vellender for
their not inconsiderable help. I would also like to thank Alison Sharpe.

I would like to acknowledge and thank the following students for supplying
sample answers: Wilonja Mutebwe, Abukar Haji Jimale, Darejan Chitashvili,
Kais Abdaly, Akram Moosavi, Nisreen Shaker, Ibahim Almeriy and all the
students at Reache Northwest.

The publishers would like to thank all those who participated in the
development of this project, with special thanks to Mary Jane Hogan, Liz Hunt,
Debra Emmett, Rachael Roberts and Alison Sharpe.

The author and publishers would like to thank the following for permission to
reproduce the following copyright material:

University of Leicester and Dr Jane Wellens for an extract adapted from "Face-
to-face or Facebook? Can Online Networking Sites Help New Students Settle
Into University?" by Dr Jane Wellens http://www2.le.ac.uk/ebulletin/news/press-
releases/2000-2009/2008/05/nparticle.2008-05-12.9320634382, reproduced with
permission;

Extract from 'Why exactly is this ride so thrilling?' by Roger Highfield copyright © Telegraph Group Limited 2006, first published in The Daily Telegraph
10.10.046, reprinted by permission of the publisher;

Extract from 'The world's rubbish dump: a garbage tip that stretches from Hawaii to Japan' by Kathy Marks and Daniel Howden copyright © The Independent 2008, first published in The Independent 05.02.08, reprinted by permission
of the publisher;

PARS International Corp for an extract abridged from "Why Should We
Be Friends?" by Kate Baker, Newsweek, 9 August 2008, copyright © 2008
Newsweek, Inc. All rights reserved. Used by permission and protected by the
Copyright Laws of the United States. The printing, copying, redistribution,
or retransmission of the Material without express written permission is
prohibited;

Extract from 'MBAs: The end of testing times?' by Nick Jackson copyright ©
The Independent 2008, first published in The Independent 17.04.08, reprinted
by permission of the publisher;

Design Museum for an extract abridged from 'Giles Gilbert Scott, Architect
(1880-1960)' http://www.designmuseum.org/design/giles-gilbert-scott copyright
© Design Museum;

Extract from 'Graffiti: Street art – or crime?' by Arifa Akbar and Paul Vallely
copyright © The Independent 2008, first published in The Independent
16.07.08, reprinted by permission of the publisher;

ABC-CLIO, LLC for an extract from Culture and Customs of Mozambique
by George O. Ndege. Published by Greenwood Press, copyright © 2006,
reproduced with permission of ABC-CLIO, LLC;

Excerpt from "The Great Barrier Reef" www.environment.gov.au copyright ©
Commonwealth of Australia, reproduced by permission.';

PARS International Corp for an extract abridged from "E-Zpass was just the
beginning" by Ken Belson, New York Times, 2 March 2008, copyright © 2008
The New York Times. All rights reserved. Used by permission and protected by
the Copyright Laws of the United States. The printing, copying, redistribution,
or retransmission of the Material without express written permission is
prohibited;

PARS International Corp for an extract abridged from "Why Money Doesn't Buy
Happiness" by Sharon Begley Newsweek, 15 October 2007 www.newsweek.com,
copyright © 2007 Newsweek, Inc. All rights reserved. Used by permission and
protected by the Copyright Laws of the United States. The printing, copying,
redistribution, or retransmission of the Material without express written
permission is prohibited;

National Gallery of Art for an extract from 'Xia Dynasty, Bronze Age China
c.2000-771 BCE' from The Golden Age of Chinese Archaeology, Part Two, p12.
Written by Brian Hogarth, Director of Education, Asian Art Museum of San
Francisco, with Carla Benner, National Gallery of Art, Washington. http://
www.nga.gov/education/chinatp_pt2.htm copyright © 1999. Board of Trustees,
National Gallery of Art, Washington;

The Geological Society of London for an extract abstracted with permission
from Earth in Our Hands – Coastal Erosion by Cally Oldershaw, published by
The Geological Society of London and available at www.geolsoc.org.uk.

IELTS answer sheets reproduced with the permission of the IELTS partners.

These materials may contain links for third party websites. We have no control
over, and are not responsible for, the contents of such third party websites.
Please use care when accessing them.

Although we have tried to trace and contact copyright holders before
publication, in some cases this has not been possible. If contacted we will be
pleased to rectify any errors or omissions at the earliest opportunity.

The author and publishers would like to thank the following for permission to
reproduce their photographs:

Alamy/Alaska Stock LLC p75, Alamy/Anglia Images p89, Alamy/Arco Images
GmbH p73(background), Alamy/Bill Bachman p109, Alamy/Roger Bamber
p100, Alamy/Bob Bartree p18(cl), Alamy/Serge Bogomijako p34, Alamy/
Mark Boulton p72(4), Alamy/Bubbles Photography p160(bl), Alamy/Caro
p140, Alamy/Cobo Images p172, Alamy/Michael Dwyer p145, Alamy/Bob
Ebsen p13(tr), Alamy/Elly Godfrey p48(tl), Alamy/Jeff Greenberg p96, Alamy/
David Harding p30(tc), Alamy/IML Group p190, Alamy/Images and Stories
p155, Alamy/Stephen May p48 (r), Alamy/Christophe Diesel Michot p30(tl),
Alamy/Adrian Mutit p98, Alamy/Papilo p72(3), Alamy/Parker Photography
p57, Alamy/Photos 12 p6(tl), Alamy/Pictorum p92, Alamy/The Print Collector
p194(cr), Alamy/Alex Segre pp8,180, Alamy/Colin Spics p121, Alamy/Carol &
Mike Werne, Alamy/Janine Weidel Photography p92, Alamy/Woodystock p158;

Ancient Art and Arcitecture p21

BRAND X pp76(background), 164(tr), 183(cr)

Business Objects 2 p110

Creatas p18(cr)

Corbis pp30(tr), 164(cr), Corbis/Bettman p140 (cl), Corbis/Blutgruppe p60(tr),
Corbis/Bruno Barbier/Robert Harding World Imagery p87, Corbis/Ron Chapple
p182(cr), Corbis/Creative p6(tr), Corbis/Richard Cummins p43, Corbis/epa p63,
Corbis/Stephen Frink p168, Corbis/Walter Geiersperger p184, Corbis/Vladimir
Godnik/Moodboard p6(tc), Corbis/Blane Harrington III p51, Corbis/Martin
Harvey p118, Corbis/Hulton Deutsch Collection p50, Corbis/ Chris Hellier
p56, Corbis/Robbie Jack p140(br), Corbis/Issei Kato/Reuters p65, Corbis/
Serge Kozak p92(tr), Corbis/Geng Lei/Xinhua Press p182(cl), Corbis/Robbie
Lewis p141, Corbis/Will & Demi McIntyre p6(cr), Corbis/ Jens Nieth p33(cr),
Corbis/Michael Prince pp92(cl), 183(br), Corbis/Ben Radford p199(r), Corbis/
Jose Fistu Raga p182(tl), Corbis/Redlink p116(3), Corbis/Stapleton Collection
p140(tl), Corbis/Jurnasyanto Sukarno p48(cl), Corbis/Ryoichi Utsumi/Amana
Images p13(c), Corbis/Tom Van Sant p104, Corbis/Uli Weismeier p30(cl),
Corbis/William Whitehurst p194(l)

Digital Vision p167(tr)

Grapheast pp 25, 116(4)

Heritage Image Partnership p85

Image Source pp82, 152(tr),164(tl), 181

Itek Colour Graphics ltd p106

Photodisc p72(2)

Photolibrary/Walter G Allgedwer P199(l), Photolibrary/The British Library
p104(bl), Photolibrary/Keith Brofsky p13(tc), Photolibrary/Michael Brooke
p119. Photolibrary/Peter Cool p116(5), Photolibrary/Pascal Deloche p152(tl),
Photolibrary/JTB Photography p167 (tc), Photolibrary/Christian Kober
p167(tr), Photolibrary/Nick Hufton p122, Photolibrary/Imagesource p178
Photolibrary/Albery Klein p60(tl), Photolibrary/Mermet p160(br), Photolibrary/
Dod Miller p196(l), Photolibrary/Lee Peterson p52; Photolibrary/Boutet Jean-
Pierre p6(cl), Photolibrary/Stewart and Cynthia Pernide p140(tr), Photolibrary/
Photononstop pp72(1),100(cl), Photolibrary/Ingram Publishing p18(tc),
Photolibrary/Felipe Rodriquez p33(br), Photolibrary/Tim Rosenthal p13(tl),
Photolibrary/Jose Añtonio Sancho p148, Photolibrary/Michael Szrdny p13(cr),
Photolibrary/Jennifer Thermes p104(t), Photolibrary/Nicolas Thibaut p194(tr),
Photolibrary/White p60(c), Photolibrary/Gerhard Zwerger-Schoner p116(2)

Rex Features/Bill Bachman p116(1), Rex Features/Jonathan Hardle p146,
Rex Features/Israel Images p73(t), Rex Features/Image Source p196(r), Rex
Features/Sipa Press p152(cl), Rex Features/Sunset p152(cl), Rex Features/
Times Newspapers Ltd p182(tr)

Science and Society Picture Library/Science Museum p18 (tl,tr);

Superstock p19.

Charts reproduced with the kind permission of:

Earthtrends.wri.org p175

Faber-Castell p81

Florida Trend.com p69

Gallop.com p203

Hitwise UK p15

Macmillan Publishers Ltd pp38, 134

Office for National Statistics pp38, 190, 191, 129, 130

Scientific American p68

The United Nations (World Population Prospects: The 2006
Revision,Vol1,Comprehensive Tables, United Nations, New York 2007, United
Nations Sales No.E.07.XIII.2) p132.

Picture Research by Cath Dunn, Polka Dot Studios.

Printed and bound in Thailand.

2014   2013   2012   2011   2010
10   9   8   7   6   5   4   3   2   1